The Lioness Roared: The Problems of Female Rule in English History

Charles Beem

THE LIONESS ROARED

First published in 2006 by   *Cau*
PALGRAVE MACMILLAN™
175 Fifth Avenue, New York, N.Y. 10010 and
Houndmills, Basingstoke, Hampshire, England RG21 6XS
Companies and representatives throughout the world.

PALGRAVE MACMILLAN is the global academic imprint of the Palgrave Macmillan division of St. Martin's Press, LLC and of Palgrave Macmillan Ltd. Macmillan® is a registered trademark in the United States, United Kingdom and other countries. Palgrave is a registered trademark in the European Union and other countries.

ISBN 1–4039–7203–6

Library of Congress Cataloging-in-Publication Data
Beem, Charles.
   The lioness roared : the problems of female rule in English history / Charles Beem.
      p. cm.
   Includes bibliographical references (p.) and index.
   ISBN 1–4039–7203–6 (alk. paper)
      1. Queens—Great Britain—Biography. 2. Mary I, Queen of England, 1516–1558. 3. Anne, Queen of Great Britain, 1665–1714. 4. Elizabeth I, Queen of England, 1533–1603. 5. Victoria, Queen of Great Britain, 1819–1901. 6. Matilda, Empress, consort of Henry V, Holy Roman Emperor, 1102–1167. 7. Monarchy—Great Britain— History. I. Title.

DA28.2.B44 2006
941.009′9—dc22   2005054454

A catalogue record for this book is available from the British Library.

Design by Newgen Imaging Systems (P) Ltd., Chennai, India.

First edition: April 2006

10 9 8 7 6 5 4 3 2 1

Printed in the United States of America.

CONTENTS

ACKNOWLEDGMENTS

The origins of this project lay in my attempt, as a doctoral student, to answer a number of questions not addressed in the conventional literature describing the history of female rule in England. In the fall of 1991, as I began my Ph.D. at the University of Arizona, I asked a visiting instructor teaching a course on Modern Britain why George of Denmark failed to become king of England. In response, the instructor smiled nervously through the long uncomfortable pause that usually accompanies the inability to provide a satisfactory answer to a student's question. Later on in that semester, I asked the same instructor what factors motivated Queen Victoria to refuse to dismiss her bedchamber ladies in May 1839. Once again, I received a less-than-satisfactory answer. This is not to suggest that this particular instructor was less than qualified to teach a course on Modern Britain: as I began searching through books and articles for the answers to my questions, I realized that I had to formulate them myself.

Had I known at the onset how daunting it would be to research and write this project, I probably would not have attempted to digest the multiple historiographies and methodologies necessary to begin the formulation of a comprehensive model for a historical examination of English female rule. Ten years later, now that it is done, I would like to acknowledge a number of people who have helped make this book possible. First and foremost, Laura Tabili, who pushed me constantly to search deeper and wider in my sources and analysis, as well as Richard Cosgrove and Helen Nader: a dream team of a dissertation committee. I am also indebted to Carole Levin for the enthusiastic support she has offered for this project. Last but not least, I offer my heartfelt thanks to Jay Brown for his unflagging support, emotional and otherwise, over the many years I endeavored to research and write this work. Many other individuals have offered me their assistance in researching this project. The staffs of the British Library in London, and the Huntington Library in San Marino, California, were invaluable in helping me locate many of the primary documents used in this study. I would also like to thank the staff of the Nantucket Athenaeum for locating a number of secondary works cited in this book. My most pleasurable research was performed at the Royal Archives at Windsor Castle, and I would like to thank Lady Sheila Bellaigue for her kind assistance. I would also like to thank anonymous readers for *Sixteenth Century Journal* and *Historical Research*. Portions of this work have appeared in a different form in *Canadian Journal of History* (vol. 39, December 2004), and are reprinted with their kind permission. Finally, I wish to acknowledge the permission of Her Majesty, Queen Elizabeth II, to make use of materials from the Royal Archives at Windsor.

THE LIONESS ROARED:
INTRODUCTION

Now, loving subjects, what I am, ye right well know. I am your queen, to whom at my coronation, when I was wedded to the realm and the laws of the same, you promised your allegiance and obedience unto me.[1]

So roared Mary I of England, in the midst of a formidable rebellion against her authority as monarch. Even John Foxe, the Protestant martyrologist who created the enduring image of "Bloody Mary," marveled, for one brief historical moment, at the exercise of kingly authority emanating from this diminutive, thirty-nine-year-old unmarried woman.[2] As England's first ruling queen, Mary forcefully reminded her subjects that she was their legitimate monarch, capable of mastering her own and England's destiny. Unlike her male predecessors, the kings of England, Mary I was compelled to justify to her subjects why a woman should be holding an estate and wielding an office that formerly had been occupied only by men. Simultaneously proclaiming herself her kingdom's wife and demanding the obedience of her kingdom's subjects, Mary I demonstrated a response to the opponents of her rule that was contradictory in its premises yet remarkable in its attempt to project a gendered representation of womanhood upon the historical template of English kingship.

This study is concerned with the particular problems faced by English female rulers that arose on account of their gender. Female rulers throughout English history held an office otherwise occupied overwhelmingly by men, and did so in societies held together by gendered hierarchies of a social and political nature, that placed women of all social classes outside the formal and public realms of royal politics and government. From the Norman Conquest to the twentieth century, the spectacle of a female ruler represented the theoretical clash between a female inclusive rule of royal inheritance and male dominated systems of duly constituted authority.

The study of the female ruler, then, comprises an analysis of a dynamic nexus of ideological and structural confrontation, and properly belongs in the historical context of English kingship.[3] Analyzing this historical process, the erection of a viable model of female rule within a male dominant political culture, requires a significant semantic shift in our understanding of the nature of kingship. In European history, from the fall of the Roman Empire to the present day, political structures and cultures through time have commonly construed kings and queens as complementary but distinct, socially constructed gender roles for men and women.[4] As kings possessed sovereign regal power, so did queens, on occasion.[5] But be it king or ruling queen, both types of rulers were described by contemporaries as ruling kingdoms. The quasi-religious and juridical sovereignty vested in kingship was gendered male; the kings of England were represented as lions, whose image threatened blazingly from the royal arms.[6] Thus, when a woman was vested with the sovereignty of kingship, the state did not temporarily become a queendom; the lions of England did not suddenly shed their manes upon the accession of a female ruler. Instead, hereditary systems of royal inheritance in England and other European states occasionally allowed women to hold the office of king, as they did for little boys, senile old men, and lunatics.

Nevertheless, although little boys and lunatics were considered to be less desirable occupants of the kingly estate and office, they were still recognized as kings.[7] But that other alternative form of kingship, the female variety, has not usually been accorded this recognition. Instead, the gendered nature of the English language has compelled us to call the ruling women of English history queens.[8] This situation has carried with it significant interpretive repercussions. In the historiography of European kingship, regnant queenship has not usually been considered a form of kingship, and is mostly examined right alongside other forms of queenship and female power: queens consort, female regents, dowager queens, and other royal women able to exercise effective political power.[9] In English history in particular, the vernacular cognates of the Latin *rex* and *regina*, reinforced gendered perceptions for generations of historians. The etymology of the word *cyning*, king in Anglo-Saxon, denoted a cunning, wise, and potent leader.[10] In contrast, the Anglo-Saxon term *cwen*, which evolved into the English word queen, simply described the wife of a king.[11] Nevertheless, when the first English female kings appeared in the sixteenth century, contemporaries could not comprehend any other way to describe them but as *queens*, even though they recognized that such women had inherited kingly sovereignty. Even today, deeply rooted conventional usage compels us to describe female monarchs as queens. Over the course of English history, as this study demonstrates, it took considerable efforts of resourcefulness for female rulers to invest their performances as queens within the meaning of kingship.

While a number of male kings in English history failed in their roles and suffered deposition, all of England's female sovereigns— from Mary I to Victoria—died in their beds, wearing their crowns.[12] A comprehensive explanation for why ruling women succeeded through time in creating acceptable models for female rule in the face of perennial systems of male political dominance, is nearly absent from the body of English constitutional and political studies. This study shall further this process, begun by recent gender based studies of Elizabeth I, discussed later in this introduction, with an examination of a series of specific problems peculiar to England's queens regnant. When we examine the public careers of female rulers through the historical prism of English kingship, they are more properly identified as female kings. As women performing a male gendered public role, female kings had to face additional gendered burdens in order to maintain their position at the top of the social and political hierarchy. This fundamental fact informs all the chapters that follow.

This study proposes to take the long view of female rulership as a particular category of English kingship and political development. Such a process requires an understanding of a wide variety of historical voices through time that provide the sources describing the successes and failures of female rulers in English history. As noted feminist scholar Gerda Lerner has remarked, such a view can have a unique impact on the understanding of women's history, by facilitating the comparison of different stages of cultural, social, and political evolution, and their effects on the public roles played by men and women.[13] Only then can an attempt at a comprehensive historical model for female rulership be fashioned. At first glance, constitutional and political studies seem far removed from the social and cultural studies that have formed the forefront of feminist-inspired historical work. In recent years, however, feminist scholars have emphasized the need to integrate women's history into the older and established interdisciplinary categories of political, diplomatic, and constitutional history.[14] Such an approach can reinvigorate political and constitutional studies. The contemporary political historian can no longer work in the vacuum of traditional politics alone: society, culture, and economics must inform and shape the findings of political history if they are to have relevance in our present day society. In order to accomplish this task, political historians examining female rulership must expand their historical horizon to include contemporary understandings of manhood and womanhood, kingship and queenship, and their place and impact in a given social and political hierarchy. This process requires the utilization of gender as a mode of historical inquiry.[15] Accordingly, we wish to note that gender is an unstable analytical term; its meaning is hotly debated among feminist historians and other social scientists.[16] For the purposes of this study, the use of the term gender implies a description of socially constructed differences between men and women, manifested in the public roles played by male and female historical actors. Thus, the gendered aspects of this study are concerned with identifying the means by which England's female kings through time manipulated and transcended the social and political limitations imposed upon their gender, in order to possess the estate and execute the office of king.

This study, then, combines the methodologies of political history and women's studies. The task of integrating the history of women into a more balanced historical perspective is challenging. Perhaps the most crucial concern inherent in analyzing the role of the female ruler is the fact that most English historical records describing them were written by men for men.[17] The mixed emotions of male commentators through time reveal the contested nature of female kingship. Although female kings satisfied the structural need to follow a female inclusive rule of royal primogeniture, their existence contradicted socially constructed notions of manhood that, until the twentieth century, did not perceive women as equals, much less superiors, in the public arena of politics.

Assigning a name to describe ideological structures of male dominance through time also involves entering an arena of discursive controversy. A number of scholars employ the word patriarchy to describe an overall system of male dominance at work in Western societies going back to classical Greece and Rome.[18] This usage of the term patriarchy has been challenged by a number of scholars who point out that patriarchy was a not a monolithic leviathan that hovered unchanged over the course of European medieval and early-modern history. Instead, it was the interaction of many patriarchies, entrenched in multiple political and social processes, specific in time and space, which posed specific challenges to female rulers over the course of English history. That said, this study proposes to expand the scope of English political history through gendered analysis of female rulership against the backdrop of constantly evolving systems of male dominated governance.

The issue of class also figures prominently in this study. Systems of male dominance were not the only recognizable systems that oppressed women: in preindustrial English societies, women of the peasant and urban proletariat were oppressed right alongside the men and children of these classes. But the social class that yielded female rulers was that of the aristocratic elites, itself a series of class formations experiencing dynamic change throughout English history, evolving from the rough and ready twelfth-century Anglo-Norman tenants-in-chief to the urbane aristocratic Whig politicians surrounding the youthful Queen Victoria.[19] Like all social classes, aristocracies are bisected by gender. As the kinswomen of powerful male elites, royal women existed in close proximity to the sources of political power in the state, and often exerted considerable informal power within royal governments.[20] But for most of these women, such power was exercised through the auspices of legitimate male authority, in their positions as elite male appendages, which enabled them to represent their kinsmen in the public realm of government.[21] The really difficult feat, then, was for a woman to obtain and hold onto recognition of wielding power in her own right, and in doing so, possessing the sovereignty of kingship.[22]

All of England's regnant queens accomplished this goal: this study proposes that these women, for all their other failings, were bold pioneers who ventured past the ideological and structural restraints of male dominance.[23] With the notable exceptions of Elizabeth I (1558–1603), and Victoria (1837–1901), the careers of England's other female rulers, the Empress Matilda, "Lady of the English" (1141–1147), Mary I (1553–1558), and Anne (1702–1714), are not usually considered to have achieved such a feat.[24] Denied recognition of their uphill battle to wield power in a male dominant society, Matilda, Mary, and Anne have been perennially dismissed as victims of their female gendered inadequacies.[25] The following narratives of how these women came to establish themselves within male dominant political structures, fragmented and unrecognized in conventional historical political studies, both recognizes their historical agency and reveals the unique evolution of female kingship in English constitutional history. Like other alternative forms of kingship did, female rule changed the way monarchy represented itself to its subjects. As medieval royal minorities placed additional stresses on the maintenance of royal authority, female kingship was even more far removed from archetypical forms of kingship epitomized in English history by Henry II, Edward III, and Henry V, kings renowned as warriors and lawgivers. The basic methodological concern of this book, that female rulers were significantly more handicapped in their attempts to rule by social and legal constraints than men, has only recently been articulated.[26] English kingship was fashioned almost entirely from socially constructed male roles: military leader, dispenser of justice, representative of God, and father.[27] Indeed, until the emergence of contract theories of governance in the seventeenth century, English kingship existed as the summit of idealized private and public roles for men.

While social and economic relations between men and women were inherently unequal, they were viewed as complementary in preindustrial European societies in a variety of socioeconomic contexts, such as the relationship between a king and a queen consort.[28] The execution of the public role of king was not performed in any form of all male vacuum. Kings throughout English history possessed mothers, wives, and daughters who influenced and wielded power informally through them. While the ideologies of female subordination in medieval and early-modern European societies found justification in biblical injunctions, Aristotelian and Platonic philosophy, and commentaries in Roman law, a number of scholars have demonstrated the cleavage between didactic literature that prescribed "proper" womanly roles, and the actual experiences of women in history.[29] Still more scholars have demonstrated the means by which women of all social classes in European history sought to breach or circumvent structures of male dominance.[30] As historical agents, women achieved their socioeconomic goals by various strategies that included both resistance and accommodation to patriarchal structures in society and government. As this study demonstrates, this was also true for all the female rulers examined in the chapters to follow.

Until the late nineteenth century, female rulers in England constituted the single exception to the socially and legally gendered subordination of women. Most daughters and wives lived their lives as *femes covert*, represented in the public sphere of law and government by their male kinsmen or wards.[31] However, it was possible for an aristocratic woman, such as the fifteenth-century Margaret Beaufort, mother of Henry VII, to obtain the status of *feme sole*, a woman unrestrained in the ownership of property and in her public dealings by any male guardian.[32] But this was as close as any medieval or early-modern English woman came to breaching the structural barriers of male dominated forms of politics and government until the sixteenth-century appearance of the female king. Given this fact, the emergence and consolidation of female rule constituted a complicated and controversial process. Although scholars have argued against the existence of a "public sphere" in preindustrial English societies, male dominant political systems rarely recognized women as legitimate participants in what we shall nonetheless term the public spaces of political, military, and sacerdotal activities.[33] The construction of female kingship, then, was a gender-bending process, drawing through time upon contemporary notions of manhood and womanhood embodied in the distinct gendered roles of kingship and queenship.

Both were symbols of power. The origins of female rule in European history emerged from the power that women wielded in the various Germanic kingdoms that arose from the breakdown of the Western Roman Empire. Scholars have argued that the lack of clear distinction between public and private realms of social and political interaction present in the kinship based structures of the Franks, the Visigoths, and the Anglo-Saxons in England allowed women to exert political power within these structures.[34] The seventh-century commentator Gregory of Tours duly recounted the exploits of savage Merovingian queens, while early Anglo-Saxon queens achieved prominence primarily by encouraging the spread of Christianity and the foundation of monastic establishments.[35] The power of abbesses also has been noted as an example of legitimate political role for women.[36] But with the exception of abbesses, who functioned as manorial lords, elite women in Anglo-Saxon society only exercised authority derived from their male kinsmen: fathers, husbands, and sons.

But informal power wielded through kinship structures was fundamentally different from a woman's formal possession of regal power. While the exercise of informal power derived from male kinsmen constituted powerful precedents for female rulers to follow, a woman's sole possession of the regal estate and office in medieval and early-modern England and Europe had its roots in the development of the hereditary principle as one of the primary determinants of royal systems of succession. This principle, one of many that determined Anglo-Saxon successions, slowly gained credence from the Norman Conquest to the thirteenth century, as theories of feudal military tenure hardened into systems of landed inheritance.[37] This process benefited women in material ways. In the realm of private law, women as *femes coverts* enjoyed considerable protection for their incomes as widows, in the form of jointures, marigatum, and dowers, which occasionally allowed forceful women the opportunity to chart their own individual destiny.[38] Among the elite strata of English society, women also developed the ability to inherit and will real and moveable property as well as feudal tenancies.[39] Nonetheless, in general, a woman's heritable property reverted to her husband's control after marriage, so that any alteration or alienation had to be formally performed by her husband. Only in the case of a widow powerful enough to stave off remarriage could she enjoy the fruits of her inheritance unhindered, such as the thrice married Lucy, Countess of Chester, who, in 1129, paid Henry I of England for the right not to marry again.[40]

But in the case of a royal inheritrix, the inheritance of property became bound up with the transmission of sovereignty. Over the course of the High and late Middle Ages in England, royal women transmitted hereditary claims to the crown derived from their fathers to their male descendants.[41] Ultimately a woman's status as a royal inheritrix was that of a flesh-and-blood transmitter of that ultimate form of property, the crown, making her reproductive capabilities a heritable commodity, or, as Gayle Rubin termed it, "a traffic in women," filling the occasional gaps in a patrilineal royal succession.[42] Such practices came to inform the emergence of post–Norman conquest succession patterns in England. Early-Norman successions were only loosely based on a hereditary principle, as the sons of William the Conqueror battled over their father's Norman and English patrimony. Only with the third Norman king, Henry I (1100–1135), was there an attempt to construct a female inclusive principle of primogeniture as the primary determinant of the succession.[43] The recipient of this plan, Henry's only legitimate heir, his daughter Matilda, failed to gain her political inheritance. However, the success of Matilda's son, Henry II, in gaining the English crown created the precedent of female transmission of a hereditary right to the throne.

Henry II, the first English king to conceptualize himself as a lion, based his claim to kingship on the right of his mother to pass on a royal claim derived from her father to her next male heir. With a succession of two centuries of uncontested lineal male heirs, however, the theory of a female inclusive system of royal primogeniture remained in constitutional mothballs.[44] With the death of Henry III in 1272, and the immediate and uncontested accession of Edward I, a system of succession based squarely on heredity settled comfortably into place with the maxim "the king is dead, long live the king."[45] Though disturbed by Richard II's 1399 deposition, as well as the fifteenth-century Wars of the Roses, a female inclusive system of primogeniture reemerged to determine the succession under the sixteenth-century Tudors and the seventeenth-century Stuarts. However, the primary circumstance that put such a system into practice was the momentary lack of viable adult royal males. Even to this day, the advent of a regnant queen in England remains a default mechanism for a system of hereditary succession that still favors men over women.[46]

The Problems of Female Rule

The following chapters are studies that attempt to fill the gaps in the conventional historical literature describing the evolution of English kingship. These studies are separated by large blocks of time, and confront four separate historiographies, a discussion of which shall appear in each separate chapter. The first chapter examines the career of the Empress Matilda in her public role as "Lady of the English" (1141–1147). Historians have long considered Matilda's career a convenient explanation for why female rule was not possible in twelfth-century England. Recent historiography has emphasized the logistical, rather than the ideological, hurdles Matilda needed to clear to make good her claim.[47] But absent from recent studies of Matilda is an analysis of her nearly successful strategy to make herself a female king.[48] Specifically, this chapter demonstrates the means by which Matilda attempted to create a viable public representation that existed completely separate from her status as a wife and a mother. By analyzing the method by which Matilda signified herself in her charters and grants, this chapter demonstrates how Matilda drew from conventional precedents of female representation in European feudal societies to create a model of singular identity in twelfth-century England. Similarly, by examining the unconventional course of Matilda's marriage to Geoffrey Plantagenet, Count of Anjou, described in contemporary monastic chronicles, this chapter reconstructs Matilda's quest for recognition as a sovereign female feudal lord. Unlike Matilda, the next woman to battle for the English crown succeeded in her attempt. Chapter 2 surveys the gendered ambiguities and controversies surrounding the accession of Mary I in 1553 as England's first female king. In the four hundred years separating the lives of Matilda and her descendant Mary I, the ability of a woman to transmit a hereditary claim to the throne became established in English constitutional theory, as Lancastrian and Yorkist heiresses alike provided the hereditary claims of that parvenu Royal House, the Tudors. In the middle of the Tudor sixteenth century, due to a lack of male Tudor heirs, this ability evolved into a woman's right to possess the crown in her own right, which was negotiated and enshrined in a series of parliamentary statutes.

The statutory triumph of female succession rights, however, still needed to be put into practice within a male dominant political culture. Lawyers, theologians, and politicians alike railed that Mary I's possession of kingly sovereignty challenged both common law dictums concerning women's status as well as deeply embedded notions of acceptable social roles for women, unmarried and married, that previously had not inhabited the public realm of politics and government.[49] This chapter explains how Mary I confronted and attempted to resolve the gendered challenges to her rule as an unmarried woman in the first year of her reign, as she and her government negotiated her marriage to Philip of Spain. Mary I's attempt to inhabit the role of king within an acceptable model of sixteenth-century womanhood reveals her as a resourceful historical actor whose endeavors created powerful precedents for her much more celebrated successor, Elizabeth I, to follow.

The relationship between marriage and a woman's exercise of regal power is central to chapter 3, in this case the marriage of Anne Stuart, later Queen Anne, and Prince George of Denmark. The means by which Queen Anne negotiated the relationship with her husband in the context of marriage has never been subject to any historical analysis, yet it is crucial to our understanding of the evolution of female kingship. Her reign immediately followed that of her royal brother-in-law, William III (1689–1702), who exercised regal power at the expense of his wife, Anne's sister, Mary II, as a result of the Glorious Revolution's settlement of the crown. Unlike her sister, however, Anne reigned alone as an autonomous female ruler despite her married status. As the husbands of two English royal heiresses, William III and George of Denmark presented a spectacular contrast in the gendering of regal power within the context of marriage. This chapter demonstrates how Anne utilized her unambitious husband as a political proxy during the course of her career as a royal heiress, during which socially prescribed roles for women barred her from formal participation in politics. As the subordinate partner in a decidedly public marriage, Prince George served as his wife's eyes and ears in the seats of power that his gender and social status afforded him. But once Anne became queen, with full access to male gendered political power, she consented to the political emasculation of her husband, as she enjoyed universal recognition as a female king reigning alone. George's public role as Queen Anne's husband created the precedents for the modern position of prince consort, a uniquely subordinate male status in an otherwise still male dominant political society.

The final chapter confronts gendered problems of an entirely different nature. While the other chapters are studies of tough, tested, mature women during the course of their public careers, chapter 4 revisits the Bedchamber Crisis of the youthful Queen Victoria. As an unmarried teenaged monarch, Victoria confronted the paternalistic concerns of male politicians who did not consider her capable of fully exercising her royal prerogative. Yet, as this chapter demonstrates, Victoria took her male contemporaries in government by surprise as she capitalized on her own understanding of the strict gender distinctions between male and female social and political roles that characterized Victorian society, and brought down a proposed change of governments. The analysis of the Bedchamber Crisis presented in this chapter reveals a much more politically astute Victoria than has previously been depicted. Furthermore, the Crisis provides a previously unnoticed example of the way female kingship confronted processual changes in both government as well as gender relations between men and women in nineteenth-century British society.

Combined, the following chapters reveal a variety of strategies developed through time that established female rule as a viable form of kingship. In this process, an additional dimension of the exercise of kingship, peculiar to female kings, is uncovered.

Recent gender based studies of Queen Elizabeth I of England have pointed the way toward uncovering the historical processes at work in the gendering of female sovereignty. As the following historiographical essay demonstrates, explaining the impact of gender on Elizabeth's ability to rule has bedeviled historians for generations. As gender analysis has transformed our current understanding of Elizabeth I's ability to rule a male dominant state, so it is possible to reinvigorate the study of Elizabeth's less celebrated colleagues as female rulers, and in doing so, expand the scope of British political and constitutional history.

Elizabeth I: The Gender Queen

This book does not include an original study of Elizabeth I's reign. However, in her position as the archetype English female ruler, Elizabeth I has long crowded the centerstage among gender studies concerning the nature of female rule in England, in marked contrast to Matilda, Mary I, and Anne. She cannot and should not be removed from discussion in this study, and her reign will provide a number of reference points in the chapters to follow. However, the reader may refer to the various primary and secondary sources found in the notes of the following essay for a fuller understanding of Elizabeth I's reign. But in the meantime, a brief survey of the evolution of Elizabethan historiography will suffice to demonstrate the emergence of a model of historical analysis that adequately explains Elizabeth's singular role in English history. Indeed, explanations for Elizabeth's successes and failures through time have reflected changing perceptions of socially constructed gender roles for men and women in the public spaces of civil and political societies.[50]

The pioneering efforts of recent gender based studies of the reign of Elizabeth I (1558–1603), crown centuries of historical debate concerning her place in history. It is hardly surprising that the fabled Virgin Queen would be an obvious starting point for feminist historical studies of female rule. In light of late-twentieth-century feminist historical theories and methodologies, Elizabeth I continues to challenge historians to explain the success that her historical reputation enjoys in the popular cultures of contemporary Western societies.[51] Indeed, the historical record of Elizabeth's reign provides, to the twenty-first-century observer, an irresistible landscape for gender analyses, as the historiography of her reign graphically betrays generations of confusion and ambivalence toward the concept of female rule.

The major difference between Elizabethan gender studies and those offered in this study is that describing the impact of Elizabeth I's gender on her rule also involves explaining, or arguing against, what is usually considered a success story. Although either feminine inadequacy, or male dominant resistance to female rule has often explained the relative failures of other ruling queens, such a simple and easy approach will not do for Elizabeth I, as a number of formidable historians through time have often considered her to be the most successful also. Indeed, as David Starkey (2000) has noted, most of Elizabeth's biographers cannot help but fall in love with her![52]

Yet, in toasting her achievements, political historians in general have had difficulty squaring Elizabeth's success as queen with the fact that she was a woman, subject to pressures to reconcile acceptable female behavior with the office of king. In fact, a number of eminent scholars of Tudor history have identified this fundamental problem but lacked a methodology with which to pursue it.[53] Inevitably, Elizabeth has been described as a woman quite unlike other women, a Renaissance Athena, who emerged upon her accession as queen fully prepared to dominate the male preserve of politics, as the Goddess Athena sprang from the head of Zeus, fully possessed of the wisdom and experience that was her mythological stock-in-trade.[54] But examining her reign in the larger historical context of female rule, historians are challenged by Elizabeth to explain why she succeeded while other female rulers failed. Thus, it has become clear to feminist historians that Elizabeth, whose immense historical figure towers above the rest of England's kings, demands an historical analysis to explain her ability to transcend the limitations imposed on her gender.[55]

Long before feminist scholars introduced the term gender analysis, historians from the Victorian era to the present day have been groping for a mode of analysis that explains Elizabeth's success as a female ruler within the context of a male dominant society. Elizabeth, of course, ranks among England's greatest monarchs. However, the most successful of the male kings of England—Henry II, Henry V, or Elizabeth's father and grandfather— do not have their successes explained as unusual for the male gender. Instead, it is implicit in historical studies that successful male kings embodied male gendered virtues and abilities; only when less successful male kings lost their thrones was there a discussion of their deficiency of masculine kingly power. For this reason, scholars have not yet subjected male English kingship to any form of gender analysis. In contrast, historians throughout the twentieth century have moved toward the conclusion that Elizabeth's mastery, or lack of it, had to be explained within the context of her gender, that is, of how a woman was able to confront, manipulate, and transcend the structures of male dominated politics. This process has been under a constant state of refinement among historians since the Victorian era.

The body of historiography concerned with Elizabeth is voluminous; the sampling of works discussed in this essay was chosen to chart the evolution of gender analysis as a historical means to explain Elizabeth's ability to rule. Much of this work in the past, often by women historians and biographers, is concerned with reaching a ravenous popular audience that continues to digest accounts of the fabled Virgin Queen.[56] In these works, Elizabeth is usually cast in her most recognizable role, as a Renaissance Athena, whose mastery of politics and male politicians, usually described in rich detail, is unquestioned. Indeed, it is the very stuff that makes Elizabeth such a compelling historical figure. These writers perpetuate the conventional images of Elizabeth that have existed in Western culture for centuries: vain, imperious, well dressed, a skilled diplomat, and both an idealized romantic figure and a quasi-religious icon adored by her people.

Like popular biographers, the vast majority of historians who have written about Elizabeth I considered her reign to be a success story. This process began with William Camden, the first of a long line of historical well-wishers, whose *Annals Rerum Anglicarum et Hibernacum Regnate Elizabetha* was first published in the reign of Elizabeth's successor James I.[57] Camden did not consider Elizabeth's womanhood, as he understood it, to be a barrier to her success as monarch. Instead, Camden's explanation for Elizabeth's success drew from a variety of justifications for female rule, a process that had actually begun during the reign of Elizabeth's predecessor Mary I, England's first female king.[58] Camden considered Elizabeth providentially endowed with intellectual and leadership qualities usually denied women. Other contemporary commentators, such as John Aylmer and Sir Thomas Smith, noted that the state itself, as a mixed constitution composed of king, lords, and commons, served as a brake upon Elizabeth's womanly shortcomings, another form of justification for Elizabeth's successful exercise of regal power within male dominant political structures.[59] Camden's work still remains a valuable primary source, and its power is measured by its influence upon narrative histories of Elizabeth's reign over the course of the seventeenth and eighteenth centuries.[60] However, the progression from providential to material worldviews accompanying the European Enlightenment effectively removed the hand of God from reputable explanations for Elizabeth's success. At the same time, the gender formations resulting from the historical processes of industrialization and urbanization affected the evolution of Elizabeth's historical reputation.[61] Nineteenth-century Victorian middle class ideology detached women from the economic and productive roles that they had performed in preindustrial societies, and assigned them to the private and domestic sphere of the home and the family. Accordingly, Elizabeth's role as a queen and a woman in a material world increasingly affected historical explanations of her performance as monarch.[62] To Agnes Strickland, whose *Lives of the Queens of England* was published over the course of the 1850s, Elizabeth was examined in the same historical context as England's queens consort, and suffered in the comparison. To Strickland's disapproving Victorian eye, Elizabeth, like the Empress Matilda, displayed blatant masculine characteristics, such as intellect, cunning, and energy, in effect transgressing acceptable female behavior.[63] In contrast, Strickland sympathized with Mary I's womanly limitations, without suspecting that Mary might have consciously manipulated multiple constructions of conventional sixteenth-century womanhood in order to establish an acceptable model of female rule.

Strickland's contemporary James Anthony Froude also used contemporary notions of gender to knock Elizabeth off the pedestal of historical greatness.[64] Unable to ignore Elizabeth's female sex, Froude minimized her success by his emphasis on her natural female failings: her indecisiveness, her distaste for military glory, as well as her legendary temper. As Froude viewed historical agency as gendered male, he credited Elizabeth's ministers, particularly William Cecil, and a male dominant state, for the successes of Elizabethan England, writing, "It was not however the ability of Elizabeth, it was the temper of the English nation which raised her in her own despite to the high place which she ultimately filled."[65] Strickland and Froude used different strategies to disparage Elizabeth's performance, but both used contemporary notions of gender to accomplish this feat, placing Elizabeth in the same categories as Matilda, as a gender role transgressor, and Mary I, as a queen limited by her womanly failings.

The noted twentieth-century Tudor scholar G.R. Elton considered the first truly modern biography of Elizabeth to be Mandell Creighton's *Queen Elizabeth* published in 1899. Unlike Strickland and Froude, Creighton set out to write a success story. In doing so, Creighton detached Elizabeth from any identification with sixteenth-century womanhood, contrasting Elizabeth's abilities with those of her siblings who preceded her on the throne: the underage Edward VI, "the prey of self-seeking and unscrupulous adventurers," and the pathetic Mary I, "an appendage of Spanish power," perpetuating the conventional interpretation of Mary as the powerless tool of her husband, Philip of Spain.[66]

In Creighton's model, Elizabeth, as a woman like her sister, is just as much a kingly abnormality as her siblings. But Creighton's Elizabeth, after waiting in the treacherous wings of her sister's reign, simply bursts on the scene in his narrative, as our familiar Renaissance Athena, "exceptionally fitted to occupy the post of ruler."[67] Creighton put Elizabeth on a Victorian pedestal, reminding the reader that as a woman her success was more glorious than that of her more successful male predecessors. Indeed, references to Elizabeth being a "Queen *and* a woman" appear routinely throughout the text, without a clue as to what the phrase "a Queen and a woman" actually means.[68] Part of the problem was that Creighton was unable to see one woman as queen moving through a variety of public and private spaces, but visualized a split personality constantly shifting between performing what he perceived as the contradictory roles of ruling queen and woman.[69]

Thirty years later, J.E. Neale, in his still influential *Elizabeth I* (1934), also wrestled with the genie of Elizabeth's gender. Neale's Elizabeth was also a success story, contrasting her reign with those of Matilda's and Elizabeth's predecessor, Mary I, in a by then time-honored fashion.[70] To Neale, Matilda's historic failure to gain the crown was "nearly as decisive against a female sovereign as any Salic law."[71] Although Mary did actually sit on the throne, her reign was an abject failure, ruined by her slavish feminine emotion.[72] In Neale's narrative, Elizabeth existed in marked contrast to those earlier womanly defeats. Thus, Elizabeth's political successes are explained by her ability to rise above her supposedly biological imperfections as a woman, something Matilda and Mary were unable to do. Conversely, Elizabeth's shortcomings as a monarch are explained by other, unmistakably "natural" feminine traits. This model created heightened dramatic contrast and complexity for Neale's narrative, as he notes, "The country had already made its first experiment of a woman ruler; it was anything but a happy augury for the second."[73]

Neale delighted in contrasting Elizabeth's abilities with those conventionally attributed to women in post-Victorian social mores, citing her superlative humanist education as the primary means by which she overcame the natural limitations of her gender. So far so good, but Neale could not resist documenting initial disbelief, by Chief Minister William Cecil and Philip II of Spain, that Elizabeth could rule effectively unaided, noting that, "However they disguised their belief, statesmen held government to be a mystery revealed only to men."[74] So, bolstered by her rigorous education and keen mind, which was capable of harnessing her feminine emotions, Neale's Elizabeth emerged as the dark horse, winning the race between herself and the male politicians who wished to dominate her.

But if she won the race, Neale still explained Elizabeth's political stumbles along the way squarely on the stones of natural feminine deficiency. Echoing Creighton, Elizabeth's skill at womanly "guile and dissimulation" largely explained her success in foreign policy, while her "resolute, irritating parsimony" was the true "secret of her greatness."[75] Conversely, Elizabeth's less savory feminine characteristics also account for her failing: her lack of decisiveness and penchant for procrastination implied a decided lack of male gendered boldness and confidence. Like Creighton, Neale was unable to reconcile queen and woman in constructing his success story:

> Her reign had silenced the old blast of the trumpet against the regiment of women. Hated by her enemies, feared or loved by her subjects, at times the utter despair of her councilors—she could be all of these, but no one could deny her success.[76]

Mid-twentieth-century political historians accepted Neale's rather embryonic gendered premises, but saw no need to expand upon them any further.[77] G.R. Elton, discussed earlier, made a grand statement of his own regarding Elizabeth's greatness and its relationship to her gender:

> Elizabeth's character was of steel, her courage utterly beyond question, her will and understanding of men quite as great as her grandfather's and her father's. She was a natural-born queen as her sister had never been—the most masculine of all the female sovereigns of history. At the same time she nourished several supposedly feminine characteristics.[78]

This is a strong pronouncement on the gendered qualities of Elizabeth's rule, yet the deeper analysis one would expect from such a statement never appeared in any of Elton's voluminous studies. Instead, he makes occasional references, noting that "her parsimony has already been explained as the careful housekeeping of a poor queen," a gendered reference to a woman's "natural" abilities at housekeeping.[79] Yet Elton, noting the very same qualities in Elizabeth's grandfather Henry VII, saw no need to apply any gendered quality to his assessment of the parsimonious first Tudor. But about any problems that Elizabeth faced because of her gender, Elton is nearly silent, making only one more reference to the gendered qualities of her rule:

> Tudor rule depended in the first place on a full, even fulsome, recognition of the prince as the visible embodiment of the state. Elizabeth maintained this tradition by carefully cultivating her own appeal as a queen and a woman.[80]

Elton was seemingly unaware of the contradiction in his gendered explanation for Elizabeth's success as both masculine and feminine, and unable to explain the difference between queen and woman. Like Crieghton's, Elton's Elizabeth was a split personality, torn between queen and woman; as he concluded his brief discussion of the topic: "What really matters, of course, is Elizabeth's ability in politics—her standing as a Queen rather than her pretty obvious failings as a woman."[81]

But in the final two decades of the twentieth century the gendered aspects of Elizabeth's rule took on a much deeper complexity, as critiques of the Whig school of historiography grasped gender as an analytical weapon. In his 1988 work, *Elizabeth I*, Christopher Haigh concocted a form of historical affirmative action, and considered the particular problems Elizabeth faced as a female ruler:

> The reign of Elizabeth saw a constant testing of the political power and the political skills of the Tudor monarch. Her task could hardly have been more difficult. And she had to achieve all this despite an appalling political handicap; she was a woman in a man's world.[82]

Haigh identified three major gendered problems that Elizabeth faced. First, he recognized that she had to deal with considerable pressure to settle the succession, either by marrying or by naming a successor, both of which Elizabeth resisted doing the duration of her childbearing years. Second, he recognized Elizabeth's initial inexperience as a statesman, and her endless endeavor to compel her councilors to obey her judgments and accept her policies. Finally, Haigh acknowledged that Elizabeth was constrained by socially constructed appropriate roles for women; that "she had to find an image of monarchy that was appropriate for a woman yet which invited obedience."[83]

Haigh was much more interested in distancing himself from such wild celebrants as Neale than in articulating a gendered analysis of Elizabeth and her reign. Yet Haigh's Elizabeth is much less the success story, suggesting that it was her gender that held her back from total success. Haigh's Elizabeth is presented nearly in abstract, her personality stripped away. Instead, choices and non-choices, policies and the lack of thereof, portray Elizabeth as a conservative, suspicious, high-wire act whose very survival was the rational end in itself.

Haigh's gendered thoughts on Elizabeth occur only in his conclusion; as in David Loades's studies of Mary Tudor, such questions come as an afterthought, not to be worked into any other aspect of the study.[84] Still, Haigh offered the sense that Elizabeth's position as a woman changed through time, that she remained constantly on guard against threats, emanating from her male counselors and parliaments, to her prerogative. In Haigh's view, Elizabeth's gender served as a brake upon otherwise considerable talents as a female ruler, rather than the vague and undeveloped asset articulated by Creighton and Neale.

As Haigh injected a thoughtful consideration of gender into Elizabethan political studies, feminist historians had already begun to reassess Elizabeth's performance within the context of gender analysis. This analytic shift also questioned the "Elizabeth as success story" model; in a ground-breaking 1980 article, historian Alison Heich lambasted Elizabeth for her nonfeminist accommodation to male dominant political structures.[85] In response, Susan Bassnet, in her 1988 work, *Elizabeth I: A Feminist Perspective*, argued that understanding contemporary notions of gender present in Tudor society was crucial to interpreting Elizabeth's responses to the encroachments of a male dominant political society to her prerogative.[86] In doing so, Bassnet implicitly accused historians from Strickland to Neale of presentizing their own contemporary notions of gender and imposing them upon their assessments of Elizabeth's performance, while making the case that social history should form an integral part of Elizabethan political studies.[87]

Two works of the 1990s, Susan Frye's *Elizabeth I: The Competition for Representation* (1993) and Carole Levin's *The Heart and Stomach of a King* (1994), aptly represent the marriage of social and political history that Bassnet advocated.[88] Both scholars made their approach to the realm of politics from the beachhead of early-modern European social history and literary studies; their works attempt to flesh out those gendered categories of Elizabeth's reign, acknowledged but only hinted at, in the works of the aforementioned historians.[89] Discarding the dichotomy between success and failure that had long dominated Elizabethan historiography, Frye's and Levin's lines of inquiry explored topically the various significant gendered aspects of Elizabeth and her rule.

In Frye's work, the overriding issue was representation: how, as a woman and a female king, did Elizabeth's subjects perceive her? How did she wish them to perceive her? Frye's work explores the symbolism inherent in public spectacles and literary allegories to illustrate the complicated gendered pressures Elizabeth faced over the course of her reign. While political historians identified Elizabeth's chief problems as marriage and succession, the Protestant religious settlement, Mary, Queen of Scots, and the continental religious polarizations that led to war with Spain, Frye uncovered a constant battle, over the course of the entire reign, between Elizabeth and her ministers, parliaments, and politically concerned male subjects to construct an effective representation of female kingship. Reconstructing Elizabeth's coronation procession of January 1559, Frye identified competing representations of idealized female kingship, noting the numerous allegories presented to the new queen as she made her way from the Tower of London to Westminster Abbey.[90]

While Neale also took note of these pageants, and then moved on with his narrative, Frye deconstructed a contemporary account for its gendered language and symbolism.[91] In Frye's analysis, Elizabeth interacted with, and attempted to modify, coded messages from a number of competing sources, such as the chief guilds of London, and zealous Marian exiles wishing for a full-blown Protestant revival, who aimed to influence the future direction of her rule. These paternalistically coded messages, Frye argued, which attempted to mold the queen into the perfect female monarch, defined the public's perception of Elizabeth at the time of her accession: a twenty-five-year-old unmarried woman, obviously in need of masculine help and guidance.[92] Frye's analysis emphasized the power of ritual and pageantry in a society responsive to such measures for maintaining the authority of royal government, especially that of a female king.[93] The most revelatory aspect of Frye's analysis was her brief treatment of Mary I's attempts to mitigate the very same paternalistic challenges Elizabeth faced, casting Mary as a model, rather than a contrast, for Elizabeth's efforts to consolidate her authority.[94]

Carole Levin also uncovered potent evidence to demonstrate how Elizabeth's endeavor to maintain her authority as a female king was an ongoing, career-spanning process. To Levin, this was Elizabeth's greatest achievement:

> Elizabeth I was very skillful in how she represented herself and her authority as monarch. She was able to capitalize on the expectations of her behavior as a woman and use them to her advantage; she also at times placed herself beyond traditional gender expectations by calling herself king. Elizabeth was able to overcome the powerful resistance to her rule, and she did so by making evident weaknesses as an unmarried woman ruler into sources of strength.[95]

Levin attempted to deliver on what was only hinted at in Creighton or Neale, and ignored in Elton, namely how Elizabeth was able to reconcile being a queen and a woman. Or, more to the point, how Elizabeth was able to modify and transcend socially acceptable behavior for women as a female king.

Levin identified two main currents of representational imagery: those emanating from the queen herself to her subjects, and those of her subjects, manifested in parliament, literature, and public rumor, directed toward Elizabeth. In Levin's analysis, Elizabeth erected a formidable arsenal of tactics to ward off the numerous competing pressures present in sixteenth-century English society that were antagonistic to female rule, noting that "Perhaps the most vital question for Elizabeth at her accession and throughout her reign was whether as a woman she could rule successfully."[96] Levin stressed that Elizabeth's solution to this dilemma was to identify as closely as possible with the attributes of kingship, by countering the enormous pressure for her to marry by constructing herself as *king* and *queen* simultaneously.

In reaching this theoretical threshold, Levin reassembled the Elizabeth of Creighton, Neale, and Elton, torn between being a queen and a woman. But this process was complicated and contradictory. As Levin noted, taking on visual and symbolic aspects of kingship and queenship tended to confuse a society unused to such gender-bending tactics. Indeed, Levin questioned the conventional notion that Elizabeth enjoyed the blessings of nearly all her subjects in her performance as king and queen. In fact, the concept of an unmarried queen "transcended the traditional role allotted to women in English Renaissance society," and encountered hostility in popular culture.[97] Indeed, Levin asserted that "questions about her [Elizabeth's] sexuality were those asked the most intently throughout her reign."[98]

In their analyses of Elizabeth's gendered strategies, Frye and Levin briefly acknowledged Elizabeth's debt to her half-sister and predecessor, Mary I, as Elizabeth benefited from Mary's passage of the Act Concerning Regal Power, discussed in chapter 2 of this study, which declared a regnant queen to have the same prerogative as a male king.[99] As Levin identified Elizabeth's representation of herself as her kingdom's wife, which constituted one of many strategies to ward off the enormous pressure to marry, the analysis offered in this study identifies Mary as the original architect of this conceptualization of female rulership within the social constructs of sixteenth-century womanhood.

In the works of both Levin and Frye, a facet of Elizabeth's reign that previous scholars only hinted at emerges, of an Elizabeth keenly aware of paternalistic attempts to undermine her authority, and her own ability to adapt socially constructed gender roles, male and female, to bolster the unstable authority of a female king. Indeed, Levin's most important theoretical contribution was the conception of Elizabeth as king and queen simultaneously.[100] As both Levin and Frye suggest, Elizabeth's management of the gendered implications of her unique status was a full-time preoccupation, involving multiple competing and sometimes contradictory strategies. Indeed, Frye's and Levin's most potent contribution to Elizabethan historiography is the notion that Elizabeth had to work much harder than her male predecessors; to mitigate deeply embedded social antagonisms to female rule, and to construct sometimes contradictory representations of appropriate modes of female rule for public consumption. This process preoccupied Elizabeth's entire reign, and overlay all of the major problems identified in conventional political histories.

The following chapters open similar lines of inquiry for Elizabeth's less celebrated colleagues as female rulers, and demonstrate the relationship between their gendered problems and hers. This study, then, both anticipates and looks back to Elizabeth's reign. The first half of this study concerns the female rulers who came before Elizabeth. The problems of female representation in a male dominant feudal political society were just as daunting for the twelfth-century Empress Matilda as they were for Elizabeth four centuries later. As the chapter concerning Matilda demonstrates, identification with the male gendered attributes of kingship complicated her quest for kingly sovereignty. Similarly, Frye's and Levin's gendered analyses of Elizabeth's strategies of self-representation briefly acknowledged Mary I's own strategies, as England's first female king, which created a number of precedents that Elizabeth brought to fruition over the course of her forty-four-year reign. As she built on Mary's own arsenal of contradictory strategies, Elizabeth created a viable model of female rulership, benefiting the two female rulers who followed her. Indeed, both Anne and Victoria looked fondly back to Elizabeth's reign as the ultimate model of successful queenship.

Yet Elizabeth remains problematical as an archetype female monarch. In contrast to Matilda, Mary I, Anne, and Victoria (who married a year after the Bedchamber Crisis), Elizabeth defied social and political convention by never marrying, to the horror of contemporaries and the continued amazement of generations of historians.[101] Monarchs, male and female, married and attempted to provide for the succession, as all the other women included in this study attempted to do. In this sense, the other female rulers examined in this study all lived their lives as daughters and wives firmly within the boundaries of structural male dominance, much more so than the fabled Virgin Queen. Their efforts to stretch these boundaries form the subject of this study.

CHAPTER 1

MAKING A NAME FOR HERSELF: THE EMPRESS MATILDA AND THE CONSTRUCTION OF FEMALE LORDSHIP IN TWELFTH-CENTURY ENGLAND

She at once put on an extremely arrogant demeanor instead of the modest gait and bearing proper to the gentle sex, began to walk and speak and do things more stiffly and more haughtily than she had been wont, to such a point that soon, in the capital of the land subject to her, she actually made herself queen of all England and gloried in being so called.[1]

The first manifestation of female kingly sovereignty in English history occurred during the climax of the career of the empress Matilda, who pursued a sustained but ultimately unsuccessful bid to gain the English throne during the years 1139 to 1148. Matilda enjoyed a brief moment of glory, but as the preceding quote illustrates, one that caused contemporaries to both marvel at and condemn her exercise of kingly sovereignty. This chapter is concerned with how Matilda manipulated and transgressed the gendered distinctions existing between men and women in twelfth-century England, in her attempt to create a singular and viable public identity as a woman possessing the sovereignty of kingship.

For the first time, then, Matilda's public career as Lady of the English is subjected to a gender analysis. In the context of twelfth-century Anglo-Norman political society, defined later in the chapter, Matilda's moment of victory was a remarkable achievement. As the only surviving legitimate offspring of the third Norman king, Henry I (1100–1135), Matilda competed with other adult royal male challengers for her position as her father's heir. Like those of their Anglo-Saxon predecessors, the political structures of the Norman kings had not previously recognized a fixed rule of royal succession, much less the idea of a woman ruling in her own right over a military feudal society. In an attempt to impose a female inclusive rule of primogeniture upon the royal succession, Matilda's father, Henry I, compelled his vassals to swear solemn oaths on two separate occasions recognizing Matilda as his heir. When Henry I died suddenly in December 1135, however, his nephew Stephen of Blois raced to London and secured recognition as king before Matilda, newly pregnant with her third child, could do the same. Initially Matilda did nothing, but in 1139, once she completed her childbearing duties, she pursued a sustained effort to supplant King Stephen. While Matilda's second husband, Count Geoffrey Plantagenet of Anjou, mounted a successful military campaign to secure Normandy for their eldest son, the future Henry II, Matilda mounted one to secure England for herself.

Matilda landed in England in 1139, and gained the support of several key baronial leaders, most importantly that of her bastard half-brother Robert, Earl of Gloucester, her chief advisor and military commander. Matilda's forces soon held sway over most of southwest England. Following the Battle of Lincoln in March 1141, Stephen was captured and imprisoned in Bristol Castle, while a significant portion of his baronial leaders recognized Matilda as their sovereign lady and offered her their fealty. Matilda's possession of kingly sovereignty, however, was precarious; driven out of London before she could be crowned, Matilda's defeat at Winchester in October 1141 resulted in the capture of Robert of Gloucester. Trading Stephen for Gloucester, Matilda continued to hold court as Lady of the English in the southwest, minting coins and bestowing patronage. Following Gloucester's death in 1147, Matilda abandoned her career as Lady of the English and returned to Normandy, in effect bequeathing her claim to her eldest son.

While contemporaries agreed that Matilda was recognized as the sole source of royal authority for several months in the year 1141, historians do not usually consider her a queen regnant, a gendered conclusion that has denied her historical agency for centuries.[2] In contrast, Edward V, a twelve-year-old boy who reigned for a mere three months in 1483, also uncrowned like

Matilda, continues to be recognized as a king of England. Unlike Edward V, the powerless victim of the ruthless politics of his day, Matilda was the historical agent responsible for the strategy that allowed her a brief moment of success.

This chapter restores Matilda's fleeting and precarious possession of kingly sovereignty to its rightful place in the development of English monarchy. Recent studies of women of the European Middle Ages, in particular, those of royal women in English history, have informed the analysis presented here of the primary source material describing Matilda's career.[3] Undeniably, Matilda encountered problems of a gendered nature in the pursuit of her goals. Unlike those of the female rulers examined in the following chapters, Matilda's own historical voice is nearly absent from the body of narrative primary sources describing her career as Lady of the English.

Given these circumstances, reconstruction of the historical Matilda depends on the surviving commentary of her contemporaries. Twelfth-century sources describing Matilda's career were the legacy of a restricted political society. Medieval European Christian societies identified men and women as engaging in three basic categories of socioeconomic roles: those who fought, those who prayed, and those who worked. All of these categories are, of course, bisected by gender. Both men and women of the nonelite classes engaged in productive labor as peasants or artisans, or as merchants or fishermen, with specific economic household tasks allotted according to a gendered hierarchy. The vast majority of these people were illiterate; their knowledge of Matilda's career was communicated verbally, and we do not possess any commentary from the bulk of Matilda's English subjects, male or female.

For those who prayed, the secular and monastic clergy, the gendered boundaries of women were much more pronounced. As the Church consolidated its sociopolitical hold over the developing states of early-medieval Europe, women were excluded from the mystical rites of the priesthood. Although propertied women were able to enter convents and engage in intellectual activities, historians have not uncovered any commentary on Matilda from the severely restricted pool of educated women of the twelfth century.

This leaves the commentaries of the elite men who fought and prayed as the principal historical narrators of Matilda's career. Only one of the barons loyal to Matilda, Brian fitz Count, left a written record of his views on Matilda's rights that survives today.[4]

Churchmen, then, mostly monks, composed in Latin all the narrative sources for this period both in Normandy and in England. Monastic chroniclers, though well educated and aware of political developments, are not representative in general of the society in which Matilda interacted.[5] All of these historians possessed providential worldviews, assessing Matilda's successes and failures partly as reflections of God's judgment.[6] At the same time, as this book demonstrates, the chroniclers used Matilda's gender as a political weapon in their historical explanations. Matilda did have contemporary sympathizers. William of Malmesbury, perhaps the most learned man in the Europe of his time, was a fervent admirer of Henry I, and transferred his allegiance to Henry's daughter, dedicating his *Historia Novella*, finished in 1142, to Matilda's chief supporter, Robert of Gloucester.[7] Not surprisingly, the *Novella* offers the most sympathetic narrative for Matilda's career. Similarly, in his *Chronicle of the Kings of England*, Henry, Archdeacon of Huntington—another of Henry I's admirers—was antagonistic to Stephen's rule, and an ally of Matilda's by default.[8] Both Malmesbury and Huntington wrote their works in England, and personally witnessed many of the major events of Matilda's career. Both placed their descriptions of Matilda at the end of their larger narratives describing the continuities of English history from the Anglo-Saxons to the Normans, and identified her as a Dowager Holy Roman empress and Henry I's legitimate heir.[9]

Matilda's antagonist, King Stephen, also had his own historical well-wishers. The commentator most hostile to Matilda was the highly placed but anonymous cleric who wrote the *Gesta Stephani*.[10] The author revealed his sympathies in the work's title, "Stephen's Deeds": the work contained a politically motivated attack on Matilda's transgression of appropriate gender roles.[11] Other provincial English monastic chroniclers, writing in Worcester and Durham, provided commentary on the major events of Matilda's career in England.[12]

Across the channel in Normandy, however, Orderic Vitalis, an Anglo-Norman monk who was the author of the *Historia Ecclesiastica*, viewed Matilda primarily as a wife, referring to her as the countess of Anjou, rather than as an exalted empress or the daughter of a mighty king.[13] While Vitalis provided the most detailed account of Matilda's movements on the continent, his narrative castigated Geoffrey Plantagenet's campaign to subjugate

Normandy.[14] A conventionally Christian concern for peace permeated Vitalis's work; his enmity toward Matilda and her husband stemmed from their willingness to cause bloodshed to achieve their aims. Both Vitalis and Robert of Torigny, the Norman monk who also contributed to the writing of the *Gesta Normannorum Ducam*, charted developments in Normandy and Anjou in their descriptions of Matilda's career.

These monastic chroniclers on both sides of the channel provided the commentary on most of what we know about Matilda today.[15] The major chroniclers, Malmesbury, Huntington, and Vitalis, all identified themselves as historians, and used narrative and documentary sources to write their histories. Their works display a higher level of sophistication and critical skill than, say, the continuators of the *Anglo-Saxon Chronicle* writing during Matilda's day. As this book demonstrates, the distinguishing events and actions the chroniclers stopped to analyze and those they simply narrated reveal a curious blend of partisanship combined with gendered commentary on the place of women in twelfth-century society.

Not surprisingly, assessments of Matilda's career have been at the mercy, for centuries, of historians relying on the voices of this small group of male monks and clerics who monopolized twelfth-century historical writing.[16] Most modern historians of twelfth-century Anglo-Norman history have viewed Matilda's career from the vantage point of hindsight, and labeled it a failure, usually in the context of the examination of Stephen's own troubled reign.[17] Even in recent scholarly studies concerned with Matilda, there is little analysis of her strategy or of the impact of gender on the course of her career.

This study is concerned with Matilda's moment of success, and the strategy she constructed to arrive there. No woman before her, among either the Anglo-Saxons or the Normans, was recognized as possessing kingly sovereignty individually. While Anglo-Saxon royal women had wielded kingly power, it had been done in the name of male kings. To achieve her singular recognition as a sovereign female lord, Matilda literally made a name for herself, by constructing a self-representation that outwardly conformed to the dictates of male dominant political structures, while it suppressed her status as a wife and a mother, her official status in twelfth-century Anglo-Norman society.

Twelfth-century sources, both narrative and documentary, reveal the strategies discussed in this chapter.[18] Monastic chronicles provided the descriptions of Matilda's actions and movements allowing the reconstruction offered here of her relationship with her second husband, Geoffrey Plantagenet. At the same time, the analysis offered here of the chroniclers' political biases suggests that their gendered animosities were motivated by political expediency rather than deeply rooted structural opposition to female rule. But as all the chapters of this study demonstrate, women rulers still had to adapt to male dominant political structures. As the documentary sources used in this study attest, Matilda's use of her male kinsmen for representational purposes supplied the link with male kingship necessary to the casting of herself in the role of sovereign female lord. In doing so, Matilda adapted for her own purposes the means by which Anglo-Saxon queens justified their exercise of royal power.

Anglo-Saxon and Early-Norman Queenship

Matilda based her self-representation as Lady of the English (*domina Anglorum*) partly on the model of male derived female authority present in Anglo-Saxon England. Throughout the Anglo-Saxon and early-Norman phases of English history, kingship had been gender specific: kings were men, while queens, the wives (*conlatera regis*) and mothers of kings (*mater regis*), were, of course, women.[19] During this period, the process in which an individual became an English king varied widely, but the candidate was always male: no women in England prior to Matilda laid formal claim to the office and estate of kingship in her own right. Indeed, there were usually more than enough adult royal males ready and willing to assume the office of king under the later Anglo-Saxons, Normans, and Plantagenets.

Nevertheless, the exercise of royal authority was not beyond the reach of women. Royal women in Anglo-Saxon and Norman England wielded power derived from the familial role of the wife as the helpmate and supporter of her husband's public social and political roles.[20] The ability of royal women to do so went hand in hand with the increasing complexity of Anglo-Saxon kingship. Traditionally, early Anglo-Saxon kings were by nature primarily military leaders. During the Heptarchy, as kings battled each other to achieve the status of *bretwalda*, or overking, and unification under the House of Wessex, as those kings battled Danish Viking invaders, it was conventional wisdom that a king should be an adult male possessing military leadership abilities.

Women rarely served as helpmates on the throne or in the battlefield, but such practice was not unknown. As early as 672, the *Anglo-Saxon Chronicle* recalled, "when king Cenwealh of Wessex died, his queen Seaxburgh reigned one year after him."[21] In the early tenth century Alfred the Great's daughter, Aethelflaed, continued the House of Wessex's military campaign against Danish invaders. As Queen of Mercia, Aethelflaed ruled the midland kingdom herself following the death of her husband. Her fame resulted in another rare mention for a woman in the *Anglo-Saxon Chronicle*, which referred to her as the "Lady of the Mercians" as it recounted her martial exploits.[22] In Anglo-Saxon English, the term lady, *hlaefdige*, implied power, and was translated into Latin as *domina*, while *cwen*, which signified the wife of a king, translated into *regina*.[23] However, the legitimacy of Aethelflaed's exercise of female lordship was based on her relationships to both her dead husband and her underage sons.[24]

As Wessex subsumed Mercia and the other Heptarchy kingdoms over the course of the tenth and eleventh centuries, the Anglo-Saxon succession entailed a compatible combination of heredity and election. While the candidate needed to be of royal stock, or an *aetheling*, literally "king-worthy," the *Witanemegot*, or Anglo-Saxon royal council, usually ratified a winner displaying those martial characteristics that defined kingship in a warrior society. This meant that occasionally uncles, brothers, or cousins displaced the claims of underage sons of kings. While Anglo-Saxon queens, such as Eadgifu, third wife of Edward the Elder (899–924), often intervened in their son's succession struggles, their daughters were not conceived of as candidates for the throne, or even as possessing the right to transmit a blood claim to the throne.

Anglo-Saxon queenship itself, however, evolved into an occasional but formidable bastion of political power. As Anglo-Saxon kingship became more complex, incorporating judicial and religious functions, queenship became a role that transcended that of *cwen*, the Anglo-Saxon term that simply meant the wife of a king.[25] Borrowing from the continental practice of the Carolingians, Anglo-Saxon queens from the tenth century on frequently received a coronation.[26] Like their husbands, these women were anointed and consecrated. This sacralizing experience set Anglo-Saxon queens apart from the rest of the women and men of the kingdom. Unlike the anointing and crowning of kings, which had its theoretical basis in Old Testament precedent, the crowning of queens in early-medieval Europe had much more to do with legitimizing the exercise of female authority within the context of decentralized state power, in which the line between public and private acts was blurred.[27] Although the crowning of queens did not incorporate the taking of a coronation oath, or the acceptance of homage, it clearly placed Anglo-Saxon queenship within close proximity of the powers and prerogatives of kingship, closer in fact, than most of the men who surrounded medieval English kings.

During the eleventh century, two consecrated queens, Emma, consort of both the Saxon king Aethelred and his Danish supplanter Canute, and Edith, consort of Edward the Confessor, demonstrated the power queens were capable of in late-Anglo-Saxon England.[28] The daughter of Duke Richard of Normandy, Emma exerted a powerful influence on Aethelred's government, and represented English continuity when she married the Danish invader Canute following Aethelred's death. Following Canute's death in 1135, and the eventual succession of her son by Aethelred, Edward the Confessor, Emma continued to issue writs, charters, and other vernacular records as she had during the reigns of her two husbands. Emma's daughter-in-law, Edith, the queen of Edward the Confessor and sister to Harold Godwine, the last Anglo-Saxon king of England, demonstrated a fierce resolve to survive the internecine power struggles between her family and her husband. Both Emma and Edith commissioned written works describing their careers as queens.[29]

The effective power of queens such as Emma and Edith reflected the position of women in general within Anglo-Saxon society: women could possess legitimate economic and social power through the auspices of their male kinship relationships, especially widows, who were often able to harness the power and authority of their dead husbands as free agents.[30] Historians have also recently noticed a representational relationship between the status and perception of medieval European queens consort and the cult of the Virgin Mary, which continued to wax in popularity in the eleventh and twelfth centuries. During this time, as Christ began to be depicted in art as a crowned monarch, so Mary began to be depicted also as the crowned queen of heaven.[31] In medieval thought, Virgin Mary possessed considerable power, not by herself, but through intercession with Christ, who, as both son and consort, was the legitimate source of Mary's power. As

Anglo-Saxon queenship evolved in the tenth and eleventh centuries, the ability to intercede between vassals and king emerged as one of the most visible of the political powers exercised by queens consort. But Anglo-Saxon queens also entered the political arena in the context of defending their son's right to inherit amid a lack of consensus concerning succession theory.[32]

While such developments certainly enhanced the power and status of Anglo-Saxon queens consort, or *reginae*, they also further confirmed that political authority could only originate in a male king, dead or alive. Emma's contemporaries identified her not only as an individual holding the office of queen, but as the daughter of Duke Richard II of Normandy, as the wife of both Aethelred and his supplanter, Canute, and as the mother of kings sired by both of her husbands. Emma's kinship relations with a virtual parade of English kings allowed her to exercise political power for nearly four decades in the early eleventh century.[33] By the time of the Norman conquest, consecrated Anglo-Saxon queens were considered *regalis imperii particeps*, and *serenissima a deo coronata regina*, women who both assisted in and shared the exercise of royal power.[34] As Pauline Stafford has noted, Anglo-Saxon England possessed a body of precedent relating to the exercise of female political power.[35]

This situation did not change with the Norman conquest of 1066. William the Conqueror was keen to preserve the structure and power of Anglo-Saxon kingship, "to observe King Edward's laws," as he styled himself Edward the Confessor's legitimate successor.[36] The eleventh-century Anglo-Saxon monarchy, in a European context, was highly structured and centralized, rendering William, who remained duke of Normandy, a powerful Western European potentate.[37] Not surprisingly, in the tradition of Emma and Edith, the women in William's family also wielded political power and exercised patronage.[38] The Conqueror's consort, Matilda of Flanders, was crowned in 1168, continuing the Anglo-Saxon tradition of separate coronations for queens. Yet Queen Matilda was often by her husband's side as she participated in the ritualized crown-wearings William employed as a representational strategy to bolster his own authority as king.[39] Although Queen Matilda frequently served as regent for her husband in Normandy, she also sided with her eldest son, Robert Curthose, in his frequent quarrels with his father.[40]

William's formidable daughter Adele, who married Stephen, Count of Blois, also provides a potent example of female authority and independence of action firmly within the acceptable social parameters of a male dominant society. The Norman chronicler Robert of Torigni described Adele in glowing terms, noting that, "After the death of her husband Stephen, Count of Blois, Adela, daughter of William, king of the English, ruled the country nobly for some years because her sons were at the time less able to do so."[41] Torigny justified Adele's exercise of political power by reminding the reader that her kinship relations—to her father, husband, and sons—qualified her for this role performed on their behalf. Indeed, Adele handed over formal control of the county when her eldest son Theobald reached his majority, but continued to exert influence in Blois without ever making a claim to possess sovereignty in her own right.

Meanwhile in England and Normandy, the sons of William the Conqueror demonstrated a continued lack of consensus regarding the rules of succession. Although the field of candidates was limited to William's sons, the two youngest surviving sons both overrode the claims of the elder brother, Robert Curthose. In 1087 and in 1100, William Rufus and Henry I, each upon the death of his predecessor to the crown, seized the royal treasury at Winchester, and then hurried to London, to accept the acclamations of the Londoners and undergo a ritualized coronation. This pattern was highly reminiscent of the late-Anglo-Saxon kings, and demonstrated how the forms and attributes of Anglo-Saxon kingship continued into the Norman era.

Indeed, Henry I's 1100 accession was a conventional example of fluid Anglo-Norman succession patterns. However, as the most able of William the Conqueror's sons, Henry I wished to streamline the rather chaotic conditions of the recent past and ensure the smooth succession of his own chosen successor as king of England and duke of Normandy. To make rigid what was fluid required widespread recognition of a fixed rule of succession: Henry I promoted a system of lineal inheritance based on a firm rule of primogeniture. However, his own legitimacy as king was not based on this principle, a concept that infiltrated Anglo-Norman inheritance practices during his reign.[42] Instead, he based his self-representation as a legitimate king on a medieval hodge-podge of justifications: porphyrogeniture, or having been "born to the purple" after his father had become king of England, sacralization from his anointing and consecration, and the acclamation of the people.[43] Finally, Henry I secured papal recognition for his title, and convinced Pope Calixtus II to reject the claims of William Clito, the son of Henry's eldest brother Robert Curthose, in effect dealing a severe blow to the legitimacy of primogeniture.[44]

The most important aspect of Henry I's efforts to construct himself as a legitimate king was his choice of a wife. Matilda, or Edith, Henry's first consort, was a daughter of Malcolm III of Scotland, and a direct descendant of the Anglo-Saxon royal House of Wessex.[45] Their marriage was a gesture highly symbolic to the process of Norman and Saxon unity in England; Henry I desired this combined royal bloodline, male and female, to continue after him.[46] Matilda bore Henry two children who lived to adulthood: a daughter, Matilda, and a son, William, the *Aetheling*. In 1114, Henry's daughter Matilda married the Holy Roman Emperor, Henry V, at the age of eleven, spending the rest of her childhood and early adulthood in Germany and Italy, performing the office of empress, a title she bore for the rest of her life.

In the meantime, Henry I set about ensuring his son's eventual succession. Since primogeniture had yet to be fully recognized as the dominant mechanism to determine the succession, Henry I obtained solemn oaths of allegiance from his spiritual and temporal tenants-in-chief recognizing his son as his heir. In the case of Henry's son, the oaths of Henry's vassals to recognize William's hereditary rights seem to have been freely given. Yet Henry balked at the idea of crowning his son during his lifetime, which was a fairly common practice of continental kings for ensuring the succession of their male heirs.[47]

Henry did arrange an extremely advantageous marriage for his son, though, with a daughter of Count Fulk of Anjou. The match was the triumph of Henry's French policy, trumping his rivals, the Capetian kings of France, by arranging peace with Anjou and obtaining the county of Maine as the bride's dowry. Henry's son, William, however, drowned in a tragic accident in Harfleur harbor in November 1120. Although Henry had married again after his first queen's death in 1118, this union had produced no further issue, ending his hopes for a legitimate male succession, and a more expansive territorial base in France for his heirs.

There were other qualified male members of his family who could have been considered Henry I's heir, in accordance with late-Anglo-Saxon and early-Norman practice. Henry I was notorious for his brood of illegitimate children: one of the eldest, Robert, was a highly capable soldier and leader, loyal to his father, who rewarded him with the earldom of Gloucester. William the Conqueror himself had also been a bastard, but Earl Robert made no attempt to succeed his father, and eventually became Matilda's chief advisor, indicating the progress that legitimate heredity had gained in inheritance practice.[48] Another possible contender was Stephen of Blois, one of the younger sons of Henry's formidable sister Adele, Countess of Blois. Handsome and dashing, Stephen spent much of his life at Henry I's court, serving his uncle faithfully and enjoying his favor, including an advantageous marriage to the heiress of Boulogne. Still another contender was William Clito, son of Henry's elder brother, Robert Curthose, who operated as a pretender to Henry's throne until his untimely death in 1128.

Despite the existence of such adult male contenders, Henry I became determined not only to see the Anglo-Norman royal bloodline continue through his daughter, but also to recreate the more expansive royal lordship he had arranged for his son. Unlike France and other states on the continent, which observed the Salic law in their succession patterns, there did not exist in England any theoretical bar to female royal inheritance.[49] In 1125, after eleven years of marriage, the emperor Henry V died, leaving Matilda a childless twenty-two-year-old widow. Henry I immediately summoned his daughter from Germany, and marched her through exactly the same chain of events that he had arranged for his son to ensure her eventual succession. In 1127, Henry compelled his tenants-in-chief to swear to recognize his daughter as his heir.[50]

The oaths contained qualifications. First, Matilda was only to succeed if Henry had no further male issue.[51] Although Matilda's contemporaries did not consider her sex to be a structural barrier to her designation as her father's heir, the notion that an underage son was preferable to a capable and experienced adult woman more than implied the belief that a female heir, while acceptable, was still considered a default mechanism of the natural order of male kingship. In fact, Matilda's status as heir was predicated on her hoped-for ability to produce male heirs to succeed her in turn. Thus, Matilda's ability to forge a dynastic link between Henry I and the next generation of male heirs remained a key, perhaps the overriding, issue in her designation as heir. According to Malmesbury, Henry I stressed Matilda's legitimacy and her Anglo-Norman lineage in making the case to his barons for his daughter's succession.[52] So, in tandem with the decision to designate Matilda as his heir came the issue of her second marriage. In 1128, one year after her designation as her father's heir, Henry I married the now twenty-five-year-old Matilda, Dowager Holy Roman Empress, to her brother's brother-in-law, fourteen-year-old Geoffrey Plantagenet, who had recently succeeded his father Fulk as Count of Anjou.[53] In doing so, Henry I recreated the territorial consolidation that had been the basis of the marriage of William the *Aetheling* to Geoffrey's sister.

However, the first Anjou match involved Henry's male heir, in which the bride's dowry of Maine would be absorbed into the patrimony of the Anglo-Norman Empire. In the case of the second Anjou match, however, the genders of the bride and groom were reversed. Although Matilda's dowry included a number of strategically placed castles along the Norman–Angevin frontier, Geoffrey's relationship to his wife's patrimony was uncertain at the time of the marriage. For a number of the Anglo-Norman tenants-in-chief, who had skirmished with Angevin counts for generations, Geoffrey Plantagenet was not a palatable candidate for Matilda's hand in marriage.[54] Not surprisingly, Henry I conducted the negotiations for the marriage in secret following the first oaths to Matilda in 1127.[55] A number of barons and bishops, such as Henry's justiciar, Roger, Bishop of Salisbury, later considered themselves absolved from their oaths since they were not consulted on the choice of her husband.[56]

Despite the fears of the Anglo-Norman baronage, Matilda and Geoffrey did not enjoy a conventional aristocratic marriage in which the husband assumed complete formal control over his wife's inheritance. Henry I, in fact, never yielded the most valuable portion of Matilda's dowry to Geoffrey before he died. Matilda herself was apparently initially unwilling to marry a mere count, her junior by over a decade; Norman chronicler Robert of Torigni observed that Henry I "gave the empress, despite her reluctance, in marriage to Geoffrey."[57] Henry I's good friend Hildebert of Lavardin wrote to Matilda chiding her for causing trouble over the marriage.[58] The couple soon separated, and remained apart from 1129 to 1131, when, according to Henry of Huntington, an English great council repatriated Matilda to her husband in Anjou.[59] Malmesbury's version of the 1131 council meeting, however, assigned much more historical agency to Matilda:

> That year the empress also arrived on her native soil, and holding no small gathering of the nobles at Northampton received an oath

of fealty from those who had not given one before and a renewal of
of the oath from those who had.[60]

Although we have no record of the great council's agenda, it seems
likely that the council reminded Matilda that her position as heir
was predicated on the production of male heirs, which could only
occur if she cohabited with her husband.
If this was the case, Matilda eventually lived up to her part of
the bargain, but she took her time. Indeed, it took five years
following her second marriage before the future Henry II was
born in 1133 in Le Mans, followed by two more sons, Geoffrey, in
1134, and William in 1136. Any assessment of the emotional component of the reconciliation of Matilda and Geoffrey remains
speculation: the chroniclers are silent on the issue of whether
Matilda and Geoffrey grew to love, hate, or like each other. We do
know, from their movements and actions, that Matilda and
Geoffrey eventually arrived at a businesslike arrangement with a
united viewpoint toward the dynastic, geopolitical goals that had
dictated their marriage in the first place.[61]
The chroniclers are also nearly silent on the question of the role
that Henry I envisioned his son-in-law to play.[62] Contemporary
inheritance practices, however, suggested that Geoffrey anticipated his wife's political inheritance.[63] Already by this time Henry I
had recognized daughters of feudal tenants-in-chief as heiresses
for the purposes of bestowing patronage on his male supporters.[64]
Female wardships, in fact, were a cheap method of rewarding
faithful service, as when Henry I awarded the marriage of Matilda
of Wallingford, a wealthy heiress, to his vassal Brian fitz Count.[65]
In all of these cases, the heiress was only considered the transmitter of a heritable estate, as her husband assumed control of the
inheritance, in many cases possession of castles, a key military
function in feudal warfare.[66] The marriages of titled heiresses
brought increased political power to their husbands. One promi-
nent example from Henry I's reign was the marriage of Henry's
nephew Stephen of Blois to Matilda, sole heiress of Count Eustace
of Boulogne, which brought Stephen the political prerogatives of
rulership. By such general rules of inheritance for women as were
formulating in the twelfth century both on the continent and in
England, both of Matilda's husbands could have reasonably
considered themselves to be the next king of England following
the death of William the *Aetheling*.[67]

Despite such contemporary practices, there is little positive evidence to suggest that Henry I expected Geoffrey of Anjou to succeed him as king of England and duke of Normandy in place of his daughter. According to Malmesbury, the first oaths offered to Matilda in 1127, which predated her second marriage, made no mention of the status of her future husband, while the Worcester chronicler stated that Matilda "should receive the English kingdom under Christ's protection with her lawful husband, should she have one."[68] The second oath taken in 1131 also made no mention of Geoffrey Plantagenet; the oaths were taken for Matilda alone.[69] Nor did Henry I make any attempt to help his son-in-law build a power base in England or Normandy, or to incorporate him into the governance of either of these territories.[70] Geoffrey Plantagenet never received any patronage from the hands of Henry I, or even his wife's dowry, unlike the generous patronage King Henry bestowed on Stephen of Blois and Robert of Gloucester.

Such circumstantial evidence suggests that Henry I may very well have intended for Matilda to rule alone, at least in England, where the two successive oaths were sworn. Henry came from a family of strong women who wielded power; his mother Queen Matilda, his sister Adele, Countess of Blois, and his first wife Edith/Matilda, who often served as his regent in England.[71] Nevertheless, Malmesbury recorded that Henry I thought long and hard about his decision to designate his daughter as his heir.[72] While Henry took stock of his daughter's character and abilities, the continuation of a Saxon-Norman royal bloodline was equally an important factor in Matilda's designation as heir.[73] The combination of these two factors, Matilda's experience and abilities, and her Saxon-Norman bloodline, explain why Henry I could reasonably have envisioned his daughter as his primary political heir.

But Henry I's choice of Geoffrey Plantagenet as Matilda's second husband complicated his succession scheme.[74] Although Henry I had not arranged the match to make his son-in-law England's next king, Henry appreciated the expansive French holdings that his eldest male grandchild would eventually inherit: in the long term, the marriage was instrumental in uniting the patrimonies of England, Normandy, and Anjou, creating the various hereditary claims of his grandson Henry II, who eventually combined rule over all these territories, and, by virtue of his marriage to a well-endowed heiress, to the duchy of Aquitaine. As a number of scholars had argued, Henry I probably hoped he would live long enough to transmit his kingdom and duchy to his eldest grandson.[75]

But in the meantime, Henry's immediate heir was clearly Matilda. The nature of the oaths of 1127 and 1131, given to Matilda alone, constituted just one aspect of the growing perception of Matilda as a singular individual in the public realm of feudal politics and government, beyond the bounds of her second marriage. In the years between her marriage to Geoffrey in 1128 and her father's death in 1135, Matilda, in her public and legal representations, rarely chose to represent herself as countess of Anjou.[76] In the various charters and grants she attested or assisted in attesting, Matilda is referred to first as *imperatrix*, a reminder that she was an anointed and consecrated empress, the highest status a woman could achieve in Europe, followed by *Henrici regis filia*, daughter of King Henry.[77] It was, of course, a steep climb down the social ladder from Holy Roman empress to provincial French countess. Robert of Torigny acknowledged the discrepancy in social status, remarking in Geoffrey's defense, "it should not be considered wholly unworthy, not even by the empress herself, that she followed her marriage to an emperor by marrying the count of Anjou."[78] Matilda's solution to this problem, as her father's heir, was to ignore her status as countess of Anjou altogether, and lay stress on her more exalted position as empress and daughter. Even before her father's death, Matilda had already begun to erect a representational distance between herself and her second husband.

Not only was Matilda's social status far above her husband's, so was her experience in politics and government. During her first marriage, from the age of fourteen, Matilda had gained considerable experience in the tradition of Holy Roman empresses as active participants in the political process, enjoying the status of *consors regni*.[79] In the far-flung dominions of the twelfth-century empire, stretching from northern Germany to Italy, Matilda, on behalf of her husband, issued charters, decided lawsuits, and served as intercessor between her husband and his vassals.[80] Matilda was given high marks for her performance as empress; William of Malmesbury mentioned the reluctance of the Germans for her to return to England following her husband's death.[81] Ultimately, it was an experience that may have given Matilda the confidence to envision herself as more than just a conduit for the royal bloodline; her career as Holy Roman empress certainly gave her the working credentials for her father to consider her, not

Geoffrey, his primary political heir. Indeed, the representational value of her position as *imperatrix* and *Henrici regis filia* sharply drew the distinction in status between Matilda and her husband; in 1130, two years after the marriage, Geoffrey represented himself in a charter as "the husband of Matilda, daughter of the king of the English and former wife of Henry, Roman emperor," in effect acknowledging her superior status.[82]

It was a curious coincidence that during the eight-year period that Matilda was her father's designated heir, from 1127 to Henry I's death in 1135, two other queens regnant appeared on the landscape of European political culture.[83] Henry I was undoubtedly aware of the existence of Queen Uracca of Leon and Castile, while Matilda's father-in-law, Fulk of Anjou, reigned as king of the Latin kingdom of Jerusalem jointly with his wife Melisende, following the death of his father-in-law in 1133. As in the case of Matilda, these female rulers were designated by their fathers to succeed them because of a lack of male heirs. Marriages were then arranged with men who could defend their wife's title and provide for male heirs to continue the succession through the female line. From the available evidence, Geoffrey Plantagenet fits neatly in this model, as Henry I envisioned Geoffrey's primary role as propagator of the next generation of Anglo-Norman royal males.[84] While Uracca and Melisende derived legitimacy for their status as queens from both their fathers and their sons, they had to fight doggedly against husbands and sons to hold onto the effective political authority that each believed was also her inheritance. In all likelihood, Henry I did not receive positive reports about these female rulers. Contemporary chroniclers were generally appalled by their behavior, or chose to minimize their roles completely, but modern scholarship has demonstrated them to be wily, crafty queens, who for most of their careers remained one step ahead of the encroachments of their male relations.[85]

From what we do know of Henry I's intentions for his daughter, Matilda's designation as his heir fits within this general model coming into play in Europe. Henry undoubtedly viewed Geoffrey primarily as the father of his male grandchildren, but he must have been aware of the roles the husbands of heiresses usually assumed. Before her father's death, Matilda probably anticipated, at best, some form of joint rule with Geoffrey, or, at worst, the role of consort. During the early 1130s, Matilda and Geoffrey finally established some form of modus vivendi, as she settled into fulfilling the dynastic goals her father wished from this union. Matilda's childbearing years, from 1133 to 1136, were perhaps the most conventional of her married life, as she resided in Anjou as countess or in Normandy. It was at the onset of her third pregnancy, in December 1135, that Henry I died.

Matilda seemingly possessed much in her favor prior to her father's death; her status as legitimate heir, the oaths of 1127 and 1131, and the production of male heirs. Matilda's sons were highly significant, their existence allowed the prospect of female rule to be perceived as just a temporary detour from conventional male rule, and not a permanent threat to male dominant political structures. These factors may have been some comfort to an Anglo-Norman baronage that had sworn to uphold her as heir a number of times. However, the future Henry II was only two years old when Henry I died. For the foreseeable future, Henry's political heir was Matilda.

But for representational purposes, young Henry and his brothers provided a necessary link to male gendered sovereignty. According to the *Gesta Stephani*, even Robert of Gloucester considered Henry Plantagenet his grandfather's true heir: to Gloucester and doubtless other contemporaries, Matilda's possession of regal authority would be a form of regency for her son.[86] There was, of course, ample precedent for this form of female rule: Anglo-Saxon and Norman queens had wielded regal power in England on behalf of their husbands and son for hundreds of years. More recently, Matilda, the consort of William the Conqueror, had served as regent in Normandy, while the empress's own mother had served occasionally as regent in England for Henry I.[87] As both the daughter of kings (*filia regis*) and the future mother of kings (*mater regis*), there was ample precedent for contemporaries to perceive Matilda as a woman legitimately performing the functions of the royal office.

Narrative sources of the time are unanimous in taking no special notice of the anomaly of a projected female ruler. The Worcester chronicler blandly reported that Henry designated Matilda to succeed him "because he had as yet no legitimate heir to the kingdom," implying that Matilda herself would supply that necessary heir, while Malmesbury, as noted earlier, stressed Matilda's legitimacy and Saxon-Norman bloodline as the reasons why England should accept a female ruler.[88] Malmesbury reported that Henry I, on his deathbed, reaffirmed Matilda as his heir, while voicing his displeasure with her husband, "as he had irritated him both with threats and by certain injuries," which suggests that Henry may well have envisioned Matilda ruling in her own right.[89] Within the social fabric of twelfth-century England, a number of factors appeared to have been in place to pave the way for Matilda to succeed her father.

Lady of the English

Practical and logistical circumstances, however, overrode the factors in place supporting Matilda's succession. While Henry I had seemingly secured recognition for his daughter's inheritance, its execution within a male dominant political structure remained to be seen. Was Matilda to reign alone? Or was Geoffrey, or even the youthful Henry, to share authority with Matilda, or exclude her completely from participation in the affairs of government? While there is no evidence of contemporary comment hostile to any of these scenarios, this is not indicative of its absence; such views would have necessarily been muted while Henry I lived. But after Henry died, contemporaries debated the political rights of women.[90] Commentary cited by contemporaries in the final chapter of the Old Testament book of Numbers conceptualized Matilda's ambiguous position. As Gilbert Foliot, Abbott of Gloucester, explained to Brian fitz Count, the Lord commanded that, since Zelophehad had no sons, his daughters should be allowed to inherit his estate.[91] However, as Henry of Blois, Bishop of Winchester, pointed out, this biblical justification for female inheritance came with a qualification: the daughters had to marry within their own tribe in order to qualify for inheritance.[92] Naturally, Matilda's marriage to Geoffrey Plantagenet was open to interpretation on this count. However, Matilda's contemporaries, whether they supported her or not, did not consider her sex, by itself, as a legitimate justification for opposition to her position as her father's heir.

Matilda's bigger problem in December 1135 was her practical position as a wife and mother, rather than her abstract position as a woman in a male dominated society. As early as 1128, several of Henry I's chief supporters, including his justiciar, Roger, Bishop of Salisbury, considered their oaths to Matilda invalid since they were not consulted on the selection of her husband.[93] Apparently Geoffrey Plantagenet was quite aware of Anglo-Norman distaste for him, which cast a negative pall on Matilda's likelihood of retaining the loyalty of the Anglo-Norman baronage. As an insurance policy, Geoffrey had demanded custody of castles that formed part of Matilda's dowry on the Norman–Angevin border, which Henry I refused to grant.[94] At the time of Henry's death, Geoffrey was in fact assaulting Normandy's southwest fringe to gain possession of these strategic fortifications.[95] According to Malmesbury, Henry I was not at all pleased with his son-in-law in his final months. In fact, at the time of his death, Henry I had done nothing beyond securing the oaths to help ensure his daughter's accession, perhaps reflecting ambivalence concerning the rather conflicting consequences that arose from her second marriage.[96]

Matilda's residence in Anjou and marriage to Geoffrey Plantagenet constituted the most formidable of the logistical obstacles to Matilda's immediate succession to her father's throne. Yet Anglo-Norman historians have never seriously questioned why Matilda did not follow recent Norman practice, and immediately bolt for London to make good her claim.[97] At the time of her father's death she had only just become pregnant.[98] The chroniclers' comments are terse, but suggest that family obligations kept her in Anjou. Torigny noted that when Henry died, "the empress Matilda, whom he had long before appointed heir to his realm, was staying in Anjou with her husband count Geoffrey and her sons."[99] Malmesbury reported that Matilda had stayed in France "for certain reasons," while Orderic Vitalis reported that Geoffrey immediately sent Matilda into Normandy to take possession of a number of castles that acknowledged her as their feudal lord.[100] From the time of the death of Henry I, it appeared that Geoffrey considered the duchy of Normandy the most tangible and important part of Matilda's inheritance.[101] Although Matilda may have initially concurred in this decision, from hindsight it is clear that Geoffrey never seriously considered any attempt to acquire Matilda's inheritance in England. This was a big problem; Matilda's failure to immediately take possession of the crown in England opened up the playing field for alternative candidates.[102]

To become king of England in the year 1135 required positive, immediate action; although the theory of the king's two bodies had already begun to develop, the idea that an immediate succession occurred upon the death of a king had not.[103] Instead, an interregnum occurred, which ended only when the crown was placed on the next king's head. This had been the case with William Rufus's accession in 1087 and that of Henry I in 1100, both of whom overrode the hereditary claims of William the Conqueror's eldest son Robert Curthose. Although Matilda had received oaths to support her candidacy, the oaths in themselves did not make her king. Like her uncle and her father before her, Matilda needed to be physically present in London, to receive formal homage from her tenants-in-chief, to accept the acclamation of the people, and to be anointed and crowned in Westminster by the archbishop of Canterbury.[104]

Matilda made no effort to accomplish any of these essential goals. Undoubtedly, the state of her relationship with her father at the time of his death constituted a serious case of bad timing. At this time, Matilda may have been estranged from her father; Vitalis reported that Geoffrey was engaged in operations to take his wife's Norman dowry castles by force, while Torigny described Matilda's anger at her father for his failure to reconcile with one of his retainers.[105] The chroniclers are then silent on Matilda's movements and actions until October 1136, when she brought reinforcements to Geoffrey at the unsuccessful siege at le Sap, three months after the birth of her third son.[106]

One likely explanation was that Matilda balked at trying to establish her authority because she was pregnant, and considered such a state to be a liability in constructing herself as a viable contender for an office essentially gendered male. Matilda had nearly died following the birth of her second son in 1134; her ill-timed third and final pregnancy may very well have sidelined her from vigorously prosecuting her rights at a critical moment in time.[107] Such a theory remains conjecture, yet it is difficult to imagine why else Matilda, who must have been well aware of how her recent predecessors became kings, did essentially nothing to establish her claims in England immediately following her father's death. Three years later, when her childbearing duties were over, it was a different story altogether.

While Matilda remained on the continent, her cousin, Stephen of Blois, successfully exploited the uncertainties of the interregnum in the familiar tradition of the Norman kings. At the time of Henry I's death, Stephen was conveniently placed in Boulogne, the county in northeast France he ruled in right of his wife, also named Matilda, directly across the channel from Dover. Stephen immediately followed the same path that Henry I had in 1100. Stephen's actions had all the makings of a premeditated coup; according to the *Gesta Stephani*, Stephen's brother Henry of Blois,

Bishop of Winchester, secured the royal treasury, while Stephen's followers convinced a reluctant Theobald, Archbishop of Canterbury, that Henry I had effected a deathbed change of mind, and repented of the oaths to Matilda he had extracted under duress.[108] Instead, Stephen presented himself as the logical candidate, emphasizing his close blood relationship to the dead king, his soldierly qualities, and his acceptance by the people of London.[109] Most importantly, Stephen was the only candidate present in London; Theobald anointed and crowned him king on December 22, 1535, three weeks following Henry I's death. Stephen's accession entailed a combination of heredity and election in which primogeniture played no part.[110]

So, as Matilda's initial claim to inherit was based primarily on the oaths, so Stephen's was based on the invalidity of these oaths, which the *Gesta Stephani* insisted were extracted against the will of Henry I's tenants-in-chief.[111] No contemporaries mentioned Matilda's sex or the undesirability of Geoffrey Plantagenent as a reason for supporting Stephen.[112] In fact, most chroniclers, whether they sympathized with Matilda or not, made no comment concerning the propriety of Stephen's accession, and accepted it as the will of God; a *fait accompli* in the medieval worldview.[113] As they recorded the fact of Matilda's designation as heir during her father's reign without comment, so they accepted the results of Stephen's coup. Post-Whig medieval revisionism has stressed the belief that the idea of a definite constitution was foreign to the medieval mind; most contemporaries considered that chance, accident, and the providential will of God were all legitimate factors in the making of a king.[114] One scholar called the road to the throne a race; had Matilda chosen to run it, Boulogne was still closer than Anjou.[115] If she had not been pregnant, perhaps Matilda would have chanced the inevitable showdown. As it was, Stephen ascended the throne virtually unopposed in England.

Normandy, however, became the center of a contested succession, providing the context for Matilda's further development as an individual sovereign woman. Although Stephen secured his rule over England, he never fully gained control over the duchy of Normandy, which he only visited once as king, as Geoffrey Plantagenet immediately began its gradual conquest. At the time of Henry I's death, allegiance was divided between Stephen and Matilda, though much of the duchy initially favored Stephen, or his elder brother, Eustace, Count of Flanders. Geoffrey, however, was a tenacious campaigner; Normandy formed the base of his activities until 1144, when he was formally invested as duke of Normandy, a title which he passed on to his eldest son Henry in 1150, in recognition of his son's hereditary right.[116] Geoffrey's eventual success in Normandy was a straightforward example of a husband taking full control of the feudal inheritance of his wife, and passing it on to their joint male heir.[117] After 1138, when she began planning her to bid to supplant Stephen in England, Matilda herself played no role whatsoever in Geoffrey's endeavor to subjugate the duchy, nor did she ever incorporate the title duchess of Normandy into her royal style. Instead, it is clear that Geoffrey and Matilda split the fight for her inheritance into two distinct and autonomous spheres of influence, the duchy of Normandy and the kingdom of England.

During the second half of the 1130s, while Geoffrey hammered away at Normandy, Matilda had not lost sight of her rights in England. Fortunately for her, Stephen failed to become an effective successor to Henry I. Contemporaries and subsequent historians generally agree that Stephen lacked backbone and intelligence; in his efforts to stabilize his rule he used both moderation and firmness consistently on the wrong occasions. Although a number of magnates, including Matilda's half-brother, Robert, Earl of Gloucester, fearful for their estates on both sides of the channel, initially supported Stephen, by 1138 a number of disaffected Anglo-Norman tenants-in-chief began to perceive Matilda as an attractive alternative to Stephen. During that year, Stephen committed the worst of his mistakes, with the arrest and the confiscations of Roger, Bishop of Salisbury, and his nephews, Alexander, Bishop of Lincoln, and Nigel, bishop of Ely. By this time, even Stephen's brother, Henry of Blois, Bishop of Winchester and papal legate, joined the other high clerics in imploring the king to respect the rights of the Church, which he refused to do. As Henry of Huntington observed, Stephen had failed to keep any of the promises he had employed to gather support for his kingship, and these final acts "prepared the way for the eventual ruin of the house of Stephen."[118]

The year 1139, then, inaugurated Matilda's singular career as a candidate for the English throne. As she laid claim to a status and an office gendered male, Matilda began to exhibit a number of characteristics reminiscent of her father and her first husband, both of whom were notably unscrupulous in the pursuit and maintenance of their royal estate. Even before this time contemporaries had begun to take note of her unladylike forceful ruthlessness. Orderic Vitalis reported that during Lent, 1138, the countess's retainers captured Ralph of Esson, and handed him over to her. Matilda kept him in fetters "for a long time" until he relinquished his castles to her.[119] For the rest of her public career, Matilda generally eschewed the employment of recognizably feminine traits in her efforts to realize her goals.

Although Matilda did not balk at the use of force, her initial strategy was legalistic; in 1139 she lodged an appeal with the papal curia protesting Stephen's accession.[120] Soon after becoming king, Stephen had followed the final precedent of the early-Norman successions by seeking papal ratification for his title. The case that Matilda's envoy, Ulger, Bishop of Algers, presented, cited not only the oaths, but also, for the first time, the principle of hereditary right. In response, Stephen's representatives argued that Henry I's first marriage had been uncanonical, and that Matilda was illegitimate, a specious argument with no foundation in fact that ignored the oaths and sidestepped hereditary right. But Pope Innocent II, plied by Stephen's gifts as well as influenced by the fact that Stephen was already an anointed and consecrated king, refused to offer a ruling favorable to Matilda on the case.[121] Undaunted by the papal curia, Matilda continued to actively formulate plans for the pursuit of her royal inheritance. By summer 1139, Matilda's arsenal of justifications included the oaths, hereditary right, and, if military efforts were successful, the will of God, the ultimate form of royal legitimacy.

The man who supplied the force of arms Matilda required was not her husband, who held no interest in his wife's English inheritance, but her half-brother Robert of Gloucester, who had formally renounced his homage to Stephen in 1138. In September 1139, the pair sailed to England, landing on the Sussex coast. While Gloucester made his way in disguise to his stronghold in Bristol, Matilda sought refuge with her stepmother, Dowager Queen Adeliza, in Arundel castle. Faced with besieging his cousin while her half-brother was at large, Stephen granted Matilda a safe-conduct to join Gloucester in the west of England.[122] For all practical purposes, Matilda had left her husband and her three young sons, aged six, five, and three, in his custody. But for representational purposes, she cast herself in the role of a female *imperator*, the daughter of her formidable father.

Although most barons initially remained loyal to Stephen, Matilda accepted the homage of a number of magnates soon after her landing in England. These included Miles of Gloucester, later created Earl of Hereford, Brian fitz Count, Lord Abergenny, and, later on, Geoffrey de Mandeville, Earl of Essex. Others, such as Ranulf, Earl of Chester, Gloucester's son-in-law, remained aloof from both Stephen and Matilda, and exploited the opportunities that inevitably arose from a fractured royal authority. From her limited base in the west of England, Matilda immediately began to function as a reigning monarch, issuing writs, charters, grants of land, minting coins, and distributing patronage contingent on her ultimate success for its practical fulfillment. Matilda's arrival in England inaugurated the period known as "The Anarchy," in which barons played off the opposing sides of Stephen and Matilda, as they built hundreds of castles without royal license. These developments greatly destabilized the central royal government that had existed at the time of Henry I's death.

Once in England, Matilda styled her self solely as *imperatrix* and *Henrici regis filia* identifications stressing the authority and legitimacy of her position. To judge from surviving charters that Matilda issued between autumn 1139 and spring 1141, Matilda's public identity was analogous to that of a single woman, or a *feme sole*, since Emperor Henry V and King Henry I were in their graves.[123] Like the forceful widow of a master guildsman, Matilda began to wield power that relied on the symbolic authority of the dead men in her life. As her husband was completely absent, physically and symbolically, Matilda was in effect operating as a free agent, basing her authority on the symbolic power derived from her father and first husband.[124]

Not all contemporary observers, however, acknowledged Matilda's resourceful strategy to construct a representational model for the exercise of kingly power. For instance, the pro-Stephen *Gesta Stephani* rarely referred to her by name, but identified "Robert, Earl of Gloucester and his sister," or "those who favored the earl," and "king Henry's children," as if she possessed no individual identity or agency.[125] When the *Gesta* did acknowledge her individually, it was as a married woman—countess of Anjou.[126] Was this gendered? Certainly, but not for the simple reason that Matilda was a woman. Instead, it seems likely that the *Gesta* employed the generally recognized inferior status of women as a political weapon to minimize the importance of her as a formidable challenger to Stephen's throne.[127]

Matilda's actions in the heady events of the spring and summer of 1141, however, demonstrated her historical agency. Since the autumn of 1139, Matilda had established her suzerainty over western and southwestern England, with Wallingford as her easternmost outpost in the Thames valley. Although Matilda and Stephen maintained an uneasy balance of power over England, a number of barons were already exploiting the lack of centralized royal control by engaging in petty wars and seizing property.[128] The most notable of these castellans, as they were referred to, Ranulf, Earl of Chester, seized Lincoln castle at the end of January 1141. When Stephen arrived to besiege the castle, Ranulf captured him, and handed him over to Matilda, who confined him, first in honorable state, and later in fetters, at Robert of Gloucester's stronghold at Bristol Castle.

From February until late summer 1141, contemporary sources considered Matilda the master of all England.[129] With Stephen in prison, and Matilda the only source of royal authority, contemporaries considered that she had effectively gained possession of the crown; the *Gesta Stephani* referred to her as *regina*, as did the Worcester chronicler.[130] But, having no choice but to refer to her as queen, which usually denoted the wife of a king; there was not a living king in sight. None of the chroniclers mentioned Geoffrey Plantagenet at all in the context of England, nor did Geoffrey ever claim the title *rex Anglorum*. Thus, the chroniclers unmistakably broadened the concept of how a *regina* was perceived, and implied that Matilda was in fact a female king. In reality, this was not yet Matilda's formal status, though in the spring of 1141 the road seemed clear for her coronation, when her anointing and crowning would officially make her the monarch. So, between possession of the substance of power, and the rite of passage sanctifying it, Matilda, in her public, legal representations, assumed the title *domina Anglorum*, Lady of the English.[131]

Yet how she ranked the various styles in her charters and grants indicated just how Matilda wished to project the representational bases of her legitimacy.[132] *Imperatrix* always came first. Matilda's continued use of the imperial style made it perfectly clear that she was an anointed and consecrated empress. Because she already enjoyed this sacralized status, Matilda may have considered an English coronation superfluous, though she certainly realized the symbolic power that an English crowning would obtain for her.[133] *Imperatrix*, however, remained the key identity. In medieval Western

European hierarchical societies, Matilda's status as an empress in theory elevated her social and political status above all other men in England and France, and she clung to this identity for the rest of her life. As soon as she arrived in England, she began using her imperial seal, which pictured her seated alone on a throne bearing the inscription *Mathildis dei gratia Romanorum Regina*, to seal her charters.[134] Although English aristocratic women had begun to regularly use seals to attest charters and grants in the early twelfth century, their shapes were usually oval, depicting their subjects standing, usually with a *fleur de lies*, such as the seal used by Matilda's mother, Edith/Matilda.[135] This development was in marked contrast to the seals of male aristocrats, which usually depicted their subjects on horseback, symbolizing their martial prowess, indicating a gendered difference between male and female forms of representation.[136] Matilda's persistence in using her imperial seal set her apart from both male and female English aristocrats, creating for herself a singular form of identification that was meant to overawe her tenants and subjects.

Next in line and second in importance was Matilda's status as *Henrici regis filia*. This designation not only emphasized the hereditary nature of Matilda's claim, but also summoned the power that Anglo-Saxon and Norman queens consort derived from their royal male kinsmen as daughters, wives, and mothers of kings. As both heredity and primogeniture became widespread mechanisms for the transmission of feudal tenancies in the twelfth century, Matilda's dual Norman and Anglo-Saxon bloodline was continuously broadcast to her contemporaries in her representation as both King Henry and Queen Edith/Matilda's only legitimate offspring.

It was after these two that *domina Anglorum* followed. It is perhaps indicative of Matilda's sense of the underdog status of her position that she felt dependent on the combination of a number of styles to represent herself. In contrast, Stephen simply represented himself as *rex Anglorum*, in the manner of his male predecessors, as his authority was derived directly from God.[137] Similarly, Stephen's queen, also named Matilda, described herself simply as *regina Anglorum*, a status derived directly from her marriage status.[138] As *regina*, she had no need to summon up the status of any other male kinsman, since none could top the status of her husband. As a crowned and anointed queen, Stephen's consort held this status *dei gratia*, but this state of grace and potential substance of power was derived through a living, reigning king. In contrast, Matilda summoned the ghosts of two dead sources of royal male authority, and clearly felt the need to pile up her different representations to build as formidable a public status as was possible, while ignoring her married status as countess of Anjou.[139]

Scholars have offered a number of explanations for why Matilda chose to style herself as *domina Anglorum*. It has been suggested that she might have balked at usage of the term *regina*, which, translated into the Anglo-Saxon English *cwen*, implied the wife of a king.[140] The title queen, then, carried with it representational difficulties, as it was the office of king, not queen, that Matilda was seeking. In contrast, the term *domina*, or *hlaefdige* in Anglo-Saxon (lady in modern usage), was used to describe a woman exercising political and military power, such as the ninth-century Mercian queen Aethelflaed.[141] As some scholars have suggested, Matilda's use of the term *domina* may be related to a wider European usage, as *dominus*, or lord, described any number of public roles and offices men such as kings performed.[142] Yet another explanation is the convention of kings elected but not yet crowned using the title *dominus* during the interregnum before their coronation.[143] The title *domina Anglorum* undoubtedly drew from a number of meanings present in twelfth-century Anglo-Norman society, but all described a woman exercising power. As the Lady of the English, Matilda advertised herself as an individual woman capable of possessing and wielding regal power.

Indicative of this was Geoffrey Plantagenet's failure to adopt the style *dominus Anglorum*. Orderic Vitalis reported that Geoffrey, upon hearing of Stephen's capture and Matilda's triumph, "Came at once into Normandy, sent out envoys to the magnates and commanded them as of right to hand over their castles to him and keep the peace."[144] While Matilda enjoyed her moment of success, Geoffrey remained focused on Normandy, with no inclination personally to help solidify his wife's position in England. In fact, Vitalis further related that the magnates of Normandy offered Geoffrey the kingdom of England and the duchy of Normandy, on the stipulation that he free Stephen from the fetters Matilda had confined him, and grant Stephen his titles and honors held during King Henry's lifetime.[145]

Geoffrey was hardly in a position, though, to negotiate on behalf of his wife, as her fortunes reached their dramatic climax. At this point, the chroniclers appear very excited by the turn of events, describing the enthusiastic response Matilda received as she made her way through the Thames valley to Winchester.[146] Even the pro-Stephen *Gesta Stephani* remarked, "the whole of England was shaken with amazement."[147] By March 1141, Matilda had detached Stephen's brother, Henry of Blois, Bishop of Winchester, from his allegiance to the captive king, in exchange for confirming the rights of the Church.[148] The Bishop of Winchester, in the Cluniac tradition, strongly favored the Gregorian reforms for which his brother Stephen had no real sympathy, providing the key factor for his switch of allegiance. In contrast, Matilda was ostentatiously pious; denied the conventional male route of military service to build a public perception of social achievement, she chose the next best thing, by dispensing considerable patronage to monasteries and other religious foundations.[149] To Henry of Blois, in the short term, Matilda seemed like a much more acceptable candidate to the clergy than Stephen had proven himself to be.[150] In the first week of March 1141, the Bishop of Winchester called a general church council in Winchester under his authority as papal legate. There, the bishops and assembled magnates, recognizing Matilda's hereditary status, elected her "Lady of the English," offering their homage and presenting her with the crown.[151]

At this point, the pinnacle of her career, Matilda's status as *domina Anglorum* drew from a number of representational sources for the purposes of legitimizing her power. The triple representation of empress (*imperatrix*), king Henry's daughter (*Henrici regis filia*), and sovereign feudal lord (*domina Anglorum*) in her charters, starting in April 1141, was composed of two-thirds authority derived from male kinsmen, and one-third authority that did not originate anywhere else than from Matilda's reaching for and gaining recognition for possessing the crown. Legitimizing bases for Matilda's authority also formed their own trinity: the oaths given during her father's lifetime, the theory of a female inclusive rule of primogeniture, and God's blessing inherent in successful conquest.[152] The magnates and prelates at Winchester elected Matilda their lady based on a combination of all these factors, while her status as a woman proved no bar to her recognition as a female king. Indeed, Matilda's status as *imperatrix* and *Henrici regis filia* conformed to and reproduced the symbolic means by which previous English queens drew their power. This was sufficient to solidify Matilda's position as *domina Anglorum*, a status transcending these male derived forms to reflect the effective power base Matilda had constructed for herself alone; none of the chroniclers mentioned Geoffrey Plantagenet or her son Henry in their descriptions of her Winchester election. During spring and summer 1141, Matilda effectively performed the role of king. In a grant of land to Reading Abbey, Matilda was described as *imperatrix, Henrici regis filia*, and *Anglorum regina*.[153] Other grants, such as the confirmation of the possessions of Glastonbury Abbey also designated her *Anglorum regina*.[154] By describing Matilda as *regina*, contemporaries quite suddenly broadened the perception of what it meant to be a queen. Since England already had a queen, also named Matilda, sources identifying the Empress as queen tacitly acknowledged that Stephen and his consort were deposed. Most of the documentary evidence from this time, however, identified Matilda as *Anglorum domina*. Even so, in an enumeration of liberties granted to the Abbey of St. Benet, Matilda referred to *regni mei* and *coronae meae*: my kingdom, my crown.[155] As a number of scholars have suggested, Matilda might have anticipated her coronation with the use of the title *regina*, but she still considered herself to be in practical possession of the substance of power.[156]

During this time, a number of contemporary narrative sources agreed that Matilda's sudden and unexpected success went straight to her head. Matilda's most renowned modern biographer has suggested that "conduct acceptable in a powerful king . . . was not acceptable in a 'Lady of the English'."[157] This line of reasoning can be taken quite a bit further. It is clear that contemporaries expected Matilda to emulate the behavior of those women who had previously held the rank of *regina*, and act like a queen consort while performing the office of king. Most queens consort, however, did not have to consolidate recognition of their position as Matilda was constrained to do. Nearly all the chroniclers who had marveled at her assumption of power turned on her immediately.[158] Not surprisingly, the *Gesta Stephani* took the greatest exception:

> She at once put on an extremely arrogant demeanor instead of the modest gait and bearing proper to the gentle sex, began to walk and speak and do all things more stiffly and more haughtily than she had been wont.[159]

But other more sympathetic chroniclers also joined this chorus of disapproval: Henry of Huntington described her as "elated with insufferable pride" while the Worcester chronicler noted her "hard heart" as she strove to consolidate her position.[160] Had she been a man, Matilda's decidedly authoritarian style might have passed for a regal show of strength. Indeed, Matilda probably felt that if she was to hold on to her newly acquired status, she needed to behave like a king. Thus, Matilda's forward movement from recognition of her status to the execution of her office was fraught with gendered difficulties concerning how a woman ought to conduct herself.

Four hundred years later, Mary I, and to a much greater extent, Elizabeth I, found the means to combine recognizable attributes of kingship and queenship in their construction of female rulership. Either it did not occur to Matilda to add a component of queenly femininity to her construction of female kingship, or she felt she had compelling reasons to seek a nearly total identification with the attributes of kingship. Despite the claims of contemporary observers, who credit Matilda with wielding authority over all of England in the spring of 1141, Matilda's actual effective jurisdiction was precarious, centered in the south and west, while London still had not recognized the authority of the "Lady of the English." So, Matilda's Winchester election did not automatically make her a female king; she needed to occupy London and undergo a coronation at Westminster Abbey.

As she anticipated her crowning, Matilda strove to consolidate her dynastic claims and establish her authority. It seems reasonable to suppose that Matilda looked to her father and her first husband for examples of successful kingship as she did for representational purposes. Both Emperor Henry V and King Henry I were suspicious, uncompromising, relentless, and ruthless in the pursuit of their aims. Probably both would have advised Matilda to follow their example. This was exactly what St. Bernard told Queen Melisende of Jerusalem following the death of her husband: "show the man in the woman; order all things . . . so that those who see you will judge your works to be those of a king rather than a queen."[161] Much of Matilda's behavior during the spring and summer of 1141 can be explained as the emulation of male gendered kingship. But kings had the built-in advantage of female consorts to soften the more hardboiled aspects of their rule; Matilda had played that very role herself for her first husband. Nevertheless, in 1141, Matilda eschewed the feminine aspects of queenship completely, in effect negating what could have been useful symbolism to bolster the construction of her authority. But for Matilda to be perceived as a soft, forgiving, and gentle woman at the one moment she needed to consolidate her position at the top of a male dominant political society would not have been practical.

But by constructing herself as a female feudal lord, and emulating male gendered kingship, Matilda annoyed contemporary observers. The chroniclers' hostility may have been due to the fact that Matilda was claiming kingly sovereignty for herself alone, and not in association with either her husband or her eldest son. The *Gesta Stephani* described Matilda as not only arrogant, but also spurning the advice of her chief advisors, the earl of Gloucester, her uncle King David of Scotland, and the "kingmaker" himself, the Bishop of Winchester.[162] The *Gesta* implied that if Matilda had behaved as a deferential woman, and heeded the counsel of her male advisors, she could have devised a means to permanently depose Stephen, and be crowned and anointed in his place. The *Gesta* placed Matilda's ultimate failure at her own door, blaming it on her arrogant reliance on her inferior, womanly intellect and emotions. In contrast, the *Gesta* lavished praise on that other Matilda, Stephen's consort, describing her as "a woman of subtlety and a man's resolution," who undertook military resistance to the empress.[163] By stressing Queen Matilda's devotion to King Stephen, the *Gesta* justified her transgression of male gender roles, since her actions were performed on behalf of her husband:

> The queen, expecting to obtain by arms what she could not by supplication, brought a magnificent body of troops across in front of London from the other side of the river and gave orders that they should rage most furiously ... in the sight of the countess and her men.[164]

While Queen Matilda's army raged across the Thames, the Empress Matilda was negotiating with the Londoners for their supplication and her entrance into the city for her coronation.

Matilda's coronation, however, never took place. Contemporaries offered a number of explanations why. Malmesbury, after remarking on the excellent job Robert of Gloucester was doing to help establish the authority of his sister, records that the "ever suspicious and murmuring" Londoners launched a surprise attack on Matilda, who made her escape in the nick of time.[165] Malmesbury did not comment on Matilda's behavior, but lambasted the "secret indignation" of the Londoners as they "gave vent to expressions of unconcealed hatred."[166] Henry of Huntington, more vague than Malmesbury, offered a more conventionally medieval explanation:

> Therefore, either by some secret conspiracy, or the providence of God—indeed, all human affairs are directed by providence—she was driven out of London. In revenge, with a woman's bitterness, she caused the Lord's anointed to be bound with fetters.[167]

The Worcester chronicler, however, offered a more temporal explanation for the Londoners' change of heart. After dismissing Queen Matilda's plea to free her husband, the Empress also refused the bishop of Winchester's request to grant Stephen's son Eustace the honors his father held during King Henry's time. But these decisions had nothing to do with the attitude of the Londoners:

> The lady was asked by the Londoners that they might be allowed to live under the excellent laws of King Edward, and not the oppressive ones of her father, Henry. She did not listen to good advice but harshly rejected their petition, and there was great disorder in the city.[168]

Finally, the author of the *Gesta Stephani*, that arbiter of appropriate womanly behavior, offered a materialistic explanation for the Londoner's rejection of the "Lady of the English." After summoning London's wealthiest citizens before her, she demanded a tax, "not with unassuming gentleness, but with a voice of authority."[169] After listening to the Londoner's objections,

> She, with a grim look, her forehead wrinkled into a frown, every trace of a woman's gentleness removed from her face, blazed into unbearable fury, saying that many times the people of London had made very large contributions to the king, that they lavished their wealth on strengthening him and weakening her[170]

Matilda's hard-line stance, acceptable in a male king, bothered the authors of the Worcester chronicle and the *Gesta*, suggesting that contemporaries were confused by what they wanted the "Lady of the English" to do, indicating that, as a woman and a *domina*, she should behave gently like a queen rather than forcefully like a king. Combined, all the chroniclers, with the exception of Malmesbury, suggested that Matilda should have used the intercessory powers of queenship to set Stephen free, moderated the harsher aspects of her father's rule, and excused the Londoners from financial support. Although a more diplomatic approach might have helped, freeing Stephen at that moment in time would have realistically served no practical purpose in establishing Matilda's authority. And, in denying Eustace his inheritance, Matilda was only imitating the efforts of her father, Henry I, who also dealt harshly with challengers to his throne. Henry I kept his elder brother Robert Curthose in prison until he died, and prevented his nephew, William Clito, Curthose's heir, from gaining any aspect of the Anglo-Norman inheritance. Matilda wished to convince her contemporaries that she was quite capable of being a king, but their reactions betrayed hostility toward her as a woman presuming to establish kingly authority.

Matilda's timely escape from the clutches of the angry Londoners in May 1141 represented the climax of her career as *domina Anglorum*. Soon after, Stephen's brother, the Bishop of Winchester, renounced his homage to the Empress. According to Malmesbury, Matilda's refusal to grant Eustace his inheritance "enraged" the bishop. Meeting with Queen Matilda, whom Malmesbury simply referred to as "his brother's wife," Winchester was "influenced by her tears and offers of amends," and agreed to switch sides once again.[171] Although the *Gesta Stephani* also mentioned Queen Matilda's "tearful supplications," the author considered Stephen's queen legitimately possessed with a historical agency that he resolutely refused to grant to the Empress:

> The queen was admitted into the city by the Londoners and forgetting the weakness of her sex and a woman's softness she bore herself with the valor of a man.[172]

The preceding passages suggest that the chroniclers used gender as a political weapon in assigning historical agency to both Matildas. While the Empress was criticized for an unfeminine-like uncompromising stance, the queen was praised for rising above the limitations of her gender to aid her husband.

The Bishop of Winchester's defection was a major blow, as was Matilda's failure to be crowned and anointed. Although her coronation was delayed until she could reenter London, Matilda's military strength remained stable; the Worcester chronicler claimed

the Empress's forces continued to wax in strength.[173] Queen
Matilda, however, possessed a powerful mercenary army led by
William of Ypres, while the bishop of Winchester rallied support
for his brother among the baronage. On August 1, Matilda made
her way back to Winchester for the inevitable showdown. Finding
the town closed to her, she took up residence in the castle, while
the bishop of Winchester ordered a siege against the city.[174]
Although contemporaries offer conflicting accounts of just what
went on during this month and a half siege, by September 14, the
Empress had taken flight to Devizes, while Queen Matilda's forces
captured the earl of Gloucester.[175] Yet in this moment of adversity,
contemporary observers once again returned to the Empress's
side, applauding her courage and resolve; even the author of the
Gesta Stephani belatedly acknowledged her historical agency,
remarking that "The Countess of Anjou herself, (who) was always
superior to feminine softness and had a mind steeled and unbroken
in adversity."[176]

For all of Matilda's attempts to construct herself as a sovereign
feudal lord, the deal struck to trade King Stephen for Robert of
Gloucester betrayed her dependence on the military expertise
only men could supply. With Stephen at liberty, Matilda's state of
affairs was returned to the stalemate that had existed before
Stephen's capture; the "anarchy" continued until 1154, with
Stephen's death and the accession of Matilda's son, Henry II.[177]
Matilda herself maintained her status in England as *domina
Anglorum* until early 1148, when, following the death of Robert of
Gloucester in 1147, she returned to Normandy.[178] By this time, no
other moment had arrived for her such as that glorious spring and
summer of 1141, yet she maintained an unstable and shrinking lord-
ship in the west of England until her departure for the continent,
when she, in effect, bequeathed her royal claims to her eldest son.

Matilda had already begun to associate young Henry in her
grants of patronage before the rout of Winchester. Sometime in
the late summer of 1141, Henry, then aged seven, confirmed his
mother's grants in a charter, referring to her as *domina mea* and
mater mea imperatrix, in effect acknowledging her possession of
sovereignty.[179] But following Stephen's liberation, the relationship
between Matilda and her son as implied in her charters evolved
into a partnership. This was a fairly common practice for
European female rulers, but Matilda only resorted to it after
victory had been snatched from her. In 1142, in fact, Robert of

Gloucester borrowed young Henry from Geoffrey Plantagenet and brought him to England, in the hope that the physical presence of Henry I's eldest grandson could bolster support for the Empress's stalemated condition.[180] Thus, in her final years in England, Matilda increasingly associated herself in her public acts and grants of patronage with her eldest son. By 1144, Matilda and Henry began to jointly issue charters, signifying themselves as *Anglorum domina* and *filius ducis Normannorum* respectively, a retreat from the bold, solo persona she had previously constructed, but one that did not challenge her claim to sovereignty, as Henry simply signed himself the son of the duke of Normandy.[181] Instead, as her fortunes sagged over the course of the 1140s, Matilda moved toward identification with that more traditionally recognizable female role, of a queen who is also the mother of a king.

By 1147, Henry, then fourteen, had assumed control of military efforts to secure his mother's inheritance, as Matilda abandoned all hope of supplanting Stephen in England as a female king. While she dropped *domina Anglorum* from her royal style, she still declined to incorporate duchess of Normandy or countess of Anjou into her public representations. Instead, she remained, for the rest of her life, *Mathildis, imperatrix* and *Henrici regis filia*. Although her husband lived until 1151, Matilda enjoyed a mostly independent existence outside the bonds of marriage after 1139, when she had commenced with her bid to supplant Stephen.[182] In 1154, Matilda gained the "success" historians usually ascribe to her, when her son Henry succeeded Stephen as king of England, according to the terms of the Treaty of Westminster. Although the treaty implicitly recognized Matilda's right to transmit a hereditary claim to the Anglo-Norman throne, it bypassed her own claim completely.

It is entirely possible, that Matilda's "success" was tinged with regret for the failure of the enterprise occupying the most productive years of her life. Yet Henry II, the greatest of England's medieval kings, seemed to have inherited both the martial abilities of his father, who conquered Normandy, and the political creativity of his mother, who had kept alive the struggle for England. Indeed, Matilda's transition from *domina Anglorum* in England to *mater regis* in Normandy did not diminish her political influence, as Henry II employed his mother's intelligence and experience as an informal justiciar in Normandy.[183] In the years of her widowhood, until her death in 1167, Matilda enjoyed the more traditional role of *mater regis*, which accorded her the necessary male kinship relationship to render her practical authority unquestioned. Even at the time of her death, Thomas Becket appealed to Matilda's intercessory powers to effect a reconciliation with her son.[184]

Such a role was very much within acceptable bounds of womanly political power in medieval England. Indeed, Matilda lived most of her life within the conventional and structural confines of male dominance, first as a daughter, marrying in succession, an emperor and a count, to fulfill her father's diplomatic and territorial goals. At the end of her life, with her son as king of England and duke of Normandy, Matilda enjoyed the status of a de facto dowager queen, wielding power in the name of Henry II. But for nine years, from 1139 to 1148, as a woman both conversant and experienced in the socially constructed gender roles of men and women, Matilda utilized the conventional representations of men and women to transcend the limitations of her gender and construct an image of independent female lordship.

That Matilda's moment of triumph in the spring and summer of 1141 did not translate into permanent possession of the crown in no way discounts her achievement. While a long train of historians may well be correct in concluding that twelfth-century England was full of men resistant to the concept of female rule, the reasons Matilda failed to be crowned and vanquish her supplanter were not solely the cultural dictates of a patriarchal society. As England's twelfth-century succession patterns were fluid, the element of timing was an essential ingredient that eluded Matilda upon her father's death, as Stephen won the race to London that she herself refused to run, in all likelihood because of her pregnancy. When she did decide to challenge Stephen, Matilda constructed a public persona outwardly conforming to male dominant political structures. Signifying herself as Empress and king Henry's daughter, Matilda presented an image of female power drawing legitimacy from the history of English queenship. The title Lady of the English, however, signified singular possession of kingly power bearing no relationship to fathers or husbands, dead or alive.

The birth of English female sovereignty confronted gendered antagonisms in its practical application. The *Gesta Stephani* and other contemporary sources noted with disapproval the Empress Matilda's unfeminine approach to consolidating her position as *domina Anglorum*, while praising queen Matilda's manly efforts to aid her husband, suggesting that the chroniclers used gender norms as a political weapon in the construction of their narratives.

Despite her ultimate failure, Matilda's willingness to scale the practical and logistical barriers that came between her gender and the fulfillment of her goals identifies her as an active historical agent, and a major player in English medieval political society. As the following chapters reveal, Matilda's gendered problems in constructing a viable model for female rule within a male dominant political structure returned in full force four centuries later.

Chapter 2

Her Kingdom's Wife: Mary I and the Gendering of Regal Power

We do signify unto you that according to our said right and title we do take upon us and be in the just and lawful possession of the same; not doubting but that all our true and faithful subjects will so accept us, take us, and obey us as their natural and liege sovereign lady and Queen.[1]

In her accession proclamation, issued July 19, 1553, Mary I announced to her subjects the arrival of the first woman to possess and inhabit the office and estate of king of England. Prior to Mary's accession, English kings, as "lions of England," occupied a male gendered office. Mary, in effect, accepted this state of affairs as she fashioned herself into a lioness. Four hundred years after the Empress Matilda's failed attempt to consolidate her hold upon kingly sovereignty, Mary I accomplished the gendering of kingly power in the guise of a queen, representing herself to her subjects as monarch within conventional perceptions of sixteenth-century womanhood.

In the January of 1554, facing a formidable rebellion against her authority as queen, Mary declared herself to be her kingdom's wife.[2] The motivations for this strategy, which are discussed in this chapter, demonstrate how Mary I constructed a representational model for female kingship. Because she assumed the throne in her own right as a single woman, contemporaries recognized that Mary's possession of the crown had freed her from all common law restraints placed upon women. Political theory accommodated this recognition with little difficulty, as embodied in the emergent concept of the king's two bodies, which recognized an eternal, corporate, and, with Mary's accession, a genderless "body politic," which combined with the flesh and blood "body natural" of the monarch.[3] Although Mary's "body politic" was symbolically wedded to her kingdom, her "body natural" came to the throne unmarried, at the age of thirty-seven. As a woman, it was up to Mary's natural body to produce an heir for her political one. Thus Mary was constrained to take another husband, a conventional, flesh-and-blood one, so that she could fulfill the most basic function of hereditary kingship: the propagation of the dynasty.

This chapter is concerned with Mary's efforts to establish an acceptable representation of kingly sovereignty in the year between her accession and marriage to her Hapsburg cousin, Philip of Spain, in July 1554. Mary's perception as her kingdom's wife was just one of several strategies she devised to create a viable perception of a woman performing the office of king. This was a noticeable shift from the representational strategy of Mary's ancestor, the Empress Matilda. In the twelfth century, on the brink of her success, Matilda behaved like a male king, only to be roundly criticized for her gender transgression of a male gendered office and estate. The analysis offered in this chapter suggests that Mary sought to mitigate the social and political contradictions inherent in the concept of female rule, of the "monstrous regiment of women," as proclaimed loudly by a host of writers during her reign, as she sought to incorporate multiple constructions of sixteenth-century womanhood within the office of king.[4] During the first year of her reign, Mary constructed a number of gender blending representational identities, which allowed her to establish herself as an autonomous female ruler and take a powerful foreign prince for a husband.

As this chapter demonstrates, Mary did her best to cloak her possession of the crown in the trappings of an obedient and deferential woman, outwardly conforming to the didactic dictates of patriarchal Tudor political society. But behind the scenes, Mary I functioned as king of England. Although Mary never referred to herself directly as a king, she occasionally felt constrained to remind her subjects that she, as a woman, was in full possession of kingly power, "as others our most noble progenitors have heretofore have been".[5] These processes, outlined in this chapter, entailed the construction of a model of female kingship. It was the most durable achievement of Mary I's short and troubled reign. Mary's five-year reign endured bad harvests, demographic disaster, religious strife and persecution, and runaway inflation, problems that taxed the resources and abilities of Mary and her government severely. As England's first female king, Mary faced all these problems plus the additional one of creating an acceptable model of gynecocracy, or female rule, over a male dominant political culture.

As we have seen in the previous chapter, systems of male dominance in the public sphere of politics and government did not preclude the exercise of female power. From powerful, well-entrenched widows to Tudor queens consort, women exercised political and economic power over men, often in the context of their familial relationships to powerful men.[6] The question, then, is not whether a woman could exercise power in Tudor political society, but how she went about doing it. Indeed, an explanation for how Mary negotiated and achieved recognition as an autonomous female ruler has only recently begun to infiltrate the historiography of her reign. While the examples provided in this chapter all appear in the primary sources concerned with her reign, they remain scattered and uncollected in the works of modern historians, identified as either unusual bursts of energy or quaint examples of feminine deficiency, that do nothing to dispel the conventional interpretation of Mary's mediocre performance as monarch.[7]

From the time of her death in 1558, historians have generally considered Mary I, as well as her predecessor and half-brother, Edward VI, as "minor" Tudors, monarchs not in control of their reigns, which served as stormy interludes between the more glorious reigns of Henry VIII and Elizabeth I. Mary's reign was nasty, brutish, and short, and no amount of gender or other analysis can remake her into a great monarch. Derived from John Foxe's fiery pen, the historical reputation of "Bloody Mary" as a persecutor of Protestant martyrs served as dogma for the Whig tradition of historical analysis, a tragic counterpoint to the much more glorious subsequent reign of Elizabeth I, who, in Whig political theology, represented a monarch much more in tune with the true progression of religion in English history.[8]

Although religiously inspired assessments of Mary's public career as a female king have not been salutary at the hands of generations of historians, her more private life as a pious, generous, and loving woman and friend has long provided the dichotomy that has allowed popular biographers to create sympathetic portraits of a brave, stout-hearted woman swamped by her initial foray into the male dominant public sphere of politics.[9] However, the conventional image of Mary as a total political failure has been challenged in the last thirty years.[10] Particularly in the last ten years, a number of historians have identified Mary's attempts to address and resolve the gendered ambiguities surrounding the accession of a female monarch as a historical problem worth investigating.[11] Although none of them has produced a monograph, these scholars have demonstrated that mid-sixteenth-century English culture and political society considered the advent of a female ruler an extraordinary and unstable concept that needed to be fleshed out and defined in acceptable terms.

The interpretation offered here presents a multifaceted and complex depiction of Mary's abilities as a politician, as wildly erratic representations of womanhood were joined with royal proclamations and parliamentary statutes that ultimately created a wide-ranging and distorted view of female rulership. Indeed, this chapter suggests that Mary consciously created a kaleidoscope of regal representations, in an effort to address and confront all the various gendered challenges to female rule present during her reign.

As with the contemporaries describing the Empress Matilda's tenure as Lady of the English, men composed the political society providing commentary on Mary's first year as queen. However, sixteenth-century commentators represented a much more broad-based and literate political society than the small circle of twelfth-century monastic chroniclers who provided the history of Matilda's career. In this chapter we hear the opinions and commentary of Mary's privy councilors, foreign ambassadors, the members of her parliaments, as well as those of her politically informed subjects. These commentators recorded Mary's own words in their chronicles, pamphlets, and letters, while the queen's royal proclamations and parliamentary statutes reveal an even more direct exposition of her efforts to construct female gendered kingly authority. Taken together, the analysis in this chapter demonstrates how Mary I transformed her political inheritance into the reality of female kingship.

The Concept of Female Rule in England: 1148–1553

Mary I's 1553 accession was due primarily to a lack of viable male Tudor heirs, but it also benefited from four hundred years of occasional precedents bolstering the position of royal female inheritance rights. In the four hundred years following the career of the empress Matilda, royal inheritance through the female line situated itself in the English constitution. Yet for much of this time the concept was dormant, as primogeniture emerged as the primary, but not sole, determinant of the royal succession. This mechanism did not exclude women, as Matilda's precedent made abundantly clear, but from the accession of Henry II in 1154, to the forced abdication of Richard II in 1399, a nearly unbroken line of Plantagenet males succeeded by a lineal progression of primogeniture.[12] Even so, a curious incident from the reign of Edward I (1272–1307), in which the king extracted an oath from the husband of his younger daughter to safeguard the succession rights of his elder daughter, reconfirmed recognition of a female inclusive rule of succession.[13]

A century later, the accession of the Lancastrian Henry IV in 1399 derailed the strict hereditary succession of the crown, and renewed the question of the succession rights of royal heiresses. At the time of his deposition, the childless Richard II recognized as his heir his cousin, seven-year-old Edmund Mortimer, Earl of March, the grandson of Philippa of Clarence who was the heir of Lionel of Antwerp, the second eldest son of Edward III (1327–1377).[14] However, March's succession rights were swept aside in the popular reaction against Richard II, which brought about the accession of Henry IV, the heir of Edward III's third eldest son, John of Gaunt.

In the big picture, though, fourteenth- and fifteenth-century England routinely disposed of unacceptable kings, regardless of their hereditary legitimacy. While Henry V's success in ruling enhanced the legitimacy of the House of Lancaster, Henry VI's (1422–1461) failure called it into question. By 1453, the loss of Lancastrian France, the utter poverty of the crown, and the lack of a male heir once again opened up debate on the succession. Three years earlier, the Speaker of the House of Commons was thrown into the Fleet prison for a motion on the floor of the Commons to recognize Richard Plantagenet, Duke of York, Philippa of Clarence's direct heir, as Henry VI's successor.[15] In 1460, York made explicit his superior royal claim derived through the female line, as he told a Yorkist dominated parliament, "though right for a time rest and be put to silence, yet it rotteth not nor shall it perish".[16]

While modern scholarship has clearly demonstrated that the Wars of the Roses (1455–1487) entailed much more than the purely dynastic struggle chronicled by sixteenth-century Tudor propagandists, the succession rights of women was at the core of the House of York's claim to the throne.[17] In 1461, Yorkist claimant Edward IV deposed the decrepit Henry VI. In turn, after the Lancastrian male royal line was extinguished at the Battle of Teweksbury (1471), unreconciled Lancastrians turned to Henry Tudor, Earl of Richmond, the son of Margaret Beaufort.[18] Tudor's chances of gaining the crown were remote until the death of Edward IV in 1483, when Edward's brother, Richard, Duke of Gloucester, usurped the crown. This act, and the subsequent disappearance of the sons of Edward IV, fractured the House of York, allowing support to mushroom for Tudor, a Lancastrian exile in Brittany since 1471. When Henry Tudor invaded England in August 1485, and Richard III was killed during the Battle of Bosworth Field, Tudor was proclaimed king by the judgment of God.

The House of Tudor

As the third usurping king of the fifteenth century, Henry VII needed more than God's blessing to stabilize a monarchy whose effective authority had been compromised by dynastic struggle. It was the succession rights of women, in fact, that lent a considerable bolster to Henry's legitimacy as king. Before his accession, Henry VII had vowed to marry the eldest daughter of Edward IV, Elizabeth of York, to unite the bloodlines of York and Lancaster. But Henry was careful not to marry the heiress of York until after the meeting of his first parliament, which ratified his title, and the right of his heirs, male and female, to inherit. However, the hereditary nature of Henry's title was ambiguous: his mother, a Lancastrian heiress, and his wife, a Yorkist heiress, both possessed superior hereditary claims to his own. Instead, as an adult male, Henry informally absorbed the hereditary rights of his kinswomen in a straightforward common law fashion.

Unlike their Plantagenet forebears, the Tudors had problems producing male heirs capable of surviving to maturity, which made female succession rights a primary dynastic issue throughout the first half of the sixteenth century. Henry VII's eldest son, Arthur, died at the age of sixteen in 1502, shortly after his marriage to the

Spanish princess Catherine of Aragon. This left the Tudor dynasty hanging by the thread of Henry's only surviving son, the future Henry VIII. Henry VIII (1509–1547) was, of course, famous for many things, including his six wives, and the English Protestant Reformation, both rooted in his intense desire to be succeeded by a male heir of his body. Henry's first wife was the Spanish princess, Catherine of Aragon, the widow of his elder brother. All of Catherine's sons were either stillborn or died soon after birth; only a daughter, Mary, born in 1516, survived. By the middle of the 1520s, it was clear that Queen Catherine had entered menopause. In 1527, Henry VIII began exploring the option of divorcing Catherine, so that he could marry his mistress, Anne Boleyn, and obtain direct male heirs.

Until the passage of the First Act of Succession in 1534, which removed her from the succession, Princess Mary constituted her father's heir.[19] This anomalous status did not deter negotiations for her marriage, which commenced soon after her birth. For most of the sixteenth century, England constituted a second rate European power; Henry VIII's continental diplomacy shuffled routinely between support for France, England's perennial enemy, and the polyglot empire of Catherine of Aragon's nephew, Charles V, King of Spain and Naples, Duke of Burgundy, and Holy Roman Emperor.[20] As a small child, Mary was first betrothed to the French dauphin, and, in the early 1520s, to her Hapsburg cousin, the emperor Charles. Both sets of negotiations took into account the possibility that Mary might succeed her father. During the negotiations for the betrothal to Charles, Henry reportedly called together the chief justices of King's Bench, as well as Stephen Gardiner, Bishop of Winchester, and the Garter King of Arms, and asked them what the status of a female ruler's husband would be in England. One of the justices replied, "Mary's husband could not call himself king by right, because the crown lay outside the bounds of feudal law. She could grant him the title and style of king, though, if she chose."[21]

The justice's opinion was perhaps the first consideration of a point previously moot in law, and points to the ambiguous nature of a female succession in Tudor political thought. One option was to find Mary a royal husband and raise him in England to be king. In 1524, Henry's chief minister, Cardinal Wolsey, considered marrying her to the king's underage nephew, James V of Scotland.[22] While such a marriage could have united England and Scotland one hundred and fifty years earlier than it occurred, Henry's conditions insisted that James be raised in England as an Englishman.[23] While these negotiations fell through, following Emperor Charles's 1525 victory at Pavia over Francis I of France, there was never any suggestion that Mary, as Henry's heir, would rule England as a female king.[24] Instead, the negotiations implicitly recognized James as Henry's political heir, if the Scots could be enticed to hand over their boy king to Henry. This they were understandably reluctant to do.

The Scottish negotiations, however, represented the climax of Mary's position as her father's heir. According to contemporary chronicler Edward Hall, it was the French, negotiating once again in 1528 for a marriage between Mary and the dauphin, who raised questions concerning the validity of Henry's marriage:

> It is well done to know whether she be the King of England's lawful daughter or not, for well known is it that he begat her on his brother's wife, which is directly against God's law and precept.[25]

Henry VIII's quest to secure a divorce from Catherine of Aragon transformed into the English component of the Protestant Reformation, as Henry and his chief minister, Thomas Cromwell, articulated a revolutionary response to papal intransigence. During the first half of the 1530s, the Reformation Parliament passed legislation severing papal authority in England while recognizing Henry VIII as supreme head of the English Church. The First Act of Succession, passed in 1534, recognized the legitimacy of Henry's second marriage to Anne Boleyn. The act bastardized Mary as it recognized Henry's second daughter, Elizabeth, as statutory heir. These events greatly complicated Mary's position within the European royal marriage market as the Protestant Reformation progressed through the next two decades.[26]

Until she ascended the throne, Mary endured her anomalous position as an unmarried daughter and sister of English kings. To Henry VIII, the gains of the Reformation justified sacrificing the diplomatic advantages of marrying his eldest daughter to a European prince. But to Mary, the Reformation represented everything that had gone wrong in her life, the dissolution of her parent's marriage and her own statutory bastardization, which rendered her poison on the European royal marriage market. Although Mary eventually submitted to her father and acknowledged her degraded status, she secretly clung to the Catholicism of her discarded mother until the time she became queen.

Elizabeth also endured statutory bastardization following her mother's execution in 1536 and the passage of the Second Act of Succession, which recognized as heirs the children of Henry VIII and his third wife, Jane Seymour. In October 1537 Jane produced Henry's long-awaited son, Edward, but died twelve days later of complications. Henry's subsequent three marriages produced no further children. By 1543, four years before his death, Henry VIII was in the same position as his father forty years earlier, with two daughters and one underage son. In 1544, the Parliament passed the Third Act of Succession, which restored Mary and Elizabeth to their place in the succession, following, of course, their underage brother. The Act was noticeably vague: while it recognized the right of both daughters to inherit, it was silent on whether they would hold the office of king. However, the Act empowered Henry VIII to designate conditions upon his daughter's possible succession and to designate further heirs by his will.[27] In December 1546, one month before his death, the final version of Henry's will reconfirmed the succession rights of his daughters. But, as Mary and Elizabeth were unmarried in 1546, the will required their marriages to be approved by Edward's regency council if they wished to succeed their brother.[28] In contrast, the will made no mention of Edward's marriage, since his future wife would play the conventional role of queen consort.

But the status of Mary's and Elizabeth's future husbands was much more ambiguous. If Henry VIII intended his daughters to occupy the office of king, he nevertheless placed constraints on their rights to inherit to which previous English male heirs had never been subjected. The marriage clauses implied the belief that, sooner or later, Mary and Elizabeth would marry, and that, should either of them succeed their brother, their husbands could lay a claim to kingship based upon common law marriage rights.[29] Neither the Third Act of Succession nor Henry VIII's will addressed the knotty question of Mary's or Elizabeth's status as heir within the context of marriage. Although they failed to define the political status of a royal inheritrix or her hypothetical husband, the Henrician succession statutes were detailed in their efforts to provide for the furtherance of the Tudor dynasty through the female line, should Edward VI fail to produce direct heirs of his own.

Following Henry VIII's death in 1547, Edward VI's minority governments failed to find husbands for the Tudor sisters. Part of the problem was the religiously polarized state of continental politics, as the Counter-Reformation sought to reverse the gains of European Protestantism. But just as important, choosing husbands for Mary and Elizabeth also involved designating such men as potential heirs to the English throne.[30] Consequently, Mary and Elizabeth enjoyed an anomalous status as unmarried statutory female heirs during their brother's reign (1547–1553). Despite this status, Mary and Elizabeth were still women, and, like all other women, were accorded no official role in the minority government of their brother. Had they possessed husbands during their brother's reign, such men could have conceivably laid claim to political significance on behalf of their wives, or served as their political proxies, since Mary or Elizabeth were prohibited from playing any formal role in government.[31] The perception that marriage to either Mary or Elizabeth brought with it the potential of obtaining the English crown was implicit in the Henrician succession statutes, which did not consider the notion that a royal heiress could defy male dominant political theory and rule unaided by a husband, or not marry at all.[32]

In the absence of constitutional precedent and political definition, Mary's and Elizabeth's unmarried states probably served to bolster public recognition of their status as royal heiresses, since it was unclouded by the complication of defining the status of husbands. As single women, Mary and Elizabeth were the formal wards of their underage brother's government. But for practical purposes, both sisters existed as powerful, independent female magnates during Edward VI's reign, endowed with considerable land and income inherited from their father.[33] Both, in the manner of an aristocratic widow, personally ran large-scale itinerant households and developed provincial affinities of a quasi-political nature. Although, in a formal sense, Mary and Elizabeth were both denied a recognized role in the public sphere of government, their status as their brother's heirs gave them a political luster that Edward VI's minority government could not ignore.[34]

Mary was well aware of the potential of her position. While Elizabeth cultivated the image of a perfect Protestant princess, in line with her brother's developing religious convictions, Mary became a high profile adherent to the old religion, symbolizing Catholic defiance to the radically Protestant Acts of Uniformity passed by Edward VI's parliaments.[35] On her rare visits to London to attend her brother's royal court, Mary traveled ostentatiously, escorted by large companies of liveried retainers, publicly displaying the rosaries outlawed by parliamentary statute.[36] Although Mary's religious preferences were embarrassing to her brother's government, they held no long-term political implications as long as Edward achieved maturity and begat heirs.

However, in the spring of 1553, as fifteen-year-old Edward VI began to waste away from tuberculosis, the specter of Mary Tudor's accession hung heavily over the government of John Dudley, Duke of Northumberland, who functioned as a strongman behind the outwardly conciliar minority regime. Mary's relationship with her brother's government had slowly deteriorated from the beginning of the reign, as she clung to her Catholicism while Edward had embraced the Calvinist Protestantism that spurred the religious changes of his minority government.[37] Although the diplomatic pressure of Charles V undoubtedly helped save Mary from prosecution for violating the two Acts of Uniformity passed by Edward's parliaments, Mary's own defiant and uncompromising stance toward Protestantism sent a clear message to her dying brother's government.

Edward VI's final acts constituted a last-ditch effort to contain female royal inheritance within acceptable parameters of structural male dominance. Unable to reconcile himself to the succession of his Catholic sister, Edward attempted to divert the succession to an avowedly Protestant candidate, his cousin Lady Jane Grey.[38] This plan neatly coincided with Northumberland's desire to retain power beyond Edward's death.[39] In May 1553, fifteen-year-old Jane Grey married Northumberland's youngest son, Guildford Dudley. Like her cousin Edward VI, Jane was fervently Protestant, and Northumberland clearly planned to continue ruling through his underage daughter-in-law. Edward did not live long enough, however, to call a parliament to ratify his desired changes to the succession. Instead, he drafted in his own hand a "Device for the Succession," issued as letters patent, which he and Northumberland browbeat his councilors into endorsing.[40]

The "Device" betrayed Edward's own fears of a female succession, which went beyond Mary's Catholicism. The "Device" justified the exclusion of Elizabeth also with the statement that they might marry aliens and subject the realm to foreign domination. Yet even in allowing Jane Grey to succeed, the letters patent diverted the succession to Jane "and her heirs male."[41] With Jane married to an Englishman, and hopefully soon to bear sons, Edward attempted to circumscribe the terms of her succession in order to redirect the crown to a male heir as soon as humanly possible. The "Device," however, was deficient in law: Mary and Elizabeth had been successively bastardized and reinstated in the line of succession by statute law; only statute law could remove them once again. Edward's jurists rejected the "Device" outright, but the dying king and Northumberland compelled the privy council to endorse the plan to alter the succession.[42]

Nevertheless, all contemporary sources agreed that Northumberland was powerfully placed to pull off the coup.[43] Like her ancestor the Empress Matilda, Mary had to fight for her right to inherit. Edward VI died on July 6, 1553. His death was kept secret, While Northumberland sent word to both his sisters to come to London immediately. Both sisters, however, were informed of their brother's death, and acted independently to protect themselves. While Elizabeth remained at her manor at Hatfield, Mary, the statutory heir, fled to her estate at Kenninghall in East Anglia. In the meantime, Jane was proclaimed queen in London, to very little popular fanfare or support. While contemporaries assumed Queen Jane would be a pawn in her father-in-law's hands, she surprised everyone by her announcement that she might make her husband a duke, but not king.[44] Thus, a fifteen-year-old young woman made the first positive pronouncement on the prerogative of a female royal heiress; she was queen, but her husband was definitely not king until she made him so, echoing the opinion of Henry VIII's jurist.

England's Sovereign Lady and Dutiful Wife

Support for Jane was lukewarm, and confined to the capital city. In a number of shires and corporations, however, recognition of Mary's hereditary and statutory rights arose rapidly.[45] At her headquarters at Framlingham, Norfolk, nobility and gentry flocked to her banner, as Mary wrote to Edward's council in London, commanding them to recognize and publish her lawful accession.[46] Unlike the Empress Matilda four centuries earlier, Mary launched an immediate challenge to the efforts to set aside her claim. In response, Northumberland headed an armed force that evaporated as Mary's now-swelled forces made their way to London.[47]

On July 19, Northumberland himself proclaimed Mary queen in Cambridge, the same day Mary's accession proclamation was published in London. On August 3, Mary entered London in triumph, accompanied by Elizabeth, While Northumberland and Jane Grey were imprisoned and later executed in the Tower of London.

These developments marked the first occasion in which a woman wielded royal authority in her own right, that is, not derived from the formal authority of a living male kinsman, since the Empress Matilda's brief tenure as *domina Anglorum*. Indeed, Mary was able to avoid the practical and logistical barriers that had plagued Matilda in 1135. The most obvious difference was that England was no longer a continental power. With the fall of Bordeaux in 1453, Calais was all that remained of the Angevin Empire upon Mary's accession. While Matilda, living in Anjou with her husband, would have had to travel several hundred miles and cross the channel to make good her claim following her father's death, which she failed to do, Mary resisted the temptation to flee England during her brother's reign, despite continual pressure on her to conform to the Edwardian Reformation. Mary's physical presence in England upon her brother's death, amid the safety of the mostly Catholic gentry of East Anglia, allowed her to formulate an immediate response to Jane Grey's accession.[48]

Mary's lifelong residence in England allowed her a totally English identification. Although Mary took pride in her royal Spanish heritage, derived from her mother, her position as Henry VIII's eldest daughter carried the same representational force in Tudor society as the Empress's identification with her father four centuries earlier. While Mary and Elizabeth put much stock in their positions as Henry VIII's daughters, upon their accessions this status was not clouded by any foreign elements that the xenophobic English commonly found distasteful. Indeed, Mary's cousin and former fiancé, the emperor Charles V, sixteen years her senior, doled out fatherly advice to Mary, suggesting she create the perception that she was "a good Englishwoman, wholly bent on the kingdom's welfare".[49] Mary's position as Henry VIII's eldest daughter carried with it an almost automatic esteem and respect from her subjects that eluded Matilda upon her father's death. While the Empress was unable to declare herself queen in England following Henry I's death, Mary did so in July 11, four days after Edward's death.[50] Unlike the Empress, restrained by a husband

and three small sons, the unmarried Mary chose decisive action. The imperial ambassadors explained her success in a letter to Emperor Charles V, noting, "there is a custom here that a man or a woman who is called to the crown must immediately declare him or herself king or queen".[51]

In the same communication the envoys considered Mary's chances "well-nigh impossible".[52] Within days of Edward's death, however, Mary had presented herself to her kingdom as England's legitimate monarch. Since she was unmarried, there was no ambiguity concerning Mary's immediate and personal exercise of regal power. As the East Anglian gentry and nobility arrived at Framlingham castle, offering their homage to the queen, they provided the first English example of a male dominant political society ready to accept a woman as their monarch since Matilda's elevation as *Domina Anglorum* in 1141. Indeed, as one contemporary eyewitness described the process, "Once Mary was indeed proclaimed undoubted queen of England, one would not believe how rapidly and in what large numbers both gentleman and ordinary folk gathered from the shires."[53]

Although Mary's unmarried state during her father's and brother's reigns made her "the most unhappy lady in Christendom,"[54] it paid her representational dividends upon her accession: as the unmarried adult daughter and sister of dead kings, it was simply impossible for any man to claim Mary's wardship, which formally lapsed into abeyance upon her brother's death.[55] Indeed, Mary's accession proclamation made this fact abundantly clear in its assertion that Mary was both a queen and a sovereign lady, which emulated the royal style of English kingship.[56] As Mary entered her capital city of London, English political society had no other option but to recognize that the royal office and estate had completely and unambiguously devolved upon her alone.

Mary and her sister Elizabeth were, in fact, the last of the direct Tudor line. Edward VI was the last male Tudor, While Henry VII and Henry VIII had either executed or imprisoned the vast majority of the male descendants of the House of York. Of last two of these, Edward Courtenay was freed by Mary, and the other, Reginald Pole, eventually became Mary's archbishop of Canterbury. Neither possessed the means nor the desire to supplant or displace Mary in the royal succession. The utter lack of legitimate male challengers of any kind considerably eased the process of recognizing Mary's accession. Indeed, it should be emphasized that the most powerful political affinity enjoyed by any individual in the summer of 1553 in England was that of Mary herself, an affinity that had come together in recognition of her efforts to claim her statutory and common law rights as her brother's heir.

The absence of the practical and logistical concerns that had dogged the Empress Matilda, in particular, the lack of adult royal male challengers or an unpalatable foreign husband, allowed the formal and theoretical bases of Mary's legitimacy to triumph over Edward VI's efforts to alter the succession. Indeed, Mary possessed many more tangible forms of legitimacy than had the Empress, whose initial claim was based upon a series of oaths of allegiance. Instead, Mary possessed statutory recognition of her title, enshrined in the Third Act of Succession and her father's own will, even though she legally remained a bastard on the statute books.[57] But an equally powerful source of legitimacy was widespread acceptance of the basic common law right of the daughter to inherit her father's and her brother's estate (kingship in the sixteenth century entailed both an office and an estate). Although her staunch Catholicism unnerved her Protestant subjects, most Englishmen nonetheless considered it just that Henry VIII's eldest daughter succeeded by common law right, "as sister of the late king Edward VI, and daughter unto the noble Henry VIII."[58]

But all these factors simply secured Mary's recognition as Edward's heir. As the new monarch was crowned and seated on her throne, the need to alter aspects of her male gendered office became apparent. Mary's immediate task was to construct a viable public representation of a woman in possession of the regal office. The obvious model Mary chose for this task was English queenship. As Susan Amussen has argued, contemporaries perceived the stability of the Tudor kingdom to be based on the interdependent relationship between hierarchy and patriarchy, reflected in the analogy between the state and the family.[59] Mary's task, then, was to inhabit her role as a female ruler without seriously damaging the structure of male dominant political theory. While Mary conceptualized her occupation of the regal office in the recognizable form of an English queen, queenship before her accession had been a status conferred by marriage to a king. In contrast, Mary was a sole queen who, in the first year of her reign, lacked a king, the means by which queenly power had previously been legitimized.

The anomaly of a sole queen became apparent at Mary's coronation.[60] Prior to her accession, nearly all postconquest English queens consort had been crowned in ceremonies usually conducted separately from their husbands'.[61] These crownings, however, did not include a coronation oath, the offering of homage, and the other symbolic gestures that accompanied the investiture of kings. The coronations of consorts did, however, include such rituals as the creation of Knights of the Bath, as did the coronations of kings, the gendered difference being that kings personally bathed naked with the newly created knights, While queens, obviously, did not.

This was the first instance where Mary's gender transformed the performance of the kingly role.[62] Even before her decisive victory over Northumberland, as she inspected her troops at Framlingham, Mary quickly shed any connection with the image of a virago: one contemporary eyewitness recalled "her womanly reticence" to engage in military affairs.[63] Whether Mary's behavior was a representational strategy is impossible to ascertain, but she did avoid what the empress Matilda's commentators considered to be her fatal mistake. Instead of assuming the masculine kingly behavior that had so incensed Matilda's contemporaries, Mary drew attention to her status as a pure and virginal unmarried woman.[64] Male kings had little use for virginity as a representational strategy (with the notable exception of Edward the Confessor), but for Mary it served as an immediate means to cloak her possession of kingship within a powerful image of sixteenth-century womanhood.[65] A virgin queen, then, could hardly lash around in a ritualized bath with knights she herself had created with her kingly power. Instead, emulating the procedures surrounding the coronations of queens consort, Mary delegated the more intimate aspects of this ritual to the earl of Arundel.[66]

The coronation ritual itself, though, was symbolic of a number of male gendered roles, military, judicial, and religious, which were clearly associated with kingship. So, was Mary to be crowned in a fashion similar to her male predecessors? The answer, according to one contemporary account, was yes.

> [Mary] was girt with a sword as when one is armed a knight, and a king's scepter was placed in one hand, and in the other a scepter wont to be given to queens, which is surmounted by doves.[67]

Other contemporary sources remarked that Mary's coronation festivities were very much "according to the olde custome," a reference to pre-Reformation rituals, which made no distinction between the coronations of kings and queens consort.[68] In all like-lihood, what they were describing was a blend of both. Unlike her male predecessors, who rode to their coronations dressed in pur-ple velvet, Mary was transported in a litter, dressed in white cloth of gold, with her hair free-flowing, as a maiden on her wedding day.[69] Mary's coronation provided the spectacle of the crowning of a king in the symbolic packaging of English queenship, allowing her to accept the homage and popular acclamation that symbol-ized the transfer of political power to kings, While simultaneously offering herself as England's bride in the fashion of queens consort.[70] Later in her reign, Mary clearly identified her coronation as her wedding to the realm, something none of her male predecessors would have dreamed of doing.[71]

Thus, perhaps the first representational innovation of Mary's reign was the recognition that, because she was unmarried, she was king and queen at the same time, representing with her twin swords the martial majesty of kingship and the peaceful serenity of queenship. Mary's coronation ritual clearly placed her at a gender-role crossroads in terms of choosing representations of kingship to present for public consumption. Recent studies concerned with contemporary perceptions of gender difference suggest that the assumption of masculine traits by women was a viable path to social acceptance in a society that gauged masculinity and femininity according to recognizably male or female behavior, rather than purely biological difference.[72] As we have already seen, Mary had no intention of playing the virago, as the Empress Matilda had done four centuries earlier. Instead, Mary's initial strategy was perhaps the safe route, to identify female kingship within the context of socially constructed sixteenth-century womanhood. The gender blending experience of her coronation suggests it was not too far of a conceptual leap for Mary to later conceive of herself as England's wife.

As we shall see, Mary never forgot that she alone possessed the full prerogative of kingship. But for public-relations purposes, Mary's emphasis on the queenly side of her office came much more naturally to her, as she immediately embraced a regal but virginal and pious femininity in her attire and public demeanor, beautifully bejeweled as she scrupulously attended mass.[73] The nearest model for this form of public display was the queenship of her mother, Catherine of Aragon. The youngest daughter of

Fernando and Isabel of Spain, Catherine, as a dutiful daughter, impressed her parent's continental interests upon Henry VIII's foreign policy in the early years of her marriage. Indeed, Catherine possessed considerable informal power, derived from her husband's confidence in her abilities, in the first decade of her marriage, serving as regent during Henry VIII's early continental escapades.[74] But in her public representations, Catherine created the impression of a dutiful, supportive, and deferential wife, although in private she often confronted and defied the king on a number of issues, most importantly their divorce. Like her mother, Mary chose to shroud her political power in the public package of a pious, regal, and submissive woman, sincerely disposed to acts of charity, and quite willing to play the part of intercessor and forgiver.[75] This formula had worked famously for Catherine of Aragon, who had been an extremely popular queen consort.

As Mary adopted what she considered to be the appropriate gendered public role, that of a regal yet gentle and mild countenance of a queen, she did not initially inspire fear among the governing class of men as her sister did in 1558.[76] Instead, a number of contemporaries considered her what she appeared to be, a middle-aged single woman with no experience in practical politics desperately in need of the assistance of the wisdom and experience of men. Indeed, soon after Mary's accession, imperial ambassador Simon Renard summed up what has since become the standard statement on Mary's political skill: "I know the queen to be good, inexpert in worldly matters, and a novice all around".[77]

It has been suggested that the low opinion of Mary's abilities given by ambassadors, such as Renard and his French counterpart, Antoine Noialles, represented gendered posturing on Mary's part: playing the inexperienced woman as a political strategy.[78] Such posturing was probably tinged with sincerity: Mary's education had stressed the conventional subjection of women to men.[79] Not surprisingly, Mary usually assumed a modest, deferential demeanor in her public audiences with ambassadors and councilors. Similarly, in public presentations, Mary flaunted her position as a virginal unmarried woman. These strategies allowed Mary to adapt salutary aspects of chaste and modest queenship within the office of king, as she touched for the "king's evil" and distributed considerable alms to the poor.[80] This process constituted a considerable public-relations coup, which shielded the exercise of regal power through the symbolic personifications of a woman performing a properly submissive role. Contemporaries such as Renard considered the practical source of English political power to exist within Mary's privy council, rather than emanating from the queen herself.[81] It is entirely possible that Renard's opinions conformed neatly to the queen's own conception of how her subjects would most favorably view female rule.

Indeed, Mary engaged in public displays of womanly submissiveness. According to the imperial ambassadors then resident in England, Mary beseeched her privy council on her knees that "She had entrusted her affairs and person to them, she said, and wished to adjure them to do their duty as they were bound by their oaths."[82] Mary's privy councilors, for their part, were decidedly prone to factionalism, consisting of holdovers from her brother's council, tainted with complicity in the Jane Grey affair, but needed desperately for administrative continuity. Other members were trusted members of Mary's household as princess, men without experience in politics and accustomed to taking orders from their mistress.

The men of ability on the council, then, were the Edwardian councilors, the "politiques," such as William, Lord Paget, William Paulet, Marquis of Winchester, and Sir John Mason, men Mary, understandably, did not wholly trust. Paget especially embodied the problems Mary encountered with her privy council, as he remained critical of Mary's executive deficiencies behind her back, tactics which, Mary reminded him and her other councilors, they would not have attempted under her father. Paget later opposed her government's religious measures in parliament, and, after Mary married Philip of Spain, advised her husband to take charge of affairs and coach the queen to present his policies to the council as if they emanated from her.[83]

Mary's modern biographers have often noted her failure to weld together a capable and productive privy council. Not surprisingly, Mary placed her initial trust in her cousin, the emperor Charles. Charles had in fact done little to ameliorate Mary's condition during Edward VI's reign beyond issuing diplomatic threats. However, his staunch Catholicism and stance as a disinterested fellow monarch created the conditions for Mary to seek his counsel throughout the course of her reign. While Mary sought to create a perception of her relationship with her council appropriate to her gender, she also sought the appropriate stance in her diplomatic relationships with the emperor, assuring Charles's

English ambassadors that "after God she desired to obey no one but your Majesty, whom she regarded as a father."[84] In other words, Mary employed multiple models of womanly submission to establish what she considered to be an appropriate working relationship with her various counselors, both foreign and domestic.

But Mary's show of compliance with the outward forms of feminine subordination became infinitely more complicated by her decision to marry and bear heirs, the most primary responsibility of hereditary kingship. The complications arising from this decision revealed Mary's complex approach to creating acceptable representations of female rule. Mary, as king and queen, would have to bear her own heirs. Soon after her accession, Mary's symbolic husband, the English kingdom, represented by the men who served in Mary's government and parliaments, immediately turned to the question of the succession and its corollary, the queen's marriage. Although Mary herself began to consider her possible options soon after her accession, she frequently advertised her personal desire to remain in her chaste state, which represented an idealized form of womanhood. In her first interview with the imperial ambassadors, July 29, 1553, Mary emphasized her personal desire to remain in a state of unmarried chastity.[85] Despite this public stance, there is no positive evidence to suggest that Mary ever seriously considered the option of reigning as an unmarried virgin queen.[86] Indeed, Mary needed to produce a direct heir, despite her age and ill health, in order to perpetuate the Catholic restoration she was attempting to achieve. In choosing a husband, Mary possessed two basic options: she could either marry an English peer of royal lineage, or a foreign prince.

The battle over the choice of Mary's husband provoked further dissention with the privy council, which eventually erupted into a fierce rivalry between the Edwardian politiques, led by Paget, and Mary's lord chancellor, Stephen Gardiner, Bishop of Winchester. Like the queen herself, Gardiner was a battle-scarred survivor of the Reformation, having spent most of Edward VI's reign as a prisoner in the Tower of London. Also, like the queen, although Gardiner had outwardly acquiesced to the Henrician religious settlement, he had since become a fervent supporter of a Catholic restoration. Gardiner and the queen clashed, however, over the choice of her husband. Gardiner favored his fellow prisoner in the Tower, the Catholic Edward Courtenay, Earl of Devon, a direct descendant of Edward IV. Contemporary sources indicate that

Courtenay enjoyed popular support as a possible male consort, but he was nearly twenty years Mary's junior, and quickly proved to be a feckless and irresponsible embarrassment.[87]

There is no evidence, in fact, to suggest that Mary considered marrying an Englishman at all. Courtenay was the only Catholic royal peer of marriageable age. Instead, like the vast majority of her predecessors as kings of England, Mary preferred a foreign match, as she considered a number of eligible and Catholic Hapsburg princes, including the recently widowed Prince Philip of Spain.

The most descriptive chronicle of Mary's marriage negotiations came from the lively and detailed pen of the imperial ambassador, Simon Renard, whose dispatches claimed he had captured the queen's ear soon after her accession. In this capacity, Renard served as a conduit between Mary, the emperor, and the intended bridegroom, the emperor Charles's son, Prince Philip of Spain. This group, along with Paget, began the negotiation process behind the backs of Mary's privy councilors, most of whom favored a domestic match, in autumn 1553. Mary's role in the negotiations was decidedly duplicitous; the success of this policy is fully reflected in Renard's diplomatic dispatches, which proved enormously influential in constructing the historical image of Mary's alleged political mediocrity. In London at the time of Edward VI's death, Renard and his diplomatic cohorts were taken completely by surprise at Mary's success in gaining her political inheritance, having been prepared to treat with the regime of Jane Grey.[88] Mary's courage and decisiveness during the events surrounding her accession apparently made little impact on Renard's assessment of Mary's abilities. Renard's dispatches constantly attributed Mary's political shortcomings to conventional feminine deficiency, as he related his advice to her to Emperor Charles in August 1553,

> (she should be) mindful of the fact that (the) great part of the labour of government could with difficulty be undertaken by a woman, and was not within woman's province, and also that it was important that the Queen should be assisted, protected, and comforted in the discharge of those duties.[89]

The emperor Charles also suggested to Mary that she needed a husband to shoulder the burden of governance for her. While the queen did not challenge these viewpoints, and indeed, began contemplating marriage soon after her accession, she personally never made any mention of a womanly need to hand over the political burdens of her male gendered office to a husband prior to her marriage. Instead, from the Queen's point of view, it was the issue of the succession that was primary in her decision to marry, as she stated in January 1554:

> For God, I thank him, to whom the praise be therefore, I have hitherto lived a virgin, and doubt nothing, but with God's grace, I am able so to live still. But it, as my progenitors have done before, it may please God that I might leave some fruit of my body behind me to be your governor.[90]

While Renard continually insisted to the emperor that he held the queen's confidence, it is quite possible that he failed to grasp that Mary's naïve and inexperienced demeanor may have been what she perceived to be a politically correct posture for a female monarch.[91] As a matter of policy, Mary needed to provide for the succession, in order to perpetuate her projected catholic restoration. But outwardly, Mary wished to create the impression that her kingdom, represented by her councilors, had chosen a husband for her, while she privately pledged to Renard and the emperor that she would be a dutiful wife to Philip following the marriage. Indeed, in January 1554, the emperor wrote assuredly to Philip, "The Queen assures us in secret it shall be done according to your desire."[92] But at the same time, Mary privately prodded the ambassador for assurances that a foreign marriage would not compromise the prerogatives of English kingship. But once the betrothal went public, Mary and her council attempted to cloak her role in this process in the outward forms of submissive prenuptial maidenhood.

The idea of a Spanish husband for Mary was not greeted with enthusiasm in England. One contemporary observed, "this marriage was not well thought of by the commons, nor much better liked of many of the nobility."[93] In the final months of 1553, the London rumor mill was grinding out grist against the proposed match in the form of pamphlets and handbills. One, entitled *"Certayne Questions Demanded and Asked by the Noble Realme of Englande of her true naturall children and subjects of the same,"* summed up English fears for their supposedly defenseless Queen. Perceptions such as these revealed the weakness of Mary's public persona, that of a female monarch outwardly conforming to appropriate public roles for women. While the pamphlet identified yet another representation of Mary, as the mother of her subjects, it nonetheless sought to challenge her maternal right to take the husband of her choice. Indeed, the pamphleteer's greatest fear was that the queen's husband would overpower her, seize the government, destroy the nobility, and plunder England in the fashion of William the Conqueror.[94] While English political society had initially accepted Mary's sovereignty in the form of queenship, one of the perceptions arising from this recognition was that, if Mary took a husband, such a man would naturally enjoy a position of strength within the royal marriage, in accordance with contemporary understandings of the relations of power between man and wife.

Keenly aware of this general supposition, Mary's privy council also did not initially embrace the Hapsburg match. While Mary generally had very little success in creating consensus among her councilors, it is clear that only the force of her royal will brought her councilors in line with her choice of a husband, which was presented to them as a fait accompli.[95] Mary's role in the marriage negotiations, in fact, revealed the difficulty of maintaining a subordinate, womanly, queen like persona while simultaneously wielding the power and authority of kingship. This took considerable effort, as parliament, echoing the fears of the pamphlet described above, also challenged Mary's right to choose her husband. In November 1553, the Speaker of the House of Commons warned the Queen that Philip would lord it over the English, carry the Queen out of the realm, and try to seize the crown if she predeceased him.[96] According to Renard, Mary responded that,

> She would marry, but found the second point very strange. Parliament was not accustomed to use such language to the Kings of England, nor was it suitable or respectful that it should be so.[97]

Similar to Gardiner and Paget's machinations within her council, the speaker's temerity in lecturing the queen demonstrated Parliament's belief that an unmarried queen, quite unlike an unmarried king, should play a subordinate role in her marriage negotiations and take advice from her realm's representatives.[98] Mary's stern answer to the Speaker complicated her official cover as a subordinate woman being guided into marriage by her male councilors. Although she invoked the authority of kingship to chastise the speaker, she continued to insist to parliament that her councilors, rather than herself, had chosen Philip to be her husband. Indeed, when provoked, Mary set aside the demur demeanor of queenship to identify with the power of kingship, later reducing Gardiner to tears when she accused him of coaching the Speaker. But his encounter with the Queen brought Gardiner finally in line with Mary's resolve to marry Philip. Paget, who was continually searching for political leverage against Gardiner, had secretly supported the marriage from the beginning, as Gardiner had persisted in advocating Courtenay as a possible husband.[99] Although Mary labored to line up her councilors in support of her marriage, she was clearly at pains to make sure the Speaker's objections were addressed in the treaty negotiations.

Mary impressed these concerns on Renard. While Renard continued to emphasize his lack of confidence in Mary's abilities, stressing that marriage would allow her to "be relieved of the pains and travails which were rather men's work than the profession of ladies," Mary's response indicated an attempt to negotiate a separation between her duties as Philip's wife and her responsibilities as her kingdom's wife:

> She would wholly love and obey him to whom she had given herself, following the divine commandment, and would do nothing against his will; but if he wished to encroach in the government, she would be unable to permit it, nor if he attempted to fill posts and offices with strangers, for the country itself would never stand such interference.[100]

It is surprising that Renard, who labored to convince his imperial masters of Mary's supposed need for firm Hapsburg male guidance, should be the one contemporary observer to reveal Mary's reservations concerning Philip's future role as her husband. Indeed, six years before John Aylmer published his defense of female rule, *A Harborowe For Trewe Subjects*, Mary implicitly identified herself in the role of the biblical judge Deborah, as she clearly delineated the lines between her future position as a dutiful wife and her continuing role as England's chief magistrate.[101] Indeed, Mary's role in the marriage negotiations betrayed the problems involved in combining the symbolic role of wife to her kingdom with the realities of conventional marriage. On the one hand, she warned Renard that the marriage must not constitute any threat to her royal prerogative.[102] But at the same time Mary was busy constructing a publicly normative role of a woman whose marriage was being negotiated for her. Indeed, Mary told the imperial ambassadors publicly that it was "not seemly for a woman to speak of or negotiate her own marriage, so she would not meddle in it," reflecting the injunctions of Juan Luis Vives, in his work *The Instruction of a Christian Woman*.[103] The dictates of appropriate gender roles also guided Mary's councilors, as the ambassadors further related;

> The council informed us that they did not advertise her to sign (the marriage treaty) before his highness has done so, for custom prescribes that the husband shall speak first, not the wife.[104]

While Mary clearly took an active but behind the scenes role in the negotiation process, she took pains to create the public perception that her privy council was negotiating on her behalf without her participation. Opposition to the marriage among her subjects, in parliament, and within her own council, however, severely compromised and complicated this process.

Unlike his prospective bride, who participated actively in the negotiations behind the scenes, Philip simply gave his assent to his father's request that he go through with the marriage, taking no part in the negotiations and assuring his father, "I am so obedient a son that I have no other will than yours, especially in a matter of high import.[105] Waiting patiently for his Spanish and Burgundian inheritance, Philip lacked the diplomatic finesse of his father, who took considerable interest in the negotiations. Nor did Philip, who never bothered to learn the English language, have any understanding of English laws or customs. Not surprisingly, Charles kept Philip on the sidelines as he anticipated Mary's possible concerns, writing to Renard in September 1553 that,

> This might be met by giving an assurance that the affairs of the kingdom should be conducted by the Queen, and by her Councillors, Englishmen, without permitting that anyone else . . . should have any part of them, or hold any office.[106]

The emperor clearly had no interest in making Philip a bona fide king of England in place of Mary. The marriage treaty's articles without question were highly favorable to the English interest. Charles's magnanimity, however, represented a realpolitik assessment of Mary and her councilors attitudes toward a foreign marriage. Considering Mary's age and health, the Emperor had doubts concerning her ability to bear children. However, the marriage could (and did) carry short-term benefits for Charles's continual balance of power struggle with Valois France. As Northumberland had shifted English policy toward alignment with France in the final years of the previous reign, it was critical to imperial interests that English foreign policy shifted back to a policy of friendship with Spain and the Empire.

By the end of November 1553, a draft marriage treaty acceptable to both sides was concluded. The gendered qualities of the marriage treaty were provocative. A number of drafts exist; the one initially approved by the emperor and Mary's privy council at the end of 1553 severely circumscribed Philip's rights and privileges as the husband of a ruling queen.[107] While Philip was accorded the courtesy title of king, and was invited to assist his "consort" in the task of government, his title would lapse upon the queen's death. Philip was also required to relinquish all claims to dispose of English patronage, and to observe "the kingdom's laws, privileges, and customs."[108] The treaty also outlined the succession rights of any children born of the union; similar to Henry VIII's will, the succession rights of daughters were hedged with marriage qualifications. While "males and females to be born of the marriage are to succeed to their mother's right to the kingdom of England," the treaty further stated,

> if no male issue, but female issue only, is the fruit of this marriage, then the eldest daughter shall succeed in the dominions of Lower Germany and Burgundy, provided she does not choose for her husband . . . a man who is neither native to England nor of Lower Germany.[109]

The version eventually ratified by Parliament also prohibited Philip from inducing his wife's kingdom to intervene militarily in the Hapsburg/Valois conflict.

Most unique about the marriage treaty was the failure to provide a dowry. For women of all propertied classes in sixteenth-century Europe, a dowry was a seemingly essential part of any marriage contract; when Henry VIII married his younger sister Mary to Louis XII of France in 1514, the bride brought a dowry of 200,000 crowns of jewelry and moveables.[110] Similarly, when Henry VIII married his fourth wife, Anne of Cleves, in 1540,

Anne's brother, the duke of Cleves, gave Henry a dowry of 100,000 florins. Henry further required that Anne's succession rights to Cleves be ratified, not only by Anne's brother, but also by her sister's husband, the duke of Saxony.[111] Both of these treaties were textbook examples of conventional foreign marriage alliances. Even as late as 1542, when a possible marriage between Mary and a son of Francis I was briefly discussed, both Mary's dubious place in the succession and the amount of her dowry constituted the main impediments.[112] On Philip's side, his previous marriage negotiation prior to Mary's was with a Portuguese *infanta*, which fell apart over Philip's refusal to accept the bride's paltry dowry.

In contrast, it appears that in 1553 the English and imperial negotiators clearly understood that the bride was much more than just a royal heiress. During the course of the negotiations, the privy council insisted that discussion of a dowry be dropped, as they held that "by English custom a kingdom must not be spoken of as a dowry."[113] As kings, like other men at all levels of English society, did not bring dowries to their marriages, so Mary came to her marriage without one. But kings did provide dowers for their wives; "King" Philip was required to provide "Queen" Mary with a dower should she outlive him. With these stipulations agreed upon, the English negotiators got the best of the gendered ambiguities of the projected marriage, driving the hardest bargain possible for their symbolic wife. In effect, on paper at least, Philip gained nothing concrete in terms of political power or financial resources, reducing his room to maneuver to the informal influence of the consort, a term the treaty assigned, ironically, to the queen. The treaty in fact was a form of pre-nuptial agreement that sought statutorily to preempt Philip's rights to any aspect of his wife's royal prerogative.

What was most significant about the treaty was its intention to make clear to a foreign suitor that the intended bride had inherited and was performing the office of king, and would continue to do so following the marriage. As Mary was known by the title queen, but performed the kingly role, so Philip would be known as king, but would, in effect, play the role of consort. Thus the treaty constituted the odd political marriage of a woman defined legally as a man, with a man treated as a woman. Philip had played no part in the negotiations; when he finally saw a draft of the treaty in January 1554, he was understandably mortified. On January 4,

Philip drew up a formal but secret disavowal, protesting, "as many times as it was necessary . . . to ensure that the power and confirmation he was about to grant should be invalid and without force to bind him."[114] Philip's basic objection to the treaty was that it went against the grain of the basic patriarchal social order as it was then understood in Europe; what a wife possessed became her husband's upon marriage.[115]

The history of the possession and exercise of female political power in Philip's family, in fact, provided contradictory examples. Philip's paternal great grandfather, the emperor Maximilian, married the heiress of Burgundy and ruled those territories as duke in right of his wife. However, Philip's other of great-grandparents, Isabel of Castile and Fernando of Aragon, presented the remarkable example of jointly shared sovereignty in their Spanish kingdoms, as Isabel successfully defended her right to enjoy her political inheritance.[116] When Isabel died in 1504, the Castilian crown passed to her eldest surviving daughter, Juana, married to Maximilian's son, Philip the Handsome. Philip took advantage of Juana's unstable mental state as he attempted to rule Castile until his own death in 1506. Following Juana's alleged mental collapse, Fernando ruled his daughter's kingdom as regent until his own death in 1516, while Charles V kept his mother incarcerated for the duration of her long life, while in theory ruling jointly with her.[117] The emperor, however, employed the women of his family in the administration of his empire, particularly his aunt, Margaret of Austria, and his sister, Mary of Hungary, as regents in the Netherlands.[118] If Philip recognized any precedent for female rule on the eve of his marriage, it was that, while a woman such as Mary could lawfully be a king's heir, the right to exercise the regal office depended on a woman's ability to withstand the pressure to relinquish political power to her male kinsmen, as Isabel had successfully done, and Juana had not. Based on Renard's supply of information concerning Mary's mediocre political abilities, Philip undoubtedly placed much faith in his own abilities to subvert the prohibitions of the marriage treaty.

Conversely, Mary's government took pains to convince the public that the treaty guaranteed both the queen's and England's sovereignty. Contemporary sources indicate English hostility to the match: the *Chronicle of Queen Jane* recounted the reception the imperial ambassadors received in London, "the boyes pelted at them with snowballs; so hateful was the sight of ther coming in to theym."[119] On January 14, 1554, Gardiner attempted to present the match to Mary's subjects in the best possible light:

> And he declared further, that we were moche bounded to thank God that so noble, worthye, and famouse a prince woulde vouchsaff so to humble himself, as in this maryadge to take upon him rather as a subject than otherwise; and that the quene shoulde rule all thinges as she doth now; and that ther should be of the counsel no Spanyard.[120]

Despite the efforts of Mary's government to allay the fears of her subjects, plans for rebellion were already underway. Religion was a factor, as Protestants braced themselves for Mary's projected reconciliation with Rome. Renard informed the emperor that "Although the rebels are taking the foreign match as a pretext, their real objects are religion and to favor Elizabeth."[121] But other contemporary sources point to the threat of foreign domination, which Mary's betrothal to Philip posed, as the motivation for Sir Thomas Wyatt's revolt, which erupted in the final week of January 1554. Wyatt's intention, "to resist the coming in of the Spanyshe Kynge," was one further challenge to Mary's authority from yet another set of representatives of her symbolic husband.[122]

With the desertion of the London militia, Wyatt's Kentish forces made their way to Southwark. As she did upon her brother's death, however, Mary rose to the occasion. Once again, Renard's descriptions of Mary's behavior differed from native English ones. Renard informed the emperor Mary was "quite bewildered, she said, especially as she had no men-at arms around her, nor anyone she could trust."[123] In contrast, John Foxe, the Protestant martyrologist who became Mary's most voracious historical critic, marveled at the queen's show of regal strength at the London Guildhall. In an impassioned speech to the Londoners gathered there, Mary declared herself her kingdom's wife.

> Now, loving subjects, what I am, ye right well know. I am your queen, to whom, at my coronation, when I was wedded to the realm, and the laws of the same, you promised your allegiance and obedience unto me.[124]

The guildhall speech was Mary's most explicit public identification as the wife of her kingdom. However, she turned the subordinate nature of the relationship on its head, as she cited her wedded state as a justification to remind her subjects of their "allegiance and obedience" to her, hardly the stance of a truly dutiful wife.[125] Yet Mary tempered her demand for obedience with the virtue and honor of kingship in combination with the symbolism inherent in maternal love:

> And I say to you, on the word of a prince, I cannot tell how naturally the mother loveth the child, for I was never the mother of any, but certainly, if a prince or governor may as naturally and earnestly love her subjects, as the mother doth love the child, then assure yourselves, that I, being your lady and mistress, do as earnestly and tenderly love and favor you.[126]

The Londoners cheered her wildly, as the Queen bravely revealed her decision to stay in the capital against her councilor's advice.

By February 6 the revolt was over, with Wyatt in custody in the Tower. Mary's success in providing a public display of kingly leadership, which relied upon the symbolism of marriage and motherhood, constituted a clear bolster to her by then rather sagging popularity. Nevertheless, the Queen had promised in her guildhall speech to submit ratification of the marriage treaty to her symbolic husband, "the people", as represented in parliament, a step England's male kings had never before taken. Soon after the revolt, writs were issued to convene Mary's second parliament, which commenced April 5.

The Act Concerning Regal Power

Mary's need to defend her possession of the royal office in the face of her upcoming marriage to Philip reached a definitive conclusion during the parliament of April/May 1554. The first two pieces of legislation passed specifically addressed these concerns. The second of these was the marriage treaty itself, but the first was a "curious" statute entitled the "Act Concerning Regal Power."[127] A number of scholars have attempted to explain the motivations surrounding the passage of this statute, which, among other things, declared that the queen enjoyed exactly the same royal prerogative as her male predecessors.[128] Most importantly, the Act defined Mary's queenship within the meaning of kingship, a radical but necessary departure from the queen's earlier attempt to construct female rule within contemporary perceptions of queenship.

The announced legislative program of this Parliament was notable in its brevity, concerning "the corroboration of true religion, and touching the Queen's highness most noble marriage."[129] But bubbling under the surface were a number of problems concerning the queen's title and prerogatives. Renard reported to the Bishop of Arras on January 7 that,

> People have been trying to influence the Queen to summon another Parliament during the coming lent. The pretext has been furnished by two English lawyers who have been prompted to say that by English law, if his highness marries the Queen, she loses her title to the crown and his highness becomes king.[130]

Noted Marian scholar David Loades considered this dispatch to be the motivation for the introduction of a bill that eventually became the Act Concerning Regal Power.[131] Yet, as Renard further explained,

> The pretext advanced by the lawyers was a mere invention, for the treaty that had been passed provided against such eventuality, and derogatory clauses to the same effect might make assurance doubly sure.[132]

Renard told Mary a further bill was redundant; she was already Queen, and the marriage treaty insured her against any threat to her prerogative. Nevertheless, Mary agreed to the introduction of a bill specifically defining a queen's royal prerogative, as Paget related to Renard,

> You know that when this Parliament was first talked about, we agreed with her majesty's approval that only two bills be introduced: one on the marriage, and the other confirming every man in his possession [of former Church property] and authorizing her majesty to act according to her own pleasure in the matter of her title and style.[133]

Paget's explanation for the motivation for the Act sounded considerably different from the one Renard offered the bishop of Arras, implying that Mary's councilors had divergent ideas concerning a bill to address the Queen's prerogative. While Paget sat on the conciliar committee appointed to draft legislation, one curious yet influential late-sixteenth-century narrative source named Paget's archenemy, the chancellor, Bishop Gardiner, as the author of the bill.

William Fleetwood, city recorder of London during the reign of Elizabeth I, described an alleged conversation he had with the earl of Leicester and Lord Burkhurst on a leisurely ride to Windsor in 1575, appropriately titled *Itineratum ad Windsor*.[134] In this work, Fleetwood related to his companions the origins of the Act Concerning Regal Power. In his narrative, a former adherent of Thomas Cromwell submitted an inflammatory tract to the queen, which claimed that, because all previous legal and constitutional limitations upon the royal prerogative were addressed to *kings*, and not *queens*, they did not bind the queen, implying that a queen comprised a different political substance than a king. Instead, the tract advised Mary to

> take upon her the title of conqueror over all her dominions. Then might she at her pleasure reforme the monasteries, advance her frendes, suppresse her enemies, establishe religion, and do what she liste.[135]

The tract clearly demonstrated the ambiguities arising from Mary's attempt to identify her rule within contemporary understandings of queenship, which could be construed as a form of political power fundamentally different from kingship. Fleetwood further related that Mary handed the tract to Gardiner to read, who replied, "it is pittie that so noble and vertuous a lady should be endaingered with pernitious devises of such lewd and subtile sycophants." Mary then threw the book in the fire and commanded the chancellor "that neither he nor any of his confiderates should attempt either the same or the like most lewd and develishe device."[136] Gardiner, then, at Mary's express command, drafted the bill that became the Act Concerning Regal Power, designed to make perfectly clear that Mary was subject to all the limitations on the royal prerogative to which her progenitors, the kings of England, had been subject to.

However, the *Itineratum* also contained a description of the fate of the bill after its introduction in Parliament, which sparked a lively debate on the floor of the Commons.[137] According to Renard, Gardiner and the queen took pains to return as complaisant a House of Commons as possible, not only to approve the marriage treaty but also to approve religious changes designed to facilitate reconciliation with the Church of Rome.[138] Soon after parliament was dissolved, diplomat Giacomo Soranzo wrote the Venetian Senate that, "through the assiduity employed no members were returned save such as were known to be of the Queen's mind."[139] But a few Protestants apparently slipped through the cracks. According to Fleetwood, when the bill concerning regal power was first read in the Commons, Ralph Skinner, a radical Protestant representing Penryn, opposed it. Skinner,

> did much marvel whie any man living would sett forth such a vaine lawe wherby it might appeare to posteritie that any such frivolous doubtes should be moved.[140]

Skinner's objections recalled the relative ease in which English political society had recognized and accepted the fact that their monarch was an unmarried woman, as he stated further,

> It doth appeare plainly that noe man as yet hathe been or is either soe malitious or so full of errors that so wold thinke that the queene, unto whome the dignitie royall is descended, should not as fully be intended to all intents and purposes and constructions to be of the selfe same authoritie as ever was or could be any king of England by the name of kinge.[141]

Instead, Skinner told the House, he hoped "ther be no hidden matter under this needles bill."[142] Skinner warned the Commons that if they passed the bill as is, it would allow the Queen to take upon herself the power of William the Conqueror, or Edward I, the conqueror of Wales, kings who had "seised the landes of the English people and did give the same unto straingers."[143] Skinner implied that the motivation for the bill was to provide Mary with the means to give her future husband lands and power at the expense of her subjects and their laws. According to Fleetwood, the bill was then reworked:

> This being said, the bill was committed to certaine learned men to consider of, who with some alteration brought the same into the House againe, and so after three readinges the bill did passé the House.[144]

This was where the *Itineratum* became confusing. The objections that Skinner raised to the bill, that a statutorily defined, powerful queenship would not be restrained by the limitations on kingship imposed by English law and custom, were exactly those that had supposedly motivated Gardiner to write it. Unfortunately, the first draft of the bill is not extant, but it must have lacked specific language that made clear that the queen was also subject the limitations imposed by "statute or law" on her male predecessors.[145] It is entirely possible that Skinner had read the inflammatory tract that had prompted Gardiner to draft the bill, or some version of the pamphlet discussed earlier.[146]

Once passed in its final form, and signed into law by the queen, the act certainly addressed the fears of those common law lawyers Renard had mentioned, putting to rest notions that any aspect of the royal office could be alienated by the marriage of a regnant queen. The Act also calmed the fears of MPs such as Ralph Skinner by declaring that regnant queens were subject to all the limitations restraining a king's royal prerogative. Ultimately, the Act eliminated any gendered ambiguities arising from both Mary's and her contemporary's use of the term *queen* to describe her occupation of the royal office.

While the marriage treaty was ratified without debate, it merely made explicit that the queen would continue to rule following her marriage. The Act Concerning Regal Power, however, had much more to say about the nature of the royal office than the marriage treaty itself, declaring that its articles had always been the law of the land. Undeniably, the Act strengthened Mary's legal position as a female king prior to her marriage, defining her queenship firmly within contemporary meanings of kingship. This recognition effectively and explicitly granted her the status of an honorary male within Tudor political society, which ultimately rendered Philip, once he married the queen, as a politically unstable and ill-defined male consort.

Parliament's ratification of both the marriage treaty and the Act Concerning Regal power both exposed and rectified the contradictions inherent in Mary's representational construct as a ruling queen fulfilling the kingly role. Indeed, the statutory identification of Mary's queenship within contemporary meanings of kingship complicated her attempt at a conventionally feminine approach to constructing female rule. Nevertheless, while the queen herself saw the need to protect the regal office from foreign encroachments, once parliament was dissolved, Mary returned once again to the more familiar womanly terrain of expectant bride.

Conclusion

By the time Philip arrived in England in July 1554, Mary had presented herself, and been identified by her subjects, in a number of guises of womanhood that had represented her possession of kingly power. These included, in turn, virgin, wife, and mother. Mary's wedding brought out another, as her symbolic husband, the English kingdom, transformed into her father. During the ceremony, performed in Winchester on July 25, according to the official account recorded by English heralds, "when it came to the gift of the queen, it was asked who should give her. Then the marquess of Winchester, the earles of Derby, Bedford, and Pembroke, gave her highness, in the name of the whole realm."[147] Following the marriage ceremony, John Elder, in a letter to Scotland describing the ceremony, noted that Mary put on her ring, "a plain hoope of gold without any stone in it: for that was as it is said her pleasure, because maydens were so married in olde tymes."[148]

Nevertheless, Mary's attempt to present the image of a traditional bride was combined with ritual displays that clearly demonstrated her continued possession of the kingly prerogative. This gendered confusion became immediately apparent following the marriage, as Elder described Philip and Mary's arrival at Whitehall palace, following their entry into London:

> And so the queens magestie entering that part of the court commonly called the kinges side, and the kinges highness entryng the other parte called the queens.[149]

As Elder suggests, Mary's gendered problems were far from over following her marriage to Philip, despite the statutory pronouncements and prohibitions included in the marriage treaty and the Act Concerning Regal Power.

In fact, they were just beginning. Although Mary authorized Philip's precedence before her in their now joint royal styles, she accepted the privy council's opinion that crowning Philip was out of the question.[150] Indeed, the question of whether Mary really desired Philip's active participation as king remains unresolved.[151] The marriage itself failed to achieve its dynastic goals, as Mary endured two highly publicized false pregnancies, which made her a laughing stock in the royal courts of Europe. While Philip resided in England for only sixteenth months over the course of their four-year marriage, he never became reconciled to the prohibitions on his conjugal rights inherent in the Act Concerning Regal Power and explicit in the marriage treaty. Philip did, however, manage to subvert one aspect of the treaty, as he induced Mary to intervene in the Hapsburg/Valois conflict in 1557. The result was Mary's most spectacular failure as queen, the loss of Calais, England's last remaining possession on the continent.

Indeed, the full extent of Mary's failures as monarch need not be recounted here. However, her efforts within a much larger historical context, as the initial architect of a model of English gynecocracy, constituted the most tangible success of her career as monarch. As she inhabited conventional constructs of womanhood; virgin, mother, daughter, and wife, and applied them to her own royal image as a representational strategy, Mary labored to create an acceptable model for female rule. By creating a public representation of herself as a queen subservient to her realm, Mary endeavored to remain within the patriarchal parameters of legitimized female power, avoiding the mistakes that had cost the empress Matilda her coronation four centuries earlier. By acting the part of a conventional woman, Mary may have deceived contemporaries such as Renard, who refused to view the queen's abilities beyond the conventional, contemporary constructs of feminine deficiency. Although Mary knew that she possessed full regal power, which needed to be protected from her future flesh and blood husband, the evidence presented here suggests Mary constructed a creative public image that placed responsibility for this protection on her symbolic husband, the English kingdom.

But in moments of crisis, Mary emerged forcefully from behind the screen of feminine inferiority to remind her councilors, parliaments, and subjects at large that she was their undoubted monarch, as she chose her own husband and pursued the ratification of both the marriage treaty and the Act concerning Regal Power. Mary's behind-the-scenes role in the negotiation of her marriage treaty resulted in Philip's political emasculation, as he occupied the uncomfortable position of England's only ceremonial king consort. Indeed, the marriage treaty served as a blueprint for Elizabeth I's marriage negotiations with various continental princes after she became queen.[152]

Mary's responses to the problems of female rule offered a varied set of examples for her successor, Elizabeth I, to follow or avoid. Ultimately, Elizabeth did not marry, while she proved even more adventurous in her approach to combining public representations of kingship and queenship over the course of a forty-five year reign. It was Mary, however, as England's first female king, who first began this process. Elizabeth in fact adopted wholesale Mary's public identifications as a virgin and her kingdom's wife, and invested these roles with new meaning as a strategy to bolster her own authority as monarch.[153] Elizabeth rarely referred to her sister during her own reign, but her debt to Mary's efforts to construct a model of female kingship constitutes one of the more salient findings of modern feminist scholarship.[154] In the year between her accession and her marriage to Philip, Mary triumphed against formidable odds in the plot to displace her, while creating a public image of benign queenship as she arranged for a marriage guaranteeing her autonomous sovereignty as queen. In her approach to the problems of female rule, Mary displayed a conventional yet creative response that created the initial model for the exercise of female sovereignty.

CHAPTER 3

"I AM HER MAJESTY'S SUBJECT": QUEEN ANNE, PRINCE GEORGE OF DENMARK, AND THE TRANSFORMATION OF THE ENGLISH MALE CONSORT

I am her majesty's subject, and have sworn homage to her today.
I shall do naught but what she commands me.[1]

Upon Queen Anne's accession in March 1702, the first of her subjects to offer their homage was her husband, Prince George of Denmark.[2] George of Denmark did not ascend the throne alongside his wife, as did the wives of male kings throughout English history.[3] Although Mary I had married Philip of Spain one year after her accession, their marriage treaty, ratified as a parliamentary statute, reduced Philip's role as king of England to that of a de facto consort, capable only of informal influence upon his wife's government. Nevertheless, in a social context, Philip still shared his wife's status, and enjoyed the style of king. George of Denmark, however, did not share his wife's status, and settled, apparently quite happily, into the process of creating the informal role of prince consort. The continuing evolution of the gendering of the public role and office of female king, then, disposed of the male counterpart completely. Like Elizabeth I, Anne was a queen without a king. However, quite unlike Elizabeth, she had a husband, who played the public but informal role of a loyal and obedient subject.

Amid the historical attention paid to the Glorious Revolution of 1689 and the Act of Settlement of 1701, an explanation for the constitutional demise of the male consort has never emerged.[4] The interpretation offered here suggests that George of Denmark's widely heralded insignificance was, in fact, highly significant. Queen Anne's recognition as a sole monarch, despite her married state, constituted the apotheosis of English female kingship. It was, in fact, a radical shift from the experience of Anne's sister and predecessor, Mary II, whose reign constituted the nadir of female succession in England. The Glorious Revolution of 1688–1689, which placed Mary II and her husband, William of Orange, on the throne following James II's desertion, represented a parliamentary construction of royal succession compatible to the dictates of male dominant social theory.[5] Although the convention parliament created William and Mary as joint monarchs, in recognition of Mary's hereditary right, it vested regal power in William alone.[6] Within the context of politically public marriage, Mary II performed the role of a de facto queen consort, creating an image of a dutiful and submissive yet supportive wife.[7] Mary's public conduct as queen provided a visible example of idealized female roles as formulated in seventeenth-century patriarchal discourses such as Robert Filmer's *Patriarcha*.[8] Filmer articulated an analogy between the family and the state, considering the authority of the king/husband/father over subjects and families as a divinely ordained hierarchy.[9] At the same time, Filmer's great rival, political theorist John Locke, labored to incorporate patriarchal ideology into his theories of the contractual nature of kingship. Both of these competing ideologies found expression in the Glorious Revolution settlement, as William III functioned simultaneously as a de facto parliamentary king who ruled on behalf of his wife, whose own elevation was based upon her superior hereditary rights.[10] William's and Mary's public roles as king/husband and queen/wife represented to contemporaries a conventional allocation of conjugal authority within the context of marriage.[11]

In contrast, Anne fully occupied the male gendered office of king. Even before her accession, Anne demonstrated how a woman could manipulate the structures of male dominance, in her public and private role as the dominant partner in her marriage to George of Denmark. Prior to Anne's 1702 accession, George played the role of political proxy on behalf of his wife while she was a royal heiress, performing a number of formal roles Anne could not perform herself because she was a woman. But once Anne became queen in 1702, she was no longer confined to the dictates of the social and political structures that denied women formal participation in the public realm of government. Instead, Anne's possession of the crown allowed her to transcend the limitations of her gender, as she began to perform kingly duties in the tradition of Mary I and Elizabeth I.

The question, then, is how George of Denmark's political emasculation was a symptom of the changing nature of female rulership in England. Scholars through the centuries have considered it sufficient simply to state that it was unconstitutional for George to be a king, but few have attempted to explain why this was the case.[12] As the English careers of Philip of Spain and William of Orange demonstrate, this was not necessarily the case at all. As the chapter reveals, George's relegation to the status of informal consort was due to a multiplicity of factors present in the unstable and transitory politics of post–Glorious Revolution England, as well as the unconventional negotiations of power governing Anne and George's marriage, which formed a permanent component of the Revolution settlement. George himself made no protest against his inferior status. Nevertheless, Anne attempted to mitigate George's social and political emasculation by a number of strategies to bolster her reputation as a good wife and his as an important man of affairs.

The historical examination of Anne and George's marriage offered here provides a sharp contrast to Anne's conventional historical image as a queen unable to dominate power relations in her relationships with other men and women in a public life that blurred the distinctions between social and political functions.[13] While twentieth-century historians have labored to lift Queen Anne's historical reputation from the smug disapproval of Whig historians, her husband figured little, if at all, in this process. Not since his death in 1708, when panegyrics devoted to his benign memory did brisk business on the print market, has George of Denmark been the subject of any historical study in Britain. Stuart political and constitutional studies only briefly mention George, if they do at all; he was that obscure.[14] Instead, much of the interest in Queen Anne focused on her relationships with the men of power who surrounded her, such as John Churchill, Duke of Marlborough, Sidney Godolphin, and Robert Harley, as well as the women who allegedly influenced her, primarily Marlborough's wife, Sarah Churchill, and later Abigail Masham.[15] While scholars in the past usually discounted Anne's historical agency in her political relations with these figures, much recent scholarship has demonstrated a more active and independent political role for the last Stuart monarch, whose reign straddled the crossroads of early-modern and modern forms of government.[16]

The examination of the relationship between Anne and her husband offered here furthers this process. Quite unlike the talented and grasping Marlborough or his ambitious and colorful wife, Prince George eschewed an active and influential political role during his wife's reign, and stood aside as the evolution of female kingship reached a critical threshold. Although Queen Anne is not usually ranked among Britain's most successful or capable monarchs, she clearly wore the political breeches in her marriage, without any apparent opposition from her husband. As the dominant partner in the relationship, Anne was complicit in the political process that marginalized her male consort, as she sought to possess the full prerogative of kingship. While Mary I labored to fortify her possession of kingly power prior to her marriage to Philip, and Elizabeth sidestepped marriage completely, Anne was able to enjoy all that her female predecessors, including her sister, had lacked: total possession of the royal office and a loving and supportive husband by her side. Thus, Anne avoided the marriage problem plaguing both the Empress Matilda and Mary I. From her reign forward, the precedent that a female king reigned alone, whether she was married or not, was firmly established.

George of Denmark also was complicit in the establishment of this precedent, which presents a notable contrast to contemporary notions of masculinity present in early-modern England.[17] George's failure to take advantage of his status as an elite male in a male dominant polity, married to a royal heiress and queen, is the true source of his political significance. As the Glorious Revolution incorporated contract theory into its ordering of the royal succession, it modified the conception of kingship as a heritable estate as it emphasized the role of king as an office subject to parliamentary limitations. While the force of William III's ability and personality cast a patriarchal dimension on this process, George of Denmark stood aside as his wife was recognized as both king and queen like her sixteenth-century predecessors Mary I and Elizabeth I. This is perhaps the only possible reason for trotting out to the historical stage an overweight, alcoholic, asthmatic prince, whose fondest desire always was to be left alone with his wife.

But locating the historical George of Denmark is problematic. As the husband of a royal heiress and then a queen, George of Denmark is frequently mentioned in narrative and documentary sources from the reigns of Charles II, James II, William III and Mary II, as well as his wife. But he is only mentioned: throughout his married life, George of Denmark made no substantive contributions to English domestic politics or foreign policy as a privy councilor, peer, or head of the armed forces. Few individuals, including his wife, bothered to go on record to provide any substantive analysis of his performances as privy councilor, military leader, or member of the House of Lords. Documentary and narrative sources mentioning George of Denmark present the odd spectacle of a seemingly ubiquitous presence in late Stuart political society who left little imprint upon the political society in which he lived.

Nevertheless, George's lack of personality and achievement made a significant contribution to English constitutional development, in particular to the evolution of female rule. Although George's refusal to lay claim to his wife's political inheritance or to create a political following of his own represents a decided lack of historical agency, it facilitated the evolution of the autonomous sovereignty of female rule in England. This process might not have happened so smoothly, or even at all, had George possessed even a fraction of the desire for political control that characterized his predecessors, Philip of Spain and William of Orange.

The Return of Male Kingship: 1603–1688

Anne's accession as an autonomous female king was hardly inevitable. The seventeenth century in England produced conflicting social and political discourses and theories regarding female rule. Between the death of Elizabeth I in 1603 and the accession of William III and Mary II in 1689, England experienced both the return to the conventional rule of male kings as well as the unconventional rule of parliament and Oliver Cromwell's Protectorate. Elizabeth's immediate Stuart successors hardly realized the hopes emanating from patriarchal discourses appearing at the end of her reign, which advocated a return of male kingship.[18] As the seventeenth century progressed, Englishmen forgot about their distaste for female rule that had arisen in Elizabeth's final years, as her historical reputation evolved into a model of princely mastery which neither James I (1603–1625), nor Charles I (1625–1649) came close to matching.[19]

The accession of James I was the triumph of hereditary right, but one reaffirming once again a female inclusive principle of primogeniture.[20] While Mary I and Elizabeth I succeeded by statutory and common law right, James's hereditary status as Elizabeth's closest blood relative, yet a Scottish alien, rendered his elevation a form of hereditary right more closely related to natural and divine law, something he considered beyond the scope of mere statute. Nevertheless, James prudently had his first parliament repeal the Henrician succession statutes that, by law, ignored his claim completely.

Female inheritance rights proved a double-edged sword for James I. After fifty years of female rule, the royal office had to be re-gendered for a male occupant.[21] James I was well known for embracing the identification of kings as fathers to their kingdoms, drawing the analogy between the family and the state that Robert Filmer later canonized in *Patriarcha*. On the other hand, James owed his crowns to British systems of female inclusive succession. Before his accession, James sought to augment his hereditary position with theoretical arguments favoring both female royal inheritance and the divine rights of heredity. Just prior to Elizabeth's death, Sir Thomas Craig published *The Right of Succession to the Kingdom of England*, in which he argued in favor of the utility of an assured hereditary succession over election or statutory and common law right. The work was meant to bolster James's candidacy for the English throne, but it also included a theoretical bolster to female succession rights, to overcome the stain of Mary, Queen of Scot's treason against Elizabeth. Craig's arguments favoring female rule mirrored those of John Aylmer's 1559 work, *A Harborowe for Trewe Subjects*, as they explained the occasional elevation of a woman to a throne as the providential work of God, who sometimes endowed certain women with man-like qualities.[22]

The most important part of these works for James was the divine nature of female inheritance. In a work penned in his own hand, *The Trewe Lawe of Free Monarchies* (1598), James drove home his point concerning the divine right of kings to ascend their thrones by hereditary right. James's successors as king, Charles I, Charles II, and James II also embraced divine right theory as a justification for their possession of the throne.[23] The articulation of an explicit divine right theory, however, required some modifications within the transition back to male kingship. In a parliamentary speech in 1604, James proclaimed, "I am the husband, and the whole isle is my lawful wife," reversing the theoretical relationship between monarch and kingdom that had allowed Mary I and Elizabeth I to identify themselves as their kingdom's wives.[24] Once seated on his English throne, James also cast doubts on the legitimacy of female rule, as he declared, "Precedents in the times of minors, tyrants or women or simple kings [are] not to be credited."[25] In fact, following the death of his eldest son, Henry, Prince of Wales, in 1612, James was much more concerned with preserving the possible succession rights of his son-in-law, Frederick, Elector Palatine, than those of his eldest daughter Elizabeth.[26]

Neither James I nor Charles I lived up to their patriarchal aspirations to kingship, as their political opponents utilized Elizabeth's historical reputation as a weapon against their alleged misrule over the first half of the seventeenth century.[27] In reality, Elizabeth had bequeathed a host of lingering problems, military, economic, and religious, which complicated both James I's and Charles I's relations with parliament. Charles's inability to work productively with parliament eventually erupted in civil war, which ended with his trial and execution in January 1649. Until 1660, England experimented with forms of government other than monarchy, under the charismatic leadership of Oliver Cromwell. Upon Cromwell's death in 1658, however, the Protectorate collapsed, as General Monck negotiated the return of Charles I's eldest son, the exiled Charles II.[28]

The 1660 Stuart Restoration attempted to erase the assault on monarchical authority that the civil war represented, and return the office of King to its former prestige and influence. Over the course of a twenty-five-year reign, Charles II proved himself adroit in reasserting the royal prerogatives of his predecessors.[29] However, his marriage to the Portuguese princess, Catherine of Braganza, produced no children, though a long succession of royal mistresses had borne Charles numerous bastards. This made Charles's younger brother, James, Duke of York, his heir. The Duke of York also had problems producing legitimate male heirs. Before Charles's accession, James had impetuously married Anne Hyde, the daughter of the first earl of Clarendon, Charles's chief advisor in the first years of his reign. This marriage produced two daughters, Mary, born in 1662, and Anne, in 1665, before Anne Hyde's death in 1671. Thus, upon their births, the Stuart sisters stood second and third in line to the English and Scottish thrones.

Mary and Anne Stuart came of age in a particularly dynamic period of English history. By the end of the seventeenth century, England had become a global colonial power, as it muscled its way into the new world previously dominated by France, Spain, and the Netherlands during Elizabeth's reign. The scientific revolution, represented in England by Isaac Newton, was transforming the European worldview from the providential to the material, as Charles II himself sponsored the founding of the Royal Society. At the same time, the secularized political theories of Hobbes and Locke came to inform how Englishmen perceived their relationship to the authority of the state represented by the king.

Whether Mary and Anne were aware of contemporary political debates on the nature of kingly authority and its relationship to the state remains conjecture, but neither sister was encouraged in intellectual pursuits. Both were educated in a manner befitting an aristocratic lady of the time, without any emphasis on scholarly attainments or preparation in politics or governance.[30] This situation was similar to that of Mary and Elizabeth Tudor, both of whom received no formal tutelage in the masculine arts of government. Like the Tudor sisters, Mary and Anne Stuart had to watch the political process from the sidelines, and glean what they could. However, Mary and Elizabeth had received superlative Renaissance humanist educations that rendered Henry VIII's children the best-educated monarchs ever to occupy the English throne. Because of their anomalous positions as unmarried women during their brother's reign, Mary and Elizabeth Tudor lived independent lives as educated and experienced women in complete control of their affairs, itself a form of political function.[31]

In contrast, Mary Stuart lived her entire life under conventional female coverture, first as a daughter and then as a wife, while Anne's coverture, as this chapter demonstrates, was negotiated quite differently from her sister's. Indeed, with their leisure time confined to conventionally feminine pursuits, the Stuart sisters chose decidedly different paths. While Mary excelled at needlework, Anne chose to spend much of her leisure time at the gambling tables.[32] Mary and Anne Stuart were certainly literate, but their literary remains lack the sophistication of Elizabeth, or even Mary I.[33] In terms of late-seventeenth-century standards for aristocratic women, their education was better than average, as Jonathan Swift lamented, "not one gentleman's daughter in a thousand can read or understand her own language or be the judge of the easiest book written in it."[34] Nevertheless, the thrust of their tutelage was preparation for marriage, rather than wearing a crown.

A Tale of Two Husbands

Before their accessions, Mary and Anne Stuart led the conventional lives of royal princesses. Unlike the sixteenth-century Tudor heiresses, plagued by problems of religion and legitimacy, the Stuart sisters were eminently marriageable. But despite their places in the royal succession, their marriages were negotiated for their diplomatic value as much as their dynastic potential. As the elder sister, Mary was the first to serve this purpose. In 1677, Charles II provided her with William, Prince of Orange, himself a scion of the House of Stuart.[35] On his father's side, William's family had been Stadtholders in the Netherlands for generations, heavily involved in European affairs, including three naval wars with England. In the context of late-seventeenth-century European politics, the marriage was a slap in the face to William of Orange's implacable enemy, Louis XIV of France, who received the news "as he would have done the loss of an army."[36] The marriage treaty was in several ways quite conventional, providing a dowry for Mary, as William in turn supplied a dower for his wife. The treaty did not include any explicit mention of Mary's place in the succession, but the terms stipulated that any children, male or female, born of the union would require the king of England's consent to marry.[37]

The Prince of Orange, later William III of England, was a capable, intelligent, and ambitious man, who viewed his marriage as the most tangible means for gaining England as an ally in the chronic hostilities between the Netherlands and Louis XIV's France.[38] However, Anglo-Dutch unity against the Sun King was not necessarily a priority for Charles II. Though a king popular among the mass of his subjects, Charles had been stung by the intractability of his parliaments, and, like his father and grandfather, sought means to augment the royal income without resort to parliament. Charles partly solved this problem by obtaining an annuity from his cousin, Louis XIV. Charles's secret dealings with

Louis included a promise to further a Catholic restoration in England. This was a promise that Charles never came close to delivering, but he did offer Louis the consolation of the marriage of Anne Stuart and George of Denmark, which in turn annoyed William of Orange, who considered himself to be the leading proponent of Protestantism in the royal family.[39]

As Charles II sought to balance his rather conflicting foreign entanglements, Anne's marriage was quickly arranged in an underhanded fashion.[40] Denmark was then an ally of France; Bishop Gilbert Burnet of Salisbury reported, "The marriage that was now made with the brother of Denmark did not at all please the nation, for we knew that the proposition came from France."[41] Charles II, his chief advisor, Robert Spencer, Earl of Sunderland, and the French ambassador, Paul Barillon, plotted the scheme in the late spring of 1683, while the King dispatched royal yachts to Denmark to fetch the twenty-seven-year-old prince in May.[42] A conventional treaty was drafted, but without the marriage stipulations that were included in William and Mary's.[43] Charles II initially kept his privy council uninformed about the negotiations, while the nuptials celebrated at St. James in July 1683 were decidedly low key for such a dynastically significant union.[44] While Mary had sobbed at the prospect of marrying her Dutch cousin, Anne, like so many women in all stations of English society, complacently walked down the aisle with a husband she had not chosen herself.[45]

As is sometimes the case in an arranged marriage, contemporaries agreed that love between Anne and George blossomed immediately, and continued unabated until death parted them. On paper, George seemed the ideal husband for an English royal heiress. As a younger brother of the King of Denmark, George was far enough removed from the Danish succession for contemporaries to believe that, as one saw it, "having no dominions of his own to gratify, he would have nothing else in view, but the interest of England."[46] This was in marked contrast to William of Orange. As a grandson of Charles I, and the husband of the Duke of York's eldest daughter, William early on considered the possibility of gaining the English crown in his long-range objectives.[47] George of Denmark, however, never gave any sign of recognizing such potential in his position as Anne's husband. It took some time for contemporaries to realize this; the marquess of Ormonde remarked, "It is thought the Prince will make haste to be possessed of so good a fortune."[48] William of Orange also feared that George might use his position as Anne's husband to build himself an independent power base, and challenge his own dynastic interests in England.[49] It soon became evident, however, that George of Denmark was not in a hurry to do anything.

What William and George did have in common were firm Protestant convictions. Fears of Catholicism raged over the course of Charles II's reign. Charles II was widely rumored to possess Catholic leanings while the Duke of York openly converted to the Church of Rome. Charles II's efforts to have Anne and Mary reared in the bosom of the Anglican Church, and marry them to Protestant husbands represented political expediency rather than religious convictions.[50] While Mary's and Anne's Anglicanism remained firm throughout their lives, this was not the case with their husbands'. Although George frequently attended Anglican services, he never lost his taste for Lutheranism.[51] But to Anglicans and dissenters alike, both George's Lutheranism and William's Dutch Calvinism were infinitely preferable to Catholicism.[52]

While George's Lutheran beliefs were cold comfort to his father-in-law, the Catholic Duke of York, the English nation welcomed the arrival of a staunchly Protestant husband for Anne. The marriage brought with it hopes of a Protestant succession, a factor equally important to those embryonic political parties, Tory and Whig, which emerged from the exclusion crisis of the early 1680s, which attempted to bar the Duke of York from the throne.[53] Although exclusion failed, York's second wife, Mary of Modena, had thus far failed to bear her husband a male heir, while William and Mary remained barren throughout their marriage. Thus, all eyes looked to Anne and George to perpetuate a Protestant line of succession, the single most important function George was called upon to perform.

For a man in his position, George of Denmark stood well poised to establish a reputation as an important man in the exclusively male public spheres of war and government. Warfare remained a primary and potent status symbol in early-modern England and Europe, and George came to his marriage with a reputation for valor and courage in the Danish army.[54] Soon after his arrival in England, however, George gained a reputation for near pathological shyness. Tellingly, William Blathwayt, who had been dispatched to Denmark to assist in the marriage arrangements, wrote to the Earl of Conway that, "he appeared not only a man of courage, but a quiet man, which was a very good thing in a young man."[55]

The diarist John Evelyn concurred, "A young man of few words, spake French ill, seemed somewhat heavy, but reported valiant."[56] George's shyness was compounded by his linguistic limitations, as he never overcame his thick Danish accent, causing contemporaries to discount his intelligence.[57]

The most famous quip about George of Denmark came from the lips of the congenial and fun loving Charles II, who remarked, "I have tried Prince George sober, and I have tried him drunk; and, drunk or sober, there is nothing in him."[58] From the moment of his arrival in England, George of Denmark showed no sign of any inclination to use his social position as a springboard for a political career. Indeed, soon after his marriage, George lamented, "We talk here of going to tea, of going to Winchester, and everything else except sitting still all summer, which was the height of my ambition. God send me a quiet life somewhere."[59] Not surprisingly, George did not emerge as a public figure of note in the last years of Charles II.[60] As there were no significant military engagements during this time, George's limited energies were devoted to reproductive activities. Compounding these factors, George suffered from lifelong asthma, which eventually prevented him from engaging in sustained martial activities. Instead, George and Anne settled down to a lifetime of mutual enjoyment in their pursuit of food, drink, gambling, and perpetuating the Protestant succession.

The secret to the success of their royal marriage was George's submission to the dominance of his wife.[61] Although social convention viewed the husband as the natural head of the family, contemporaries recognized that women occasionally held de facto control over their husbands.[62] According to a tract written later in the eighteenth century, "The secrets of matrimony, like those of freemasonry, are to be kept as such for this very good reason, because it is a shame to discover them."[63] According to the different categories of husbands described in this work, George fell into the category of *whissler*, "A person entirely devoted to the service of his wife, and nothing but affairs of the greatest moment can force him from her presence."[64] Quite unlike the noted philanderers Charles II, James II, and William III, George remained sexually faithful to Anne throughout their marriage.[65] George's reputation as a faithful husband may well explain why his masculinity never came under serious attack by his contemporaries, as he created a reputation for civility and honor within the context of marriage.

But to those individuals who knew him personally, George of Denmark was generally not well regarded. One contemporary in a position to know summed up George of Denmark succinctly: "He is very fat, loves news, his bottle, and the Queen."[66] Another contemporary, Sarah Churchill, who knew him quite well, commented that, "the Prince used to employ himself agreeably all day either standing upon a stairhead or looking out a window, making malicious remarks upon the passerby," concluding that, "Anne grew uneasy at the figure his highness cut in that princely amusement."[67]

While George may have desired to amuse himself away from the hustle and bustle of politics, his status as the husband of a royal heiress, mindful of the potential of her position, made this impossible. While possession of the crown itself washes away all former social and political disabilities, such as being a woman, Anne, despite her place in the succession, was still subject to the dictates of a political society that allowed only men to participate formally.[68] Like a powerful woman in any aspect of English society, Anne still needed a male representative in the public realm of government and politics.[69] For better or worse, this was the primary political task George was called upon to play for the rest of his life.

It was usually for the worse. Anne's uncle, Henry Hyde, Earl of Clarendon, recorded in his diary an episode illustrating George's lack of discipline and Anne's efforts to compensate for it. In 1690, prior to William III's Irish campaign, Clarendon's son asked to be excused from accompanying Prince George, since his own regiment had been disbanded. While George tried to persuade him to go anyway, he was apparently unsuccessful, as Clarendon further related:

> Rochester [Clarendon's brother] later went to Anne, who was already apprised of all this by the Prince. Anne said, the Prince must be waited on! Could not go on with just an equerry and groom to the Bedchamber—Rochester replied, heard Prince gave leave for Lord Falkland to stay behind for business reasons; Anne said Prince is so good natured, gave his servants leave to do anything, but Anne was angry, and hoped George would recall Lord Falkland to service.[70]

Both Clarendon's son and Lord Falkland were dismissed from their household posts for their refusals to accompany the prince, undoubtedly on Anne's orders.[71] As this episode illustrates, George lacked backbone and resolve, which his wife supplied. Nevertheless, as

Anne's political position as a royal heiress grew increasingly complicated during the reign of her father James II (1685–1688), George's role as his wife's political proxy expanded. Even during the reign of Charles II, George performed public roles Anne would have performed herself were she a man. On two occasions in 1683 and 1684, George accompanied the king to banquets honoring artillery companies, no doubt due to the prince's interest in military affairs.[72] In addition, George made numerous inspections of naval forces in 1684, accompanied by the duke of York, Lord Dartmouth, and Samuel Pepys.[73] Also, in 1684 George was created a Knight of the Garter, a prestigious honor recalling those martial qualities of chivalry rooted in England's medieval past.[74] The Garter remained the preserve of men until the twentieth century; George received it because his wife stood second in line for the throne. Thus, Anne's position as a royal heiress allowed her husband to reap honorific benefits that both pleased her and indirectly acknowledged her own status.

There is no evidence that Anne was at all concerned or jealous that her husband received public and formal acknowledgments that would have been hers had she been born a man. Anne was content to be known as the princess of Denmark from the time of her marriage to the date of her accession, just as her sister was content in her position as princess of Orange. In the domestic sphere of their households and marriages, both Mary and Anne created public perceptions as dutiful and conventional wives, as Mary I had tried to do following her marriage to Philip of Spain. But this is where the similarities between the sisters ended. As a royal heiress, Mary did not possess political ambitions, and expected her husband to exercise her political prerogatives for her when she became queen.[75] In contrast, as Anne anticipated her own "sunshine day," she clearly considered the crown as reserved for herself alone.[76] In the meantime, George definitely had a political role to play, but it was Anne who dictated policy.

With the death of Charles II in January 1685, and the accession of Anne's father, James II, George's public duties increased in their status. Although James II had no more use for George in a substantive way than Charles II had, George continued to receive formal acknowledgments of his wife's hereditary position. Soon after his father-in-law's accession, George served as Charles II's chief mourner, and was called to the new king's privy council.[77] George also inherited James's infantry regiment.[78] George undoubtedly enjoyed his military command, but he made no effort to use it as a catalyst for political prominence, nor did he insinuate himself among the king's advisors.

Thus it was up to Anne herself to create a body of political support for her hereditary status. If George received the formal recognition due his wife had she been a man, Anne's real political lieutenant was John Churchill, later Earl, then Duke, of Marlborough. Churchill's wife Sarah served as Anne's closest companion, advisor, and confidant until well into her own reign. In this group, known as the "cockpit circle," named after the apartments they occupied at Whitehall Palace, George was an honorary and nonvoting member who always supported his wife's initiatives. As Anne and the Churchills monitored the course of James II's reign, George was called upon to lend Protestant legitimacy to James's schemes to restore Roman Catholicism.

James II came to the throne in 1685 as a known Catholic. The English kingdom accepted him as such because he was old and his nearest successors were his Protestant daughters. Yet James also benefited from widespread acceptance of an indefeasible hereditary right, one of the original tenets of the Tory Party that had emerged victorious from the exclusion crisis that had rattled the final years of Charles II's reign. James's efforts to suspend the Test and Corporation Acts, however, threatened the other great Tory tenet, defense of the Anglican Church from Catholics and dissenters alike. In November 1687, James instituted a Commission of Regulation to purge corporations of members of parliament and other officials who opposed repeal. Soon after, George was appointed to a privy council committee, "to lend a spurious air of Protestant compliance," which attempted to put into effect the commission's findings.[79]

The unexpected birth of a male heir in the summer of 1688 to James II and his second wife, Mary of Modena, caused William of Orange to act upon his wife's dynastic interests. William, like Philip of Spain a century earlier, considered his conjugal rights to extend to his wife's political inheritance.[80] William, however, had the historical hindsight to recognize that the evolution of female political inheritance in England was both peculiar and particular. Also, like Philip, William did not seek royal power in England for its own sake, but for English aid in tipping the scales of the European balance of power. In William's case, marriage to James II's eldest daughter provided the best opportunity to bring England into the European coalition designed to keep the Catholic leviathan, Louis XIV of France, firmly in his cage.

William's wife Mary dutifully submerged her royal status within her husband's goals as George faithfully did for Anne. When a group of leading magnates wrote to William in Holland, asking him to come to England to facilitate the convening of a freely elected parliament, and protect Protestantism in England, the cockpit circle supported this decision. The venture initially rested on the spurious notion that the infant Prince of Wales was an imposter, smuggled into the royal bedchamber in a warming pan to ensure a Catholic succession in England. Anne refused to attend the queen's birthing, a privilege her status certainly afforded her, so she, William, and Mary could persist in publicly discounting the legitimacy of the birth, Anne's debut on the political stage that revealed her singular dynastic interests.[81]

Even before William of Orange landed at Torbay, on the Devonshire coast, in November 1688, James II was frantically endeavoring to reverse his policies in a futile attempt to save his tottering throne.[82] Once again George of Denmark was trotted out for public duty when he accompanied James II's crumbling army to Salisbury. George's presence in the royalist camp was intended to placate Anne as well as keep her from aligning with William. Lord Clarendon's account of Prince George's last encounter with James II provides yet another example of his lamentable reputation among the leaders of late Stuart society:

> James went that day as far as Andover. He was attended by his son in law Prince George, and by the Duke of Ormond. Both were among the conspirators, and would have accompanied Churchill, had he not, in consequence of what had passed at the council of war, thought it expedient to take his departure suddenly. The impenetrable stupidity of Prince George served his turn on this occasion better than cunning would have done. It was his habit, when any news was told him, to exclaim in French, "*est-il possible?*" This catchword now was of great use to him. "*Est-il possible?*" he cried, when he was made to understand that Churchill and Grafton were missing.[83]

That evening after supper, Prince George and Ormond also defected to William. James II exclaimed, "What! *Est-il possible* gone too? After all, a good trooper would have been a greater loss."[84] After James II fled to France, effectively abdicating his throne, finding a suitable role for George of Denmark in the public realms of politics and war became William of Orange's problem.

The Glorious Revolution Settlement

Once James II had left England, William summoned a convention parliament to decide the fate of the English crown. Since the convention decided to disinherit the infant prince of Wales, James II's nearest heir was his elder daughter Mary. The big difference between Mary Tudor in 1553 and Mary Stuart in 1688 was, of course, the princess of Orange's married state. William thought himself entitled to the crown, but it remained unclear in English law whether Mary's coverture as his wife extended to the crown.[85]

William's and the convention's primary problem, then, was to cloak his de facto assumption of power in some form of constitutional legitimacy rooted to previous English political practice. There was much discussion in the convention concerning the nature of James II's abdication as well as who should succeed, and by what right.[86] Thus, one of the central questions of the Convention Parliament was the current state of women's succession rights. The sixteenth-century precedents clearly pointed to the accession of a regnant queen in 1688. But both Mary I and Elizabeth I came to their thrones unmarried, so the problem of defining the role of a husband of Mary I was negotiated after she had been queen for a year, and had assumed the prerogatives of kingship. There was support within the convention for the accession of Mary alone, as well as some form of regency that still kept James II symbolically on the throne. English history abounded with relevant precedents for the convention to consider, identifying both heredity and election as legitimate means to gain the crown, such as Henry IV's 1399 accession by election and Henry VII's by conquest and subsequent dynastic union with Elizabeth of York. Even Mary I's marriage to Philip of Spain was considered a relevant precedent. Various members of the convention cited all of these as models for constructing a legitimate settlement of the crown.[87]

A key factor in William's assumption of the crown was his wife's full and unwavering support. Prior to 1688, William considered his wife's political inheritance his own.[88] Although the circumstances to claim it were unusual, William had made it perfectly clear to the leading members of the convention privately that unless he was offered the crown, he would go back to Holland.[89] In this resolve Mary supported her husband as a good wife should. When the Earl of Danby made the motion to recognize Mary's hereditary rights alone, she sent off a sharp letter to him:

> She was the Prince's wife, and would never be other than what she should be in conjunction with him; and that she would take it extremely unkindly, if any, under a pretence of their care for her, would set up a divided interest between her and the Prince.[90]

In the compromise hammered out in the Convention, and enunciated in the Declaration of Rights, it was recognized that James II had deserted the throne, while William and Mary were invited to take the crown formally as joint monarchs. However, the Declaration further stated that regal power would be vested in the king alone, leaving Mary effectively in the same position of Elizabeth of York two hundred years earlier: a royal heiress who brought a superior dynastic claim to her marriage with a royal usurper.[91] Should William outlive Mary, he was to hold the crown for the rest of his life.

The convention used Mary's hereditary status to offer William what many contemporaries believed to be a de facto elective crown.[92] If Mary provided the dynastic legitimacy, William provided a pragmatic candidate clearly in support of Protestantism, parliament, and the rule of law. What Mary lost was the opportunity to be a regnant queen, a choice that did not bother her. She was, in actuality, a queen consort. Her status was spelled out clearly in the Declaration of Rights and the subsequent Bill of Rights. Shortly after accession, Mary recorded in her journal,

> The next day after I came, we were proclaimed, and the government put wholly in the Prince's hands. This pleased me extremely, but many would not believe it, so that I was fain to force myself to more mirth then became me[93]

Mary II has rarely been credited with any historical agency concerning the outcome of the Revolution settlement, but her decision to be William's consort seems to have been a willing decision, given her indifference to politics.

In making Mary II a consort, the convention ignored the 1554 Act Concerning Regal Power, an act originally passed to define the power of an unmarried queen.[94] Indeed, during the convention, as one contemporary with a short historical memory stated it, "We will have a king, for the laws no nothing but the name king."[95] Thus, in 1690, when William returned to Holland, as he did annually for the rest of his life, parliament deemed it necessary to pass a bill vesting Mary, at the head of a nine-man council, with regal power when William was abroad. Yet the earlier precedents of female rule hung over the parliamentary debates surrounding the 1690 passage of the regency bill, which attempted to resolve the question of jointly held sovereignty.[96]

Mary II's exclusion from regal power appeared, on the surface, as the triumph of traditional and pervasive male marriage rights, but it was clearly an aberration in the evolution of female rule in England. In the Declaration of Right's provisions concerning Princess Anne, the results resembled the Henrician succession statutes. The Third Act of Succession (1544) and Henry VIII's will (1546) defined Mary and Elizabeth Tudor as heiresses capable of succeeding to the throne, and passing on their rights to their children. As both daughters were unmarried, no provision was made for their husbands, although their marriages required the approval of Edward VI's council. In 1689, Anne was already married, of which the declaration made no mention. Instead, the declaration mirrored the Tudor succession statutes, defining Anne and her children as William and Mary's heirs, without elaboration. In effect, the declaration treated Anne as politically a single woman.

Thus Williams's position as king had much more to do with parliament's ability to settle the succession than his or George's theoretical rights as the husbands of royal heiresses. Fifty years later, as emergent Whig political theory stated the case:

> For the convention did not proceed upon principles of hereditary right, but asserted the right and power of the states of the nation, in placing the crown upon the head of such of the royal family, as was thought expedient at such a juncture.[97]

In 1689, however, the Glorious Revolution was open to a variety of interpretations, including the concept of William's assumption of a "crown matrimonial" Gilbert Burnet wrote a particularly patriarchal reading of Williams's rights:

> If the next [heir] is a femme covert, then by the law of nations, which creates a communication of all the rights of the wife to the

husband, this is likewise communicated, so that here we may have still a lawful and rightful king.[98]

Other contemporaries incorporated theories of hereditary and contract kingship all within one justification. One contemporary pamphlet, while acknowledging parliament's undoubted right to reorder the succession, also argued along patriarchal lines that, although Mary was the hereditary heir, since William and Mary could not share sovereignty, William was the "natural" choice to wield the regal power.[99] Inevitably, contemporary understandings of the constitutional nature of William and Mary's accession divided along party lines: while Whigs could celebrate their pragmatic "election" to the crown, a number of Tories found it much easier to stomach an image of William as the recipient of a "crown matrimonial," wielding regal power in right of his wife, the rightful heir according to common law principles.

Nevertheless, despite the fluidity of constitutional interpretation, there is no evidence suggesting that George of Denmark made any attempt to capitalize on the obvious analogy between his position as Anne's husband and William's assumption of regal power, as the Revolution unambiguously settled the succession on his wife alone, without any mention of what his social or political status would be upon his wife's accession.

Although Anne and George had lent their support to William and Mary, Anne only reluctantly accepted William's intrusion between herself and her sister in the hereditary line of succession. Indeed, Anne's relations with her sister began to deteriorate soon after William and Mary's accession. As first in line to the throne, Anne became the focus of disaffection with William III, when the honeymoon of the Glorious Revolution abated, and the English people realized that their king was a foreigner intent on dragging England into the continental problems of the Netherlands.

As a female heiress presumptive, Anne had to formulate a political following within the formal structures of politics and government. Her position as William and Mary's heir was completely in keeping with sixteenth-century precedents, as Burnet explained:

> She [Anne] was not made acquainted with public affairs; she was not encouraged to recommend any to posts of trust or advantage; nor had the ministry orders to inform her how matters went, nor to

oblige those around her; only pains had been taken to please the Earl of Marlborough.[100]

As William Cecil served as Elizabeth I's chief advisor before her accession, Marlborough occupied the same role for Anne. But Anne also had a husband, ineffectual as he was. Regardless, George continued to represent his wife in the public sphere of politics and governance. While Marlborough served as Anne's power broker in Parliament, George was often present in the seats of power. This state of affairs served Anne's political purposes: even before William's invasion, Anne occasionally found it convenient to retreat to the role of a conventional woman uninformed about politics, as did Mary I in her own gendering of womanly political power. When her uncle, the earl of Clarendon, tried to ply her for information on William's 1688 invasion, Anne dryly remarked that "I know nothing except what the prince tells me he heard the King say."[101] In this sense, George both reaped benefits and also served as a public whipping boy for his wife, as relations between the court and the cockpit waxed, waned, and waxed again over the course of William's reign.

The reign started out auspiciously enough for Anne and George. After six years of annual failures, Anne gave birth to a son, William, in July 1689, who survived infancy. Anne, however, continued to conceive and suffer miscarriages and stillbirths for the duration of the 1690s, these taking a severe toll on her health and her mental outlook.[102] Nevertheless, as long as his son lived, George had accomplished what Philip of Spain and William III had failed to do: perpetuating the royal succession through the female line, which had not been accomplished since the twelfth-century Empress Matilda bore her three sons. As Matilda's sons had done for her, Anne and George's son reinforced their dynastic importance. William III recognized the importance of Anne's son, and created him duke of Gloucester immediately following his birth, and, in 1695, a Garter knight.[103]

The birth of his son and the political debt to his wife allowed George of Denmark to enjoy initial favor from William and Mary. On February 13, 1689, after William and Mary's acceptance of the crown, George was called to William's privy council. His presence there, however, was purely a formality, bestowed on behalf of his wife's status, as it had been during James II's reign. More substantial was George's statutory naturalization in March 1689, and his creation in April as baron of Ockingham, earl of Kendall, and duke of Cumberland.[104] George's creation as an English peer gave him a seat in the House of Lords, which he attended regularly for the rest of his life. In these respects, George can properly be viewed as a formal political proxy for his wife. George also served as a social proxy: for instance, he accompanied William to the horse races at Newmarket in October 1689, while their wives stayed behind.[105] Although William undoubtedly viewed the excursion as a political means to bolster his popularity, George of Denmark, in all likelihood, considered the races a pleasurable leisure activity.[106]

William III had little respect for George of Denmark.[107] Considering his own ambitious temperament, it is not difficult to surmise how William simply could not understand why George had no desire to follow in his footsteps. William's low regard for George was demonstrated by his refusal to bestow any form of military patronage on his brother-in-law, which his status as Anne's husband should have afforded him. One contemporary noted that George was incensed that William had not appointed him Lord Admiral of England.[108] In the summer of 1690, William personally led an expedition to Ireland, where he decisively defeated the forces of James II. George of Denmark participated in this campaign, at his own expense, accompanying William without any formal command, as his infantry regiment was disbanded after the Revolution.[109] During this campaign William III snubbed George, refusing to allow him to ride in the king's coach. While this episode can partly be explained by William III's likely aversion to George's lack of talent and initiative, his treatment of George was also perceived as a means to punish Anne for using George's presence in the royal forces to bolster the political potential of her position.[110]

The irony here is that George played no role in this process; it was the Marlboroughs who actively exploited the potential of Anne's position. Anne's relations with William and Mary had already soured by the end of 1689, when her "friends" managed to secure her passage of an unprecedented £50,000 annual grant from Parliament. The grant was a clear political defeat for William, who wished to keep the royal heiress on a tight financial leash.[111] Marlborough himself got into further trouble in 1691 when William claimed that he had learned of Marlborough's secret correspondence with James II in France.[112] As Sarah Churchill was Anne's chief lady of the bedchamber, Anne's refusal to dismiss her after Marlborough's disgrace created the rift between Anne and Mary that remained unresolved when Mary died of smallpox in December 1694. These were the conditions under which George of Denmark was constrained to conduct his and Anne's public and private affairs.

In the context of the personal nature of power relations at the court of William and Mary, George attempted to stay on good terms with just about everyone who mattered: the king and queen on one end and the cockpit circle on the other. In her own self-serving memoirs, Sarah Churchill never forgot that, despite the considerable pressure thrust upon him to convince his wife to abandon the Marlboroughs, George remained steadfast:

> His Royal Highness continued steady in his opinion to the last, notwithstanding that almost all the servants in the family, and especially those whom I brought into it, were frequently pressing him to have me removed.[113]

While George remained on good terms with the Marlboroughs during their period of disgrace, he also sought opportunities to heal the breach with William and Mary. Despite his humiliating experience in Ireland, George made one more attempt to render military service under William III. Whether George wished to gain military distinction on his own, or Anne directed him to do so, is impossible to ascertain. However, William and Mary's attitude toward George's initiative suggests it was the latter. In May 1691, as William prepared to depart for a campaign to Flanders, George asked the king leave to serve in the fleet without command. According to Sarah Churchill, William reportedly embraced George but said nothing. As George took the silence for consent, and began packing his bags,

> The king, as it afterwards appeared, had left orders with the Queen, that she should neither suffer the Prince to go, nor yet forbid him to go, if she could contrive matters, as to make his staying home his own choice.[114]

Queen Mary then tried to enlist Sarah Churchill's aid to accomplish this task, but Sarah refused to do so unless the queen acknowledged the request came from her. Finally, in a repeat of George's Irish humiliation, Queen Mary sent the earl of

Nottingham to positively forbid the Prince "not to hazard himself on board the fleet."[115] Regardless of George's military competency, William's aversion to Anne's growing political independence undoubtedly influenced his decision to bar George from active service.[116]

William's contemptuous treatment of George angered Anne, yet George continued to negotiate the troubled waters separating the king and queen and his wife. As Anne and the Marlboroughs chose to defy William and Mary, George employed his natural deference and affability to minimize the bad feelings, as he played the role of forgiver and intercessor within the royal family. In 1692, at the height of animosity between the cockpit circle and the crown, George inquired whether he could pay his respects to William prior to the latter's departure for the continent.[117] Although William had deprived George and Anne of their customary guard, and William's own guard took no notice of the prince when he arrived at Kensington, the meeting must have been a success: following the interview the drums rolled as the guards stood at attention when George took his departure.[118] Soon after William embarked, George was recalled to the privy council, on one occasion accompanying Queen Mary back to her apartments to dine with her.[119] In December 1690, when Anne's relations with William and Mary were particularly tense, George was called to the council of nine, the regency council headed by Queen Mary that ruled during William's absences on the continent.[120] George undoubtedly earned these distinctions on account of his own efforts to coexist peacefully with William and Mary and the cockpit circle.[121]

George's efforts as an intercessor between warring royal factions reflected a political role royal women usually played. Yet George somehow sidestepped contemporary attacks upon his masculinity. Although George's efforts to create a military reputation under William III failed miserably, his reputation for valor in the Danish army prior to his marriage was still well known at the time of his death in 1708. While Anne certainly cuckolded George politically in her reliance on the Marlboroughs, she was careful to preserve a public image of wifely deference and devotion to her husband. While such tactics caused friction between Mary I and Philip of Spain, it was perhaps the secret to the success of Anne and George's marriage; the unambitious but willing proxy loyally supported by his politically minded wife; an inversion of gendered roles that outwardly played to conventional expectations. As Anne and the Marlboroughs formulated policy, George was their physical representative in the enemy camp, so to speak. While William refused to give George the opportunity for military distinction, he still felt compelled to provide his heir's husband a place in government, a role that was probably contingent on George's affable policy of nonparticipation.[122]

Nevertheless, George's access to the royal court served as a valuable political conduit in the context of Anne's estrangement from it. Unfortunately, all of George's efforts to heal the breach between Anne and Mary had failed by the time of Mary's death in December 1694. During his bereavement, William once again slighted George, by denying him precedence during Mary's funeral.[123] Mary's death, however, allowed William and Anne to reach at least a public pro forma reconciliation. Indeed, from 1694 to William's death in 1702, there were few public humiliations for George, although he relinquished the military aspirations that seemed to be his only discernible ambitions.[124] George's status as the father of the duke of Gloucester, the male Protestant heir of the House of Stuart, probably softened William's later treatment of George, as the king was personally fond of the young prince.[125]

Following Mary II's death, and the remainder of William III's reign, George reflected Anne's status as the king's heir, enjoying a public reputation as a man of affairs. In January 1695, one contemporary drew attention to the animosity remaining between Anne and William, but identified George as the historical agent responsible for reconciling the two:

> Great pains are taken to bring about reconciliation between the king and the prince of Denmark; but as if it was a general peace, all the steps are taken with so many precautions and so slowly, that we have no great reason to expect a happy issue of them.[126]

Such pessimism was unfounded; George of Denmark immediately embraced William's signal marks of favor. From 1695 to 1697 George sat on William's cabinet council.[127] However, William declined to appoint George to the Commission of Justices empowered to administer the kingdom during the king's absences on the continent.[128]

William also decided not to place Anne on the commission, neither did he keep her personally informed of government affairs.[129]

On the other hand, in his final years, William allowed Anne to play the role of royal hostess in court functions such as "drawing rooms": innocuous social gatherings for which William himself hardly had the patience.[130] In public, William accorded Anne every respect due a female heir to his throne, but this recognition did not include any form of political role. On the other hand, William maintained the political fiction of George's status as an important man of affairs by providing him posts in government, giving to George what he would not to Anne. Within this modus vivendi, William and Anne, following Mary's death, maintained a guarded status quo in their political relationship to each other.

George himself was much more comfortable playing the social role of husband and father within his own nuclear family. That role, of course, also had a public dimension. In 1697, on William's return from the Peace of Rijswick, Prince George represented the king's heir as he accompanied the king in his coach from Greenwich into London, while Anne herself viewed the procession privately from a window.[131] Two years later, for the ten-year-old duke of Gloucester's pleasure, George accompanied King William as they inspected three horse troop guards at Hyde Park. George also joined William and other aristocratic males at the Newmarket horse races in the final years of William's reign.[132] Inevitably, William III found it expedient to consort in public with his heir's husband. Such demonstrations provided William with the means to indirectly acknowledge Anne's position as heir, while William was well aware that George of Denmark possessed the most benign and comical of public personas. As this popular rhyme put it:

> King William thinks all
> Queen Mary talks all
> Prince George drinks all
> And Princess Anne eats all.[133]

But although George enjoyed cordial relations with William in his final years, he also became a rallying point for parliamentary opposition to the king. In 1689, William had induced George to surrender certain properties in Denmark to the Duke of Holstein. Ten years later, William still had not recompensed the prince and princess of Denmark, another grievance Anne held against her brother-in-law. In autumn 1699, George solicited William III to settle the outstanding debt and the king requested parliament to grant his brother-in-law those funds. Although William had encountered difficulty achieving his financial objectives in this parliament, "the most violent of the opposition were desirous to gratify the Prince at the expense of the King," and the grant was carried with little difficulty.[134] Much of William's unpopularity in parliament was due to his reliance on his Dutch advisors Portland and Albemarle, and in April 1700 the House of Commons voted that a resolution should be presented to the king asking him to remove all foreigners from his councils, except for Prince George.[135]

While William could not escape his perception as a foreign king, Anne's greatest political strengths as William's heir were her native Englishness as well as the existence of her own Protestant male heir. The duke of Gloucester, however, had endured a precarious existence, suffering from cerebral swelling and convulsive fits; his tragic death on July 30, 1700, six months after Anne's seventeenth and last pregnancy ended in a stillbirth, required further definition of the Protestant succession as outlined in the Bill of Rights. Gloucester's death robbed George of his most important achievement. By 1700, George did not possess any form of political affinity or following separate from his wife, while he had long forsaken any desire to create a military reputation under William III. What was left to him was the position of father to a future king of England. Like the barren queens Catherine of Aragon and Catherine of Braganza before him, George's inability to propagate the dynasty rendered him even more politically superfluous than he already was. Increased fears of Jacobitism, resulting from Gloucester's death, plagued both William III and Anne, and were soon addressed by statute, in the Act of Settlement, passed in 1701.[136]

The Act of Settlement was a defining moment in the history of the English monarchy, as parliament demonstrated its ability, after three hundred years of trying, to order the royal succession.[137] While the Bill of Rights had acknowledged George indirectly, in his ability to sire further Protestant heirs, the Act of Settlement, passed under the assumption that Anne would no longer conceive, considered George of Denmark to be politically nonexistent as it reaffirmed Anne's sole right to inherit the crown.[138] Thus, the main purpose of the Act was to order a Protestant succession following Anne's eventual death. By settling the succession on the House of Hanover, the Act once again made explicit the dictum laid down in the Bill of Rights that the monarch must be Protestant to possess the crown.[139] Thus, when William III died on March 10, 1702,

Anne possessed a clear parliamentary title. In 1702, such a title had no connection to the common law rights of husbands or the theory of the divine right of kings. While moderate Tories could view Anne as a more-or-less true hereditary successor, Whigs could comprehend the new queen as they did William and Mary, as an unambiguously parliamentary monarch. With the death of William III then, the possible common law rights of George of Denmark to be king alongside his wife constituted an anachronism in post–Glorious Revolution political reality.[140]

George's unrecognized common law marriage rights indicated the changing nature of the royal office. For the Empress Matilda, the pursuit of the crown was the pursuit of both a feudal estate and a divinely sanctioned office, which made contemporaries nervous over the possible claims her husband might lay to the estate of English kingship. Four hundred years later, the Tudor-era Act Concerning Regal Power clearly identified kingship still as an estate and an office, while the negotiators for Mary's marriage and parliament sought to circumvent any common law or wider European claims of a prospective husband to a regnant queen's royal estate. But by 1702, kingship was identified much more as a political office.[141] The growth of bureaucratic government, and the sheer cost of financing continental and naval warfare laid to rest the anachronistic medieval ideal of a monarch able to pay for the normal costs of administration out of the royal estate. While a royal estate existed until the middle of the eighteenth century, William's reign inaugurated the evolution of the civil list, a procession of parliamentary grants to the monarch acknowledging the wide discrepancy between royal income and the cost of government. This inescapable financial reality has maintained all British sovereigns since. Thus, Anne, upon her accession, brought to her marriage a salaried position, rather than a landed inheritance. Given these developments, George's position as the husband of a regnant queen possessed no constitutional significance whatsoever, nor was there any contemporary mention of a gendered social correlation between George's status and the wives of male kings, all of whom became queens upon their husband's accessions.

Prince George of Denmark, Consort to the Queen

Once Anne became queen, George of Denmark was widely recognized as an appendage of his wife, much as Mary II was considered in her relationship to William. Unlike her sister, Queen Anne was a female king, recognized by her contemporaries as such, entirely in accordance with the gendered definitions of royal power enunciated in the 1554 Act Concerning Regal Power.[142] While the Bill of Rights had qualified Mary II's possession of royal authority, the Act of Settlement recognized Anne's sole right to inherit, as she assumed possession of the full royal prerogative enjoyed by William III, without the gendered ambiguities plaguing the Glorious Revolution's settlement of the crown.

Thus, upon her accession, it was universally recognized that Anne had succeeded alone, as John Sharpe, Archbishop of York, made clear in his coronation sermon, "Her reign alone will let us see, that it is not without great reason, that in my text Queens are joyn'd as equal sharers with kings."[143]

Similarly, while Mary II basked in a public image rooted in consortship, Anne looked back to sixteenth-century precedents for female rulership. Upon their accessions, Mary I and Elizabeth I had both constructed representations as virgin queens and wives of their kingdoms to bolster their possession of kingly authority. Such imagery did not work for a decidedly matronly and married Anne in 1702. Instead, Anne achieved immediate recognition as the mother of her country, by co-opting the patriarchal family/ state analogy. This was a logical and appropriate gendered representation, as English kings in the past had commonly represented themselves as fathers to their kingdom. This imagery was also present in the archbishop's sermon, which emphasized that "kings and queens should submit their scepters to that of Jesus Christ, and become nursing fathers and nursing mothers to his Church and people."[144] Although the archbishop's sermon clearly equated Anne's queenship with kingly power, this particular image of a familial relationship between Anne and her kingdom implied that the Queen's motherhood to her nation did not necessarily include a husband. Indeed, the coronation sermon was conspicuous in its omission of even a single reference to Prince George of Denmark.

However, while Anne's body politic was single, her body natural had a husband. It is noteworthy that Anne's accession did not produce the kind of polemical debate concerning female rule that accompanied Mary I's accession, nor the justifications for Mary II's subordinate political relationship to William III. In fact, contemporary opinion recalled arguments originally set forth in John Aylmer's 1559 work, *A Harborowe for Trewe Subjects*, citing the

Hebrew judge Deborah, "tho'a married woman and subject to a husband, reign'd over the Lord's people notwithstanding."[145] The image of Deborah, in fact, was a much more perfect fit for Anne than for the unmarried Elizabeth I; while Anne was her husband's subordinate in the domestic sphere of her home and marriage, in the public sphere of royal government she was the chief magistrate who knew no peer. In turn, George of Denmark, emulating Deborah's husband, offered no challenge to his wife's superior magisterial authority, as he stepped forward as the first peer to offer his homage, while in theory remaining the lord and master of his home. The persuasiveness of these perceptions, however, depended on George of Denmark's acquiescence.

This, in fact, turned out to be George's finest public performance. Contemporary commentary confirms that Anne and George were successful at creating such perceptions, as it recognized the distinct social and political spheres that Anne inhabited as monarch:

> [He was] an extremely kind husband, evidencing his excessive love, and yet behaving himself as a submissive subject, in paying all due respect to her majesty. His royal spouse, tho' exalted to the throne, consequently supreme over all her subjects, yet demeand'd herself with kindness and obedience towards him; the addition of three crowns not impairing her familiar affection, or a whit altering her conjugal submission to her lord's desires.[146]

George's desires, however, rarely deviated from those of his wife, as this anecdote from Anne's coronation illustrated:

> She [Queen Anne] arrived in her sedan chair at St. James's Palace in the evening, greatly exhausted. Prince George of Denmark, who was in high spirits, was in no mood for retiring. At length the Lord Chamberlain ventured to draw attention to Her Majesty's weariness, and hinted that it might be as well if he proposed retirement. "I propose!" exclaimed the Prince. "I cannot; I am her Majesty's subject, and have sworn homage to her today. I shall do naught but what she commands me." The Queen was equal to the occasion, and replied, with a smile, "Then, as that is the case, and I am very tired, I do command you, George, to come to bed.[147]

As a good wife, however, Anne labored to convince her contemporaries that she regretted the fact that her husband did not share her royal status. There is some murky evidence that, on the surface, suggests that Anne allegedly considered a plan to make George a king consort. It was conceivable for Anne to attempt to use her prerogative powers to accomplish this goal as she would with a peer. Instead, she chose to have her first parliament consider the proposition.

However, the project never evolved past the discussion stage.[148] Parliamentary records do not reveal any debates on the subject, nor did such a bill ever materialize. Sources describing Marlborough's role indicated that Anne was persuaded that it was unconstitutional for parliament to make George a king consort.[149] In his 1743 biography of Marlborough, Thomas Lediard recorded that news of a possible scheme to make George king was circulating in the "Protestant Courts of Germany, esp. Hanover, that Anne had design of proposing to Parliament the royal dignity [for her husband]."[150] One noted authority on the life of the duke of Marlborough insisted that, "it fell to Marlborough to persuade her that this could not be done," arguing that Anne's desire to present an English contrast to William would be stymied by such an effort.[151] There is also scanty evidence of an alleged Tory plot to make George king in order to subvert the terms of the Act of Settlement.[152]

What eventually did emerge from parliament was a bill granting George a whopping £100,000 annually should he outlive the queen, while also exempting him from those clauses of the Act of Settlement that prohibited foreigners from holding public office, which caused a commotion in the House of Commons. Bishop Burnet, no political friend to the Queen, provided a description for this chain of events that withheld as much as it revealed:

> Great opposition was made . . . to the passing of this clause, but the Queen pressed it with great earnestness she had yet shewn in anything whatsoever; she thoughtit became her, as a good wife, to have the act passed, in which she might be the more earnest, because it was not thought advisable to move for an act that should take Prince George into the consortship of the royal dignity.[153]

Unfortunately, Burnet did not state where this advice came from, or what its substance was. However, as Burnet suggests, it was entirely within parliament's competence to pass an act creating George a king consort. A pamphlet circulating during Anne's first parliament made a strong case for parliament to do just this.

> If we consider that his royal highness is the happy consort of our most gracious queen, for he may have a great share in her majesty's council's, and in the present ministry, we ought in prudence to pay the greatest respects which are within our power to a person so nearly concerned in the kingdom's happiness.[154]

Although the pamphlet acknowledged George's public reputation as an important man of affairs, it stressed that George's kingship would not encroach upon Anne's full possession of the royal prerogative. The author called for George's creation as king consort, "in conjunction with her majesty our present Queen; yet the administration of the regal power may be solely in her majesty."[155] To prove the point, the joint reigns of Philip and Mary, and more recently, William and Mary, were cited as applicable precedents. Philip particularly was the more salient example; while he did not possess formal political power, from the time of his marriage all statutes, proclamations, writs, and all other government documents were issued jointly in the name Philip and Mary. Philip's name always came first, undoubtedly to conform to the patriarchal social custom of a husband having precedence over his wife. The pamphlet's social logic was a conventional reflection of marital gender roles, but one that was ultimately in conflict with Anne's possession of kingly power.

Ultimately, the reason George did not become a king consort was that Anne chose not to pursue the project. The discussions were all, apparently, behind closed doors, leaving only sketchy and fragmentary secondhand evidence for the historian to assess. As a king, George would hardly have been a political threat to Anne. However, Marlborough may have convinced Anne that elevating George would violate both the Bill of Rights and the Act of Settlement, since neither statute made any provision for her husband. As Harley's correspondence suggests, George's position as a crowned king could have been exploited by nonjuring Tories and Jacobins, eager to derail the Hanoverian succession. Anne also may have felt that her possession of kingly power was incompatible with her husband enjoying the status of king. But Anne, among her copious literary remains, left no explanation for her decision, which remains, ultimately, elusive. Nevertheless, it seems reasonable to suppose that if Anne had really desired to make George a king consort, she would have pursued it as vigorously as she did the passage of the annuity act.

Although George remained his wife's subject, the annuity act clearly demonstrated the high regard she felt for her husband, and the respect for him that she expected from her subjects:

> In consideration of the natural love and affection which your Majesty bears towards the said prince and of the eminent virtues wherewith that excellent prince is endued as also with regard to the great and signal services under your majesties authority he hath performed and doth continue to perform.[156]

The entire episode is completely in keeping with Anne's own proprietary view of her political role, but it also represents a public relations scheme to bolster her popular reputation as a good monarch and a good wife. While male kings did so by emulating male gendered qualities such as martial skills and leadership ability, female kings had to emulate womanly qualities. As a married woman, Anne wished to be known as a good wife. At the same time, Anne softened the blow to George's masculinity by heralding his importance and his worth. Indeed, Anne proved to be a most generous wife. Upon her accession, Anne ensured that George enjoyed recognition as the first peer of the realm, weighted down with honors and offices that made him preeminent in the military as Lord High Admiral and Generalissimo of all English forces on land, as the War of the Spanish Succession against France was about to commence.[157]

If military distinction, rather than a crown, was George's only aspiration, his health robbed him of the fruits of his moment of glory. From William III's last years into his wife's reign, George was plagued not only by asthma, but gout and other maladies requiring persistent bleeding and blistering.[158] In August 1702, Anne and George journeyed to Bath in hopes that the waters would soothe the prince's chronic asthma. In November, as Anne's first parliament met, George was severely ill once again, as one contemporary informed his wife, "Prince George has been given over this week past of his asthma; he could not be kept awake with blisters nor cupping, so that everyone expected death each minute. He is this day much better and may last for some while, though I think not long. . . ."[159]

Anne joined both houses of parliament, November 12, 1702, to hear a sermon and prayer for George's recovery.[160] While George ultimately survived on this occasion as he had so many times in the past, he remained chronically ill for the rest of his life.

Despite George's declining health, Anne also attempted to have him named supreme commander of allied forces in Europe. Achieving this unenviable task fell to Marlborough. While Anne threatened to hold back the declaration of war against France, all of Marlborough's exertions on George's behalf could not sway the Dutch, "not only because they placed no confidence in the military talents of the Prince, but because they feared he would resist the control of the field deputies, whom they sent to the army."[161] George was reportedly incensed with Marlborough for his failure: Marlborough wrote to Lord Treasurer Sidney Godolphin in August 1702, inquiring whether "Prince George be capable of thinking soo ill of mee."[162] Anne also attempted to obtain William's office of Stadtholder for George in the Netherlands, a request to which a bewildered states-general made no reply.

Given George's lack of leadership ability and his rapidly declining health, it is unlikely that Anne really expected him to formulate war strategy. It is much more plausible to assume that the creations were symbolic, designed to make up for the slights and humiliations George had endured from James II and William III.[163] But just as importantly, the creations can also be seen as an attempt to bolster George's masculine reputation within the context of his marriage to a regnant queen. Although those close to him knew the extent of his political limitations, George enjoyed a benign yet popular reputation as an important man of affairs, which complemented Anne's own popularity with her subjects at large. As English continental commander, Marlborough on paper answered to George of Denmark; his correspondence contains numerous references to keeping George informed of military affairs, while paying him all due honor as his superior officer.[164]

In reality, George was nothing more than an official conduit of military policy. Much like a modern constitutional monarch, George went through the motions of generating official memoranda without any discernible influence on the substance of such policies.[165] Nevertheless, this activity had a purpose: what was perhaps most important to Anne was that her subjects perceived that George was an important man of affairs, possessing the illusion of power, which bolstered his public reputation as a suitable husband for a ruling queen, rather than the substance, which was beyond his competency. George remained Anne's political proxy in the House of Lords, voting reluctantly for the Occasional Conformity Bill of 1703, which he, as a Lutheran, understandably opposed.[166]

On one occasion, however, George used his prestige independently, as a means to advance the fortunes of an eminently deserving individual, Isaac Newton. Following Newton's elevation to the presidency of the Royal Society, he struck up a friendship with George, who agreed to underwrite the research costs of Newton's colleague, John Flamsteed. George's interest in science, and his esteem for Newton, eventually brought Newton to the attention of Queen Anne, who knighted him in 1705 following a royal visit to Trinity Lodge, Cambridge.[167]

This rare glimpse into George's intellectual pursuits provides a counterpoint to his indolent conventional image. Nevertheless, George continued to provide evidence of his incurably easygoing nature. Left to his own devices, in fact, George had no stomach for the harsh realities of politics, which on one occasion meant defying the wishes of his wife. In his autobiography, George's secretary, Dr. George Clark, serving as an MP in 1705, recalled how Prince George dismissed him on account of his failure to vote for Anne's choice for Speaker of the House of Commons, and the distress he felt after the deed was done;

> But then Prince George changed his mind, sent his footmen to see if Mr. Nicholas, his treasurer, had already done the deed, having changed his mind.

Even though the deed had been done, Clark further remarked that, "I had several intimations that my waiting upon him would not be unacceptable."[168] Although George's loyalty was admirable, he remained pliable and softhearted toward his servants to the end of his life.

George's tenure as Lord High Admiral also gave final confirmation of his utter lack of political and administrative discipline and competency. While George was the official conduit for all manner of business related to naval affairs, Marlborough's brother, George Churchill, a man long in the Prince's service, wielded the principal power in the council. Bishop Burnet observed that George, "Was unhappily prevailed upon to take upon him the post of high Admiral, of which he understood little; but he was fatally led by those who had credit with him, who had not all of them his good qualities." To this Burnet added, "In the conduct of our affairs, as great errors were committed, so great misfortunes had followed on them, all these were imputed to the Prince's easiness, and to his favorite's mismanagement and bad designs."[169] George's chronic inability to instill discipline and provide leadership, which Clarendon had noticed back in 1690, was fully evident during George's tenure as Lord High Admiral. Although George's personal failings were forgivable within the private circle of his family, in the glare of public opinion they became a means to attack the queen politically.

Thus, in the final year of his life George played the part of public whipping boy for his wife one last time. In January 1708, when Anne sought to create new Tory bishops, the Whigs threatened to "show up the admiralty in such a way that the Prince should be obliged to give up his post of high admiral."[170] Despite the storm, George remained devoted to his staff, notably George Churchill, as he always had to both Anne and the Marlboroughs.[171] Later that year, when Anne reached a critical phase of her relationship with both Sarah Churchill and the duumvirs Marlborough and Sidney Godolphin, George supplied her with support during a highly charged political power struggle for control of the ministry.[172]

By this time, after Anne and George had been married for twenty-five years, the distinction between personal and political assistance probably no longer existed. In a letter of June 1708, Sidney Godolphin wrote to Marlborough describing a particularly unpleasant interview with the queen:

> In short, the obstinancy was unaccountable, and the battell might have lasted till [evening], if after the clock had struck 3 [Prince George] had not thought fitt to come in and look as he thought it were dinner time.[173]

George may very well have been hungry, consistent with his popular reputation for gluttony, but it is entirely possible that George offered a practiced and polished piece of theater to rescue Anne from her impasse with Godolphin, acting as an unofficial chief of staff in the personal and political comfort of his spouse. One month later, Godolphin again wrote to Marlborough, suggesting he consult the Danish envoy Count Plessen in order to channel information through George to Anne, in the hopes of salvaging their deteriorating relationship with the queen.[174] In both cases, Godolphin supplied a rare glimpse of the extent of George's influence with his wife.

George's final year of life, then, was his political swan song, as his health worsened in autumn 1708.[175] On October 24, George died with his wife at his bedside, as she had been for several days. A number of contemporaries believed that Anne never fully recovered from the loss of her husband. Following her tragic attempts to bear children and the break with her longtime advisors and companions the Marlboroughs and Godolphin, Anne lost the one individual able to provide her with any sense of emotional well being within her domestic circle.[176]

One of Queen Anne's earliest biographers, writing twenty years after her death, recalled the national mood that accompanied the announcement of the Prince's death:

> His royal highness's great humanity and justice, with his other extraordinary virtues, had so endeared him to the whole nation, that all orders of men discovered an unspeakable grief for the loss of so excellent a prince.[177]

George had played his unique role well. As Anne was a popular queen, so was her consort. On those occasions when the English people saw their queen in public, George of Denmark was by her side, congenial and deferential. Inevitably, the English people became accustomed to the sight of a male consort to a female king. George's public persona was benign, if not comical, yet the men of power surrounding his wife offered him the constant deference that was his due as the husband of a ruling queen, at least to his face. Even before Anne became queen, George consented to play a variety of public roles, and accept public honors that would have been hers had she been a man. But once Anne became queen, George simply stood aside and made no protest as his wife was recognized as an autonomous female king. By these acts, George of Denmark represents a significant figure in the evolution of female rule. Two years after his death, William Cockburn succinctly summed up George's signal accomplishment:

> He was not ambitious to grasp of power, altho' he had the opportunity of asking what he pleas'd, being sure of all requests, yet his demands were ever attended with modesty and moderation.[178]

George's public role as the informal but beloved consort to a ruling queen hardened into political precedent. One hundred and thirty-two years after George's death, in 1840, the youthful Queen Victoria married her cousin, Albert of Saxe-Coburg-Gotha.

Following the marriage, the Whig government of Lord Melbourne was constrained to revisit the history of Anne's reign, to see just what kind of status George of Denmark enjoyed.[179] While Victoria initially wanted Albert to share the royal dignity with her in 1840, she was dissuaded by clear political precedent. Whereas George of Denmark might have had a choice in 1702, Prince Albert did not, as he created a body of political influence informally as the queen's husband.[180] Given his desire for power and influence, Albert found the role of male consort much less congenial to his talents and aspirations than George of Denmark had.

George of Denmark's consignment to the informal status of male consort represents the apotheosis of English female kingship. Mary I came to the throne in 1553 as an unmarried female heiress, whose right was upheld by both statute and common law rights of inheritance. When Mary contemplated marriage, however, her husband's possible common law rights to her royal prerogative were one of several gendered uncertainties concerning female rule that arose during her reign. But the reign of Anne, following the long reign of Elizabeth I, and the more recent Glorious Revolution and Act of Settlement, saw the public role of female king clearly defined as an office, rather than a heritable estate. Under these circumstances, George's common law rights to his wife's throne were uncertain, and needed to be invoked, something he and Anne never made any attempt to do. It was entirely possible for Parliament to have created George of Denmark as a king consort, but contemporaries left no clear explanation for why this did not occur. However, given the power dynamics of George and Anne's marriage, it is reasonable to suppose that they both agreed not to pursue this goal, and to allow Anne to enjoy a complete and unambiguous autonomy as monarch.

George of Denmark himself was apparently happy with such an outcome. While a man of ability and daring might have attempted to use his status as a queen's husband as a springboard for political power, George stood aside as the evolution of female rule discarded the male counterpart completely. While George of Denmark may still have dreamed of military glory when his wife became queen, by the time the opportunity arrived, he was old and sick. Thus his personal inclinations and energies were perfectly suited for the informal role of consort. In this one public role he excelled. In a poem included in a short history of George's life published soon after his death, a curious mixture of fact and fiction concludes with a ringing endorsement of his most successful role:

> And thus we've lost the pillar of our state,
> both good and virtuous, wise as well as great.
> The best of men, who led the best of lives.
> The best of husbands, to the best of wives.
> The best of queens ne're loved a better man.
> Then show me such another, if you can.[181]

Figure 1   Queen Elizabeth I, "The Gender Queen," Huth. 50. (28),
by Permission of the British Library.

Figure 2   Seal of the Empress Matilda, Add. Ch. 75724, by Permission of the British Library.

Figure 3   Matilda, Cotton Nero D VII, by Permission of the
British Library.

Figure 4   Queen Mary I, C. 38. g. 3, by Permission of the British Library.

Figure 5 Queen Anne, P.P. 3360, by permission of the British
Library.

Figure 6   The Youthful Queen Victoria, 10804 N. 14, by
Permission of the British Library.

CHAPTER 4

"WHAT POWER HAVE I LEFT?" QUEEN VICTORIA'S BEDCHAMBER CRISIS REVISITED

and the Queen felt this was an attempt to see whether she could be led and managed like a child.[1]

The final chapter of this study confronts a sort of monarch entirely different from the female rulers discussed in previous chapters. Mary I, Elizabeth I, and Anne were all mature, experienced women whose careers took place in the context of a politically powerful regal office. During the periods 1553–1603 and 1702–1714, these women had successfully accomplished a gendered transformation of the practical and symbolic authority of English kingship. In particular, the ability of Mary I and Elizabeth I to create a viable model of female sovereignty within male dominant political structures formed a permanent part of the fabric of English political evolution. This became clear following the Glorious Revolution, as a number of factors, discussed in the previous chapter, allowed Queen Anne recognition as an autonomous female ruler despite her married state.

One hundred and twenty-three years elapsed between the death of Anne in 1714 and the accession of the eighteen-year-old Victoria in 1837. During this time, from the accession of George I until the death of William IV, kingship appeared exclusively in the conventional male form. This period experienced both the gradual transition to constitutional monarchy as well as the gender transformations within British society which formed a major part of the social effects of industrialization, modernization, and class formation. All of these seemingly distinct historical processes collided in the Bedchamber Crisis of 1839.

This crisis has long remained a misunderstood and easily dismissed political flare up that toppled a would-be, constitutionally sanctioned change of government. On Tuesday, May 7, 1839, the Whig ministry of Viscount Melbourne tendered its resignation to the Queen after carrying a motion to suspend the Jamaican constitution by only five votes, a slim majority signaling his party's lack of confidence in the House of Commons. On the advice of her now former prime minister, and according to current political convention, Victoria offered the government to Tory leader Sir Robert Peel. Reluctant to shoulder the burden of governing without a working majority in the House of Commons, Peel asked the queen for permission to replace bedchamber ladies, with kinship ties to Whig politicians, with ladies similarly connected to the Tory party, as a display of royal support for his government. However, the queen refused, on the grounds that Peel's request was "contrary to usage" and "repugnant to her feelings." On Friday, May 10, Peel resigned his commission. To the queen's personal satisfaction, the Melbourne government returned to power until the general election of 1841. On the following Monday, May 13, the Crisis reached its political conclusion as Peel and Whig minister Lord John Russell offered their respective explanations to a wildly expectant House of Commons.

The Bedchamber Crisis caused a sensation in its day, sparking a public discourse concerning the proper role of monarchy in its power relations with parliament. At the center of the controversy was the question of gender: Victoria's position as a female monarch provoked debate concerning the political differences between male and female monarchs, and the proper application of precedent. William IV (1830–1837) was Victoria's immediate predecessor as monarch, but Anne (1702–1714) was her immediate predecessor as female monarch: precedents from both reigns concerning the allegedly political composition of the Queen's royal bedchamber came into play during the Crisis.

The Bedchamber Crisis, then, was complicated, comprising a political crisis concerning the power of monarchy within a political system undergoing a process of liberalization, and a gender crisis concerning the role of women in politics, which brought the emerging Victorian ideology of separate spheres for men and women into the glare of public opinion and parliamentary debate.

Although contemporaries were amazed by the outcome of the affair, the Bedchamber Crisis has long been considered little more than a footnote in Victorian political history.[2] To generations of British historians, the crisis constituted a trite political sideshow displaying a young, inexperienced, emotional Queen, unable to grasp the inexorable progression of parliamentary supremacy.[3] Diarist Charles Greville, no political friend to the Queen, echoed the sentiments of typical Tories, "She exhibited the talent of a rather thoughtless and headstrong girl; and [she was] secretly longing to get back her old ministers [if she could by any pretext or expedient]."[4]

Greville's assessment filtered down to the twentieth century through Lytton Strachey, the first of Victoria's modern biographers, who declared the youthful Victoria incompetent:

> Of the wider significance of political questions she knew nothing; all she saw was that her friends were in office and about her, and that it would be dreadful if they ceased to be so.[5]

The pervasiveness of this interpretation is understandable: the well-documented emotional outbursts of the still-teenaged Victoria steal the thunder from other, more subtle forms of evidence, that suggest a more complicated and multilayered crisis. Indeed, beneath the explosive clash of personalities that characterized the affair lies a gendered political debate revealing the ambiguous status of women within a parliamentary system that continued to deny them formal political representation until the twentieth century.

Only recently have historians detected the complexity of the Bedchamber Crisis. Arguments have been advanced relating the Crisis to the preceding Flora Hastings scandal, discussed later in the chapter, while even more recent analysis has attempted to probe the gendered contexts within which the Crisis took place.[6] The examination of the Crisis offered here combines political and gender analysis with one hitherto neglected aspect of the Crisis: the political evolution of the royal bedchamber.[7] This methodology, combined with an analysis of Victoria's own interpretation of the salient issues at stake, uncovers the Bedchamber Crisis as a significant signpost of nineteenth-century British political and social evolution, and reveals the youthful Victoria as a much more informed and active historical agent than previously detected.

As the Crisis demonstrated the intensely personal nature of political interactions, the primary sources examined in this study consist of the queen's letters and journal, as well as the correspondence and journals of the major politicians and political observers of the day, whose opinions betrayed the ambiguous constitutional status of the monarch, particularly of a young unmarried female monarch, in the first half of the nineteenth century.[8] Parliamentary records also reveal the contested nature of precedent as a means of resolving the Crisis, as Victoria's unique position as a regnant queen brought the emergent ideology of separate spheres into the Crisis's political debate. Far from being an insignificant political tantrum thrown by an inexperienced teenaged Queen, the Bedchamber Crisis constituted a convoluted attempt to elevate women to a formal political status within the body politic, which Victoria thwarted with a flourish of monarchical power. Thus, the true legacy of the Bedchamber Crisis consists of the ironic combination of a victory for female kingship won by an assertion of the political insignificance of women.

The Royal Bedchamber

The political evolution of the royal bedchamber formed a significant aspect of the Whig explanation for Victoria's conduct during the Bedchamber Crisis, the last occasion in English history in which male politicians recognized and assigned a political value to what was usually a prestigious but domestic post for aristocratic women within the monarch's royal household. But it was far from the first. Throughout English history, the royal bedchamber of a king was the epicenter of the royal household, itself a part of the monarch's court, the physical space where kings lived and royal power was exercised. Although formal participation in English politics and government was exclusively male dominant until recent times (except for ruling queens), both men and women, engaged in myriads of sociopolitical relationships, populated the highly politicized spaces of the royal court.[9] From queen consorts and on downward the aristocratic social ladder, women who inhabited the royal court frequently influenced domestic and foreign policies, the distribution of patronage, or enriched themselves and their families by their proximity to the royal ear.[10]

As the inner sanctum of the royal court, the compositions of royal bedchambers were necessarily gendered. Since the

Anglo-Saxon period, aristocratic men served male kings in their most intimate aspects in their bedchambers, as a corollary to their political and military status. In turn, female aristocrats reflected the status and furthered the political ambitions of their male kinsmen as they tended to the domestic needs of queens consort.[11] With the arrival of the sixteenth-century regnant Queens Mary I and Elizabeth I, a politically gendered transformation of the royal bedchamber occurred, as elite women moved from inhabiting the intimate spaces of a consort to a number of the top posts in the privy chamber of the ruling monarch. This resulted in an alteration of the symbiotic political relationship between the privy chamber and the privy council, that had developed over the course of the reigns of Henry VIII and Edward VI.[12]

As female kings and queens at the same time, Mary I and Elizabeth I considered only themselves, by virtue of their possession of the crown, exempt from the restrictions placed upon women by the dictates of Tudor political society. Although the 1554 Act Concerning Regal Power had recognized regnant queens as kings, court ladies under Mary and Elizabeth remained within the social and political bounds of Tudor society that denied them a formal role in government.[13] However, their intimate relationship with ruling queens afforded them the opportunity to indirectly and informally influence the course of politics, by obtaining patronage for their male relations or influencing the course of marriage negotiations[14]. Elite women had performed these functions for centuries, but under a female king the middleman of the queen consort was eliminated; the queen herself, surrounded by her ladies, was the font of power. In a much more malevolent yet conventional form of political influence, court ladies (and gentlemen) were a resource for gossip and slander, which served as a potent political weapon in the crowded corners of the Elizabethan court. Sir Walter Raleigh, the epitome of a grasping Elizabethan courtier, summed up his own estimation of the political power of court ladies, lamenting that they were "capable of doing great harm, but no good," in furthering the interests of men who solicited their aid in political advancement.[15]

Under Elizabeth I's seventeenth-century male Stuart successors, the bedchamber emerged as a formalized political space, as elite males once again tended the monarch in his most intimate aspects, and wielded political power from the confines of the royal bedchamber.[16] Following the Glorious Revolution of 1688, the composition of William III's and Mary II's respective royal bedchambers displayed a conventionally gendered division of labor and function, with elite males engaged in politics serving the king, while the wives, daughters, and other kinship relations of such men served the queen in a purely domestic capacity. Nevertheless, with the rise of party politics in the late Stuart era, Mary's household ladies reflected the changing political composition of her husband's governments, as William employed both Tories and Whigs as ministers. As they sewed, prayed, and laughed with their queen, Mary's ladies were political only in their representational relationship to their male husbands or kinsmen: Mary's bedchamber was a model of domesticity.[17] Nevertheless, the late Stuart development of party politics and the concept of a loyal opposition transformed the nature of bedchamber ladies, rendering them flesh-and-blood representatives of partisan politics living in close proximity to the font of power.

Such modernizing processes did not enjoy favor with William and Mary's successor, Queen Anne, whose fondest desire as monarch was a nonpartisan body politic united in its support of church and state. With her 1702 accession, the royal household once again underwent a division of offices between male and female court appointments.[18] Despite the beliefs of many of her contemporaries and subsequent Whig historians, Queen Anne also adhered to the gendered distinctions between her male and female household officers and attendants established by the sixteenth-century Tudor queens.

Much recent scholarship, in fact, suggests that Anne viewed her bedchamber attendants primarily as domestic servants.[19] Although Anne formed close personal relationships with her bedchamber ladies, such as Sarah Churchill, Duchess of Marlborough, and Abigail Masham, she was reluctant to accept political advice or tolerate political discussions with these women after she became queen, much to the chagrin of Churchill, whose eventual fall from grace was directly tied to her unceasing efforts to influence the queen politically. A stickler for court etiquette and protocol, Anne adhered to conventionally prescribed roles for men and women, and maintained a gendered distinction between her male household officers, who engaged in politics, and her female bedchamber attendants, whose primary functions were domestic, serving as her intimate companions.

Nor surprisingly, Anne saw no conflict of interest with retaining the domestic services of household ladies whose kinsmen had fallen from political favor. When Anne dismissed the duchess of Marlborough from her government at the beginning of 1711, her daughters remained employed in Anne's household until their father was also dismissed from service at the end of that year, when they resigned their positions voluntarily.[20] Similarly, when Anne decided to appoint the duchess of Somerset to be Sarah Churchill's replacement as Groom of the Stole and Mistress of the Robes, Chief Minister Robert Harley tried to block the appointment, as the duke of Somerset had gone into opposition to his government.[21] However, Anne asserted her right to appoint her domestic companions regardless of the political persuasions of their husbands, making clear her own gendered distinctions between the roles played by male and female household officers.[22]

Following Anne's death in 1714, and the succession of four male Hanoverian monarchs, the king's bedchamber became fully and formally politicized once again.[23] Under the Whig oligarchy that controlled parliament until 1760, the effective political power of the monarch to manage parliamentary politics slowly evaporated.[24] From 1760 until the accession of Victoria, despite the vigorous attempts of George III to reverse this trend, in a process one venerable historian called "the waning of the influence of the crown," royal government, still dependent on the monarch's confidence yet also subject to the will of House of Commons, was pared down in a piecemeal fashion of its ability to direct parliamentary politics.[25] This process primarily involved the management of "influence", the control of patronage networks of civil, military, and ecclesiastical offices, sinecures, and court appointments, which allowed the king's ministry to manipulate the direction of parliamentary business.[26]

The last bastion of direct royal influence, centered in the royal household, lay in the ability to control court appointments, a power George III was reluctant to surrender. However, the brief reforming ministry of the Rockingham Whigs (March 1782–April 1783) reorganized the royal household, eliminating sinecures and effectively reducing the crown's ability to dispense political patronage and influence parliamentary politics.[27] By the early nineteenth century, the assault moved on to court appointments themselves. As Melbourne later described it to Victoria, when the Whigs Lord Grenville and Charles James Fox attempted to form a ministry in 1806, "as there was nobody else," they asked the king for household changes "as a mark of confidence."[28] Despite his age and infirmity, George III remained a crusty old Tory sympathizer, removing only one appointee, Lord Sandwich, Master of the Buckhounds.[29]

Succeeding governments under the regency of the Prince of Wales (1811–1820), later George IV, attempted to expand on this precedent to tighten ministerial control over top royal household appointments. The Prince Regent, in fact, faced pressure to rearrange his household officers in 1812, when Lord Liverpool's Tory government resigned after a vote of no confidence. The proposed coalition government of lords Grey and Grenville asked the prince for household changes, declaring, "the connection of the great offices of the court with the political administration should be clearly established in its first arrangements."[30] As in the Bedchamber Crisis of 1839, the request was both personal and political; when the prince refused absolutely, the Whigs failed to secure a commission to assemble a cabinet, and the Liverpool ministry returned to power.

During the reign of Victoria's immediate predecessor, William IV, the cabinet secured control over top household appointments, including bedchamber attendants sitting in parliament. William IV made no effort to combat this development; as Melbourne later related to Victoria, "Nobody ever gave up the Household so completely as William IV."[31] Control of the household appointments was important because the men who staffed them in a male king's household were usually politicians serving in either house of parliament. Particularly when a proposed ministry did not command a comfortable majority in parliament, as occurred in 1806, 1812, as well as May 1839, the political complexion of the monarch's household officers assumed an increased significance in relation to the political balance in the House of Commons. Thus, the last Hanoverian kings faced pressure from governments, Whig and Tory, to rearrange their top household appointments in support of the party in power. This power was limited, however, to changing those household appointees actually engaged in politics. In 1834, when Peel first served as prime minister, household changes were limited to men holding seats in parliament, while Melbourne followed this model when he returned to power in 1835, leaving nonpolitical grooms and equerries in office, despite their direct or kinship connections to the Tory party.[32]

However, the political precedents relating to royal household changes that developed over the course of the 1830s were not applied to the bedchamber of William IV's consort, Queen Adelaide. Ladies with kinship ties to the Tory Party primarily populated Adelaide's bedchamber, reflecting William IV's own political tastes. During the campaign to secure passage of the Reform Act of 1832, Whig Prime Minister Lord Grey secured the resignations of those members of the king's household who opposed reform, as well as Adelaide's chamberlain, Lord Howe.[33] Grey, however, did not openly perceive Adelaide's bedchamber itself as an arena of political activity, and made no effort to purge it of women with kinship ties to the Tory Party.[34] The formal recognition of Adelaide's bedchamber as a depoliticized domestic space within the household was analogous to an emerging recognition of "separate spheres," public and political for men, private and domestic for women, in nineteenth-century British class formation.[35] However, with the death of William IV on June 20, 1837, and the accession of the eighteen-year-old Victoria, the political household of a king and the domestic household of a queen were once again combined under a female monarch.

The Gendering of Monarchical Power

The change in the monarch's gender was an event of major importance.[36] On the positive side, the image of a youthful unmarried queen, following a succession of gouty old Hanoverian kings, considered by so many contemporaries to be out of step with their times, was a breath of fresh air.[37] Although Victoria was upon her accession universally recognized as a youthful queen, as yet untarnished by participation in partisan party politics, she had in fact inherited the political prerogatives of kingship possessed by her recent predecessors. The conventional term describing Victoria's status as monarch remains queen regnant, rather than female king, which is a more descriptive term for the queen's actual political status. Although early modern statutes such as the Act Concerning Regal Power (1554) and the Act of Settlement (1701) defined the regal office as genderless, female kings were nonetheless expected to conform to socially constructed female gender roles: Victoria's attempt to wield the prerogatives of kingship during the Bedchamber Crisis, while she was an unmarried teenager, produced both condescension and consternation among her contemporaries.

Indeed, Victoria's youth and gender created the perception that she did not possess the necessary attributes to fully perform the office of king. Visually, Victoria still looked like a little girl upon her accession, standing less than five feet tall, and possessed of a round, child-like face that gave little indication of the monarch she became.[38] But her youth and sex alone were more than reason enough for contemporaries to doubt her abilities. The eminent Victorian Thomas Carlyle summed up such attitudes at Victoria's coronation:

> Poor little Queen, she is at an age which a girl can hardly be trusted to choose a bonnet, yet a task is laid upon her from which an archangel would shrink.[39]

Carlyle's impressions betrayed a fatherly feeling toward a fatherless queen.[40] To her subjects at large and her government in particular, Victoria was unmistakably a daughter who needed fatherly guidance. Whig Minister Lord Palmerston put it most bluntly, stating, "The nation will not so readily believe in the will . . . of a girl of 18 as they had been accustomed to do in the determination of men of mature age."[41] Carlyle and Palmerston were only able to base their observations upon conventional expectations of a young woman's capabilities: upon her accession, Victoria was an unknown entity to the men of power at the dawn of the era named for her. Kept out of the public view, due to her secluded upbringing under the watchful and possessive eye of her mother, the duchess of Kent, contemporaries could only assume that Victoria was desperate for mature male guidance. Unknown to the male politicians of her early reign, Victoria was trained to be both a king and a queenly consort to her future husband. Under her mother's charge, Princess Victoria received an education that stressed the study of history, politics, and religion, as well as conventionally female accomplishments, such as singing, painting, and dancing: a typical aristocratic tutelage designed to make her an appropriate wife and companion, a role she relished once she took a husband.[42] Jealous of her primary political asset, the duchess of Kent refused to allow George IV and William IV any control over the upbringing of her daughter, which in itself constituted a political victory for her over her royal brothers-in-law.[43]

The one adult male the duchess of Kent allowed access to her daughter was her brother, Leopold of Saxe-Coberg-Gotha, after 1830 King of the Belgians. Leopold's agenda for his niece was comprehensive. As a young man he had been the husband of Princess

Charlotte, daughter and heir of George IV. As a prospective male consort for a female king, Leopold, under the guidance of his advisor, Baron Stockmar, flung himself into the study of British constitutional theory and political history. Leopold apparently anticipated the kind of substantial role in his wife's future reign that had eluded George of Denmark during Queen Anne's reign.[44]

Charlotte's tragic death in 1817 sidelined Leopold's British political career. However, by the early 1830s, when Victoria's future accession seemed assured, Leopold, now king of the Belgians, put his British political education and his own experience as a monarch to good use.[45] The twin influences of her mother and her uncle instilled in Victoria a dualistic approach to her future office. Under her mother's guidance, Victoria acquired the typical outlook of her gender that drew her into the private domestic sphere shared by the aristocratic women of her household. Before and after her accession, and before her marriage, Victoria drew enormous emotional comfort from her household ladies. Thus it was up to Leopold to remind his niece that her future role as a female king would not be confined to the conventional domestic sphere of royal women, but would also encompass a singular role in the male dominated world of government and politics. In 1834, when Victoria was fifteen, Leopold urged her to study political history, warning her, "If you do not prepare yourself for your position, you may become the victim of wicked and designing people, particularly at a period when party spirit runs high."[46]

Victoria obliged her uncle, writing back to him "Reading history is one of my greatest delights."[47] Shortly following her accession, Leopold once again wrote bluntly to Victoria:

> You must study the political history of at least the last 37 years, more particularly. I had begun something of the sort with you even so back as George II, you will do well to go through the reign of George III and to follow the various circumstances which brought finally the present state of affairs.[48]

As Leopold intimated, the effective political powers of the British monarch had slowly eroded since the accession of George III. By 1837 it was a generally accepted political convention that the ministry needed the confidence of parliament and not the monarch. But it was not a fixed political rule; the monarchs of the 1830s were not the type of constitutional monarchs that Elizabeth II, a queen who reigns above the sway of party politics, is today.[49] As prince of Wales and later king, George IV moved from youthful Whig sympathies to virulent Toryism, while William IV also was a well-known Tory sympathizer. In 1834, in fact, William IV dismissed a ministry that commanded a majority in the House of Commons. While this was the last occasion when the monarch employed the prerogative to turn out a government, it was not at all certain what the precise limits of royal political propriety were.[50] Upon Victoria's accession, Walter Bagehot's relegation of the monarch to the "dignified" elements of the constitution was still thirty years away; contemporaries agreed that the crown was still a political office, yet its proper constitutional role in a political crisis was open to interpretation.[51]

Whatever the extent of her royal powers, Leopold wished his niece to retain them, writing in January 1838,

> I wish very much that you would speak to him [Melbourne] on the subject of what ought to be done to keep for the crown the little influence it may possess. Monarchy to be carried on requires certain elements, and the occupation of the sovereign must be constantly to preserve these elements, or should they have been too much weakened by untoward circumstances, to contrive by every means to strengthen them again.[52]

Leopold's advice easily served as a blueprint for Victoria's stance during the Bedchamber Crisis. Although Leopold himself was a liberal constitutional monarch, his political philosophy was not progressive. Absent from his advice to his niece was the utility of compromise in the face of unforeseen political circumstances. Leopold instead held realistic expectations that Victoria could reverse the trend of political mediocrity that characterized the reigns of her immediate predecessors. In addition to his admonitions to study political history, Leopold's letters to Victoria stressed decisiveness, steadfastness, and resolution, the most visible aspects of successful kingship. In a revealing correspondence written just prior to Victoria's accession, Leopold warned his niece that she should be "no one's tool."[53]

That Victoria took her uncle's admonitions to heart was evident during the Bedchamber Crisis. It is also clear from her journal that she took delight in certain aspects of British history, especially that of British queens, both consort and regnant.[54] By the time she became queen, Victoria was well aware that her prerogative was the same as that of male kings, recording in her journal in December 1838 Melbourne's assertion that "the king of England is always king; king in the helplessness of infancy. King in the decrepitude of age."[55] Victoria was thus aware of the concept of the "king's two bodies," encompassing an eternal, genderless, and corporate "body politic" that passed from monarch to monarch, combined with the "body natural," which, in Victoria's case, was that of a young woman.[56] Victoria could not ignore her body natural any more than her female predecessors could, and looked primarily to them for appropriate models for her role as monarch, searching their reigns for applicable precedents and historical examples, both positive and negative, upon which to construct her own version of female kingship.

Victoria's historical identification with female rulership was of her own conception: Leopold had stressed the study of recent male kingship to prepare her for her role as monarch.[57] Nevertheless, Victoria displayed unflagging interest in the careers of Mary I, Elizabeth I, and Anne, which she often discussed at length with Melbourne over the course of his premiership.[58] As an unmarried woman anticipating her forthcoming marriage, Victoria recalled the particular gendered relationship with the state that female kingship encompassed, noting that upon her marriage, "Queen Mary [I] was given away by 3 of her gentlemen, in the name of the realm."[59] Yet Victoria did not necessarily admire these women, remarking soon after the Bedchamber Crisis that Mary I was "bigoted" and Elizabeth I "tyrannical."[60] Victoria's opinion of Elizabeth I in particular displayed her understanding of the dual role of king and queen both she and Elizabeth were called upon to play, as she remarked, "Elizabeth was a great Queen, but a bad woman."[61]

The Whig view of Mary II, however, was much more appealing to Victoria, presenting a model of royal domesticity on the eve of her 1840 marriage;

> That was the great thing about Queen Mary. When he [William III] was in Ireland he could leave her with perfect safety and confidence — and she managed so well.[62]

On the other hand, Victoria was not impressed with Anne's performance as monarch. Usually identified as a "Tory" monarch, Anne's reputation in Whig historiography was that of a weak-willed woman in the thrall of her bedchamber attendants. In November 1834, Victoria wrote Leopold,

> I am much obliged to you, dear uncle, for the extract about Queen Anne, but must beg you, as you have sent to me to show what a queen ought not to be, that you will send me what a queen ought to be.[63]

At the same time, Victoria drew inspiration from Anne's accession declaration that her heart was "entirely English," after perusing a book about coronation history.[64] What this evidence suggests is that Victoria considered that the careers of her female predecessors, rather than male kings, provided the most salient examples and precedents for her to follow. Indeed, Victoria was well aware that female rulers faced handicaps because of their gender that their male counterparts did not. The disadvantages women faced as monarchs bothered Victoria, as she recalled Melbourne's gendered distinction between male and female heirs to the throne, "the title of Prince of Wales only belongs to a man, he said, there can be no Princess of Wales (in her own right)."[65] Following her 1840 marriage, Victoria also lamented her inability to arrange for her husband to share her rank, remarking "about it being so unfair that a Queen's husband should have so much less than a king's wife."[66] Such evidence suggests that by the time the Bedchamber Crisis erupted, Victoria was plainly aware that her gender changed the nature of the office occupied by her recent male predecessors.

Victoria's own perception of the gendered differences between male and female monarchs was reflected in the strict distinction she maintained between kingly and queenly duties and functions. In her kingly duties, such as conferring with her ministers, Victoria's ladies were sent away, as the queen subscribed to conventional notions concerning the intellectual inferiority of women, describing in her journal three months after the Bedchamber Crisis a social visit with the Duchess of Sunderland,

> The Duchess of Sunderland and her 2 daughters there. Talked of the Duchess caring for politics, and I could not bear women mixing in politics, and that I never talked to my Ladies about them.[67]

Although early nineteenth-century British women had already begun to form public associations to advance various reform movements, they had yet to enter formally the public sphere of parliamentary politics.[68] Victoria raised no objection to this state of affairs, and frequently recorded in her journal Melbourne's opinions on the intellectual and emotional inferiority of women, without comment or protest.[69] Melbourne, in fact, told Victoria to her face, "A woman cannot stand alone for long, in whatever situation she is in."[70] As far as other women were concerned, Victoria was in perfect agreement with Melbourne. A year later, Victoria dismissed female suffrage as "This mad, wicked folly of women's rights, with all its attendant horrors," as she considered that "God created men and women different—then let them remain in their own position."[71]

Although early Victorian working class women did not possess the luxury of absenting themselves from the public spaces of factory work, and middle and upper class women often ignored the didactic literature that sought to confine them to the domestic sphere of the home, Victoria enforced her recognition and understanding of separate spheres for men and women upon her royal court.[72] Considering herself the single exception to this rule by virtue of her possession of the crown, Victoria looked for political support and advice from men only, while her ladies served only as her domestic companions, remarking, "I was very fond of some, but that I never talked of anything that interested me much, to them."[73] Victoria's queenly intimate relationship with her ladies also occasionally veered toward the kingly, as she assumed the role of honorary male protector. Following an assassination attempt in 1840, Victoria kept her ladies in the palace until their safety could be assured, remarking, "I must expose the lives of my gentlemen, but I will not those of my ladies."[74] Victoria's relationship with her ladies was complicated, but not political in her own estimation.

Thus, upon her accession, both Victoria and the Whig government she inherited considered the staffing of a female monarch's bedchamber to be a nonpartisan process.[75] This was a conscious decision, originally urged by Leopold, and one in which the queen concurred. Victoria's first prime minister, Lord Melbourne, raised no objections to the recruitment of women with kinship ties to both major parties.[76] However, none of the ladies whose husbands or fathers were Tory peers accepted, although there is no positive evidence to demonstrate why. Although Victoria herself might have viewed her bedchamber as exclusively domestic, Tory politicians probably did not, in all likelihood reflecting a belief that having their women in the queen's bedchamber was a form of political function, and not proper when the queen's government was Whig. Nevertheless, Tories made no objections following the formation of Victoria's bedchamber, which was staffed exclusively by ladies married to or related to Whig politicians. In fact, the only complaint made concerning the composition of the bedchamber before the Crisis came from Leopold's representative, Baron Stockmar, who expressed concern to the Melbourne ministry over the allegedly "Whig" composition of the bedchamber, the only Cassandra to view the bedchamber as a potential political problem.[77] Only after the Crisis was over did Tories detect a political conspiracy alleging that Melbourne had consciously and deliberately politicized Victoria's bedchamber. Greville ruefully recalled that,

> The origin of the present mischief may be found in the objectionable composition of the Royal Household at the accession. The Queen knew nobody, and was ready to take any ladies that Melbourne recommended to her. He ought to have taken care that the female part of her household should not have a political complexion, instead of making it exclusively Whig as (unfortunately for her) he did.[78]

Greville was obviously unaware that invitations had been extended to and refused by female relatives of Tory politicians, as he unabashedly identified bedchamber ladies as possessing a recognized political function in his ex post facto condemnation of Melbourne. For Greville, Stockmar, and their male contemporaries, however, defining women as political in the context of early nineteenth-century Britain was problematic.

In the context of a male dominant political culture that denied women any formal role, the Tory conception of a formally politicized bedchamber was both novel as well as partisan. Both during and following the Bedchamber Crisis, contemporaries and subsequent historians identified Victoria's bedchamber ladies as political beings without making any distinction between activities performed by men and women that can properly be described as political. Following the 1832 Reform Act, increasing numbers of British middle class men were able vote and stand for election to local and parliamentary office.[79] Ironically, the Reform Act was the first parliamentary statute to specifically identify voting rights with men only, in effect defining women statutorily as nonpolitical beings seven years prior to the Bedchamber Crisis. Denied the franchise or the ability to sit in parliament, early nineteenth-century British women also engaged in a multitude of political activities: Chartism, supporting abolition of slavery, and demonstrating in support of Queen Caroline, the spurned wife of George IV, in 1820.[80] But in the rarified circle of the royal court, the political activities of bedchamber ladies were circumscribed. Although Queen Adelaide's bedchamber ladies may have discussed political issues with their husbands, fathers, and sons in the privacy of their homes, the queen's bedchamber was not an appropriate space for such activities. As her immediate predecessor as queen, Victoria's bedchamber emulated that of Adelaide. While Victoria's bedchamber ladies may well have held strong political views, these views only reached the queen through her male ministers, and were not discussed in her bedchamber. This situation was clear to contemporaries, as Whig Minister Lord Brougham recorded Victoria's response to the Duke of Wellington's assertion that her bedchamber ladies were political:

> It was paying her an ill compliment to suppose her ladies gave her advice on political matters. They did no such thing. They were her domestic companions. Nothing more.[81]

Although contemporaries varied in their opinions concerning the political nature of women, Victoria's own were uncomplicated and clear-cut, reflecting her acceptance of the gendering of public and private spaces for men and women that characterized nineteenth century British middle class society.

Victoria herself, however, was a politician in the manner of her recent male predecessors, but this role was played only in the male gendered public sphere of government. Her first ministry was Whig: by the time the Bedchamber Crisis erupted, Victoria was widely considered a Whig partisan. Upon her accession, Lord Melbourne immediately replaced Leopold as the dominant male figure in her life. Humorous yet extremely deferential, Melbourne possessed a personality that drew Victoria into learning the procedural aspects of kingship, while imparting to her his own sardonic version of the Whig interpretation of British history.[82] Until Victoria married Prince Albert of Saxe-Coburg-Gotha in 1840, Melbourne served as Victoria's chief advisor and private secretary, in constant attendance upon Victoria's needs, both personal and political.

Victoria's letters and journal were packed with references to Melbourne, proclaiming her gratitude, affection, and respect: Greville believed Victoria's feelings to be sexual as well.[83] While contemporaries and subsequent historians assumed that Melbourne turned Victoria into a Whig partisan, Melbourne's most recent biographer has argued that Victoria was more prone to an emotionally motivated "Melbournism" rather than ideological Whiggism.[84] Melbourne's position as the queen's advisor in her public life as king and her domestic life as queen tended to blur the line between the private and public spheres in which Victoria performed the role of monarch. The Melbourne government's resignation on May 7, 1839, forced the queen to recognize the separate spheres of politics and domesticity within which she lived her life and performed her office.

The Bedchamber Crisis

Victoria did not take the news of her government's resignation well. Lord Brougham recorded that, "[Lord John] Russell told me that when he first mentioned our intention of resigning she cried bitterly, and would not come downstairs in the evening afterwards."[85]

Greville also recorded what quickly became the talk of the town, while the Queen's journal entries confirmed her emotional state, which centered solely on the thought of losing Melbourne.[86] Melbourne, however, counseled Victoria to compose herself and prepare for the constitutional transfer of political power, telling her, "your majesty will meet this crisis with that firmness that belongs to your character, and with that rectitude and sincerity which will carry your majesty through all difficulties."[87]

That Victoria dried her tears and put her constitutional duty ahead of her personal devotion to Melbourne is well attested, even by Greville, who recorded that by the next morning "she had regained her calmness and self-possession."[88] On Melbourne's advice, Victoria summoned the elderly Duke of Wellington, the hero of Waterloo, to discuss the formation of a Tory ministry. In their first interview, Wellington suggested that its leader in the House of Commons, Sir Robert Peel, would best serve the ministry. On the same day, Wednesday, May 8, Victoria wrote to Peel, summoning him to the palace to accept her commission.

By all accounts, Peel was ambivalent about the prospect. The outgoing Whig ministry had enjoyed a modest majority in the Commons in an unstable alliance with the radicals, several of whom had voted with the Tories on the Jamaica bill. Peel thus faced the task of forming a minority government. Quite unlike

Melbourne, whose conservative Whiggism bore little resemblance to the emerging ideology that would later define the Liberal Party, Peel was a principal architect of the modern Conservative Party.[89] Like William Pitt the younger before him, Peel's primary motivation was maximizing the effectiveness of a government hampered by tradition and convention to the changing needs of an imperial state. A political modernizer who as a young man streamlined the administration of Ireland, Peel put his imaginative mind to overcoming the disability of leading a minority government. Anticipating difficulty in getting a member of his own party elected Speaker of the House, Peel prepared to reach for any viable support for his projected government. As he eyed the ladies of the queen's bedchamber, Peel revealed his own perception of how the royal household could be utilized as a political bolster for his incoming ministry.

What followed was a complex controversy of personality, precedent, and gender. Peel's own attitude toward the queen's bedchamber attendants blurred the line between the political and the personal aspects of ministerial responsibility. On the same day of his first meeting with the queen, Peel wrote to his colleague Lord Ashley:

> I remember that I am to provide attendants and companions of this young woman, on whose moral and religious character depends the welfare of millions of human beings. What shall I do? I wish to have around her those who will be, to the country and myself, a guarantee that the tone and temper of their character and conversation will tend to her moral improvement.[90]

In this letter, Peel implied that the staffing of the queen's bedchamber was his responsibility, not the queen's, suggesting the belief that Victoria was incapable of making such decisions and improvements without his assistance. Peel's attitude obviously manifested itself clearly enough: Victoria later complained that Peel attempted "to see whether she could be led and managed like a child."[91] Peel's insistence that Victoria's bedchamber ladies were capable of influencing her, morally and otherwise, marked out his belief that the bedchamber was an arena of political activity. Furthermore, Peel's interest in the moral upbringing of the queen smacked of old fashioned paternalism: Peel, who never suggested a moral reform of the courts of the elderly and morally lax George IV and William IV, considered Victoria to be much less a monarch than her uncles. This perception became a problem as he began to negotiate the process of creating a political dialogue with the queen.

Unbeknownst to Peel, Victoria's bedchamber ladies were not nearly as influential on the queen, politically or morally, as he imagined them to be. However, their domestic antics did, on occasion, carry significant political repercussions. One historian has argued that Peel's desire to improve Victoria morally came in response to an unsavory court scandal that occurred two months prior to the Bedchamber Crisis.[92] In March 1839, Lady Flora Hastings, an unmarried lady-in-waiting to the queen's mother, the duchess of Kent, was falsely accused of pregnancy, after the queen's personal physician misdiagnosed her cancerous abdominal swelling. The queen's chief bedchamber ladies, Tavistock, Portman, and Baroness Lehzen, the queen's former governess, had allegedly spread the rumors. Only when it was too late to contain the damage did Victoria offer Lady Flora a personal and private apology.

By this time the scandal had erupted into a full blown political war. Lady Flora's family blamed this affront to her honor on the moral indiscretion of the queen's chief female attendants and called for their dismissal. But despite the furious press war that raged between the Tories, who supported the Hasting's family, and the Whigs, Victoria had no intention of dismissing any of her ladies. Indeed, Peel failed to grasp the salient lesson to be learned from the Hastings scandal, which demonstrated that Victoria considered the female composition of her bedchamber above the sway of public opinion and a nonnegotiable aspect of a female king's royal prerogative, regardless of the alleged moral failings of her ladies.

Thus the fundamental conflict between Victoria and Peel was their individual perceptions of the political nature of bedchamber ladies. To Peel, bedchamber ladies threatened to influence the youthful queen both morally and politically, as the Hastings scandal so aptly demonstrated. In this sense, Peel viewed Victoria's ladies as political beings, whose chief officers should be subject to the party in power. To Victoria, this was nonsense: her household ladies were intimate companions, nothing more. Melbourne saw this situation clearly, reflected in the highly ambivalent advice he gave the Queen prior to her first discussions with Wellington and Peel. On the one hand, Melbourne urged Victoria to accept political reality and "place the fullest confidence in those to whom you entrust the management of affairs."[93] On the other hand, he advised her to stand on precedent, stating, "Your majesty had better express your hope that none of your majesty's household except those engaged in politics, may be removed."[94]

Melbourne's advice has often been taken as a scheme to win back the government, but as he himself later explained to the House of Lords, it was in the interest of making sure that Peel stuck to applicable precedent that he had counseled Victoria so.[95] Nevertheless, to the Queen, the logical conclusion was that ladies were quite obviously nonpolitical members of her household along with the men who held relatively insignificant posts such as grooms and equerries. Although Victoria entered her discussions with Peel fully prepared to turn out her chief household officers with political connections to the Whigs, she had already decided that her ladies were not on the bargaining table, as she recorded in her journal a conversation with Melbourne on May 8, expressing her fear that the Tories may want to remove her ladies, declaring "I said they dared not, and I never would allow it."[96]

In her first meeting with Wellington, on the morning of May 8, Victoria brought up the issue of household changes and her opposition to a possible dissolution of parliament.[97] The duke was taken aback; Victoria wrote, "The Duke did not give any decisive answer about it, but advised the Queen not to begin with conditions of this sort, and wait till the matter was proposed."[98]

Wellington informed Peel nonetheless that Victoria had an agenda concerning the formation of the new government, a situation Peel had not anticipated. By all accounts, Peel, despite his brilliance, was a shy, dour man, possessing little idea of how to conduct business with a teenaged female monarch. Just prior to his first interview with the Queen, Peel's friend Lady de Grey warned him, "The First impression on so young a girl's mind is of immense importance, accustomed as she has been to . . . Lord M . . . who, *entre nous*, treats her as a father."[99]

The irony here is that Melbourne's personal life was hardly an example of that of a conventional family man in an early Victorian context, and reflected the much more lax aristocratic moral tone of the regency than the image of domestic harmony that Victoria and Albert later strived to create.[100] During the first two years of the reign, Melbourne's relationship with Victoria was social and instructive, but not paternal in the usually recognized sense. In reality lacking in fatherly discipline, Melbourne had done nothing to contain the Hastings scandal nor did he counsel Victoria to find a more politic solution to a problem that became a public-relations disaster. It is reasonable to suppose that Victoria's affection for Melbourne was also based on the freedom of action that he allowed her, being the antithesis of a true father figure. Three weeks before the Bedchamber Crisis erupted, in April 1939, Victoria recorded in her diary an exchange with Melbourne concerning her self-acknowledged willfulness:

> I said I so dreaded the thought of marrying; that I was so accustomed to have my own way, that I thought it 10 to 1 that I shouldn't agree with anybody. Lord M said, "Oh! But you would have it still" (my own way.)[101]

Peel on the other hand was a conventional paterfamilias, possessed of a capable and supportive wife and family.[102] Peel's daughter Julia, in fact, was of the same age as Victoria. In his private life, Peel emulated much more an emergent ideal of masculine domesticity that redefined the father's role in the context of the private, domestic sphere of the home.[103] Considering Victoria's subsequent reaction to their first meeting, Peel obviously lacked Melbourne's polished deference, and probably brought a more conventional tone of paternal authority to a queen who had never really known a true father figure whose parental authority was able to challenge, much less override, her own will.

Peel first met Victoria later in the day on Wednesday, May 8. As Peel came to his first meeting, he knew Victoria possessed opinions concerning the composition of the government. Obviously rattled, Peel failed in his initial attempt to establish a working relationship with the queen. While Peel had the discretion not to record his own impression of the queen's behavior, Victoria reported that Peel came to her "embarrassed and put out," later remarking that "I never saw a man so frightened."[104] Peel's uncomfortable manner, which the queen found unnerving, was aggravated by the realization that Victoria did not prove to be a child-like cipher willing simply to accept his ideas.

Victoria was offended not only by Peel's manner but also by his attitude toward the proceedings. At this first meeting Victoria was prepared for a session of hard bargaining, and felt incensed that Peel was not prepared to do the same. As she had been to

Wellington, Victoria was forthright and earnest in expressing her reluctance to lose Melbourne, and clear in her wish to maintain her personal relationship with him. In turn, Peel made it clear to the queen that he was accepting office under adverse circumstances. Victoria then mentioned the household. Peel was noncommittal, but promised to return the following day with proposals for cabinet and household officers, leaving the strongest impression on the queen that he required the fullest display of royal acquiescence to his government, "that your majesty's confidential servants might have the advantage of a public demonstration of your majesty's full support and confidence."[105]

Victoria returned to an emotionally agitated state, once out of the company of the Tory politicians. On Thursday, May 9, Victoria recorded in her journal, "Got up at 10—feeling more wretched even than even before—crying and sobbing and being in despair, yet anxious to do all that was right."[106] Officially out of office, Melbourne was careful not to meet personally with the queen, but nevertheless composed prompt replies to a flurry of messages from her over the course of May 9. Melbourne's advice remained ambivalent; he wrote to Victoria that morning, "begging me not to mind Sir Robert's manner."[107] At the same time, Melbourne reiterated his advice to stand firm on the nonpolitical members of the household, but he made no specific mention of bedchamber ladies.

Victoria's meeting with Peel later that day turned the negotiations into a crisis.[108] It started off constructively. Victoria acquiesced to all of Peel's suggestions concerning the top male household posts, while he accepted hers concerning Tories she personally favored. But when Peel suggested a similar principle be applied to the principal ladies of the bedchamber, Victoria at once rejected the notion.

According to the queen, Peel tried to persuade her, without success. Victoria's ability to debate with Peel revealed her understanding of the salient issues at stake. Peel hurled a number of justifications at Victoria for his request to remove the principal bedchamber ladies, reminding her that they were the wives of the outgoing government, implying that kinship relations defined bedchamber ladies as political beings. Victoria replied that her ladies also had close kinship ties to Tories, undercutting Peel's assertion that marriage and kinship to male politicians carried with it a form of representational political power. Victoria also disputed the notion that her ladies were capable of any political influence over her, insisting to Peel, "I never talked politics with them."[109] Victoria further informed Peel that her ladies could be of no consequence to his government, and that the bedchamber ladies of a queen had never been a political concern to any previous government. In doing so, Victoria reminded Peel that while she held the kingly office, she was also a queen, and considered the personal and domestic spaces of queenship nonpolitical and beyond the scope of his ministerial power. Peel replied that she was a queen regnant, "and that made all the difference," to which Victoria replied, "not here."[110]

This exchange exposed the fatal impasse of both constitutional and gender interpretation. Later that day Victoria wrote to Melbourne, informing him that "the Queen would not have stood so firmly on the grooms and equerries," in effect conceding to Peel a right to control even the nonpolitical male members of her household. But Victoria drew a sharp gendered distinction between the men and women of her household, telling Melbourne, "but the ladies are entirely her own affair," comprising a separate domestic sphere completely removed from her male household officers.

Peel's final argument was political expediency. As the Queen's devotion to Melbourne was common knowledge, so was his inability to command a majority in the House of Commons; Peel, by requesting the removal of the principal ladies of the bedchamber, effectively asked Victoria to use her prerogative to create a novel form of royal support for his fledgling government. Peel felt that the request, in the case of a queen regnant, was a logical extension of recent precedent related to politically motivated household changes, citing "public grounds" for his requested changes.[111] In other words, Peel did not assert a definite ministerial power, but asked the queen to create a new precedent to suit immediate political needs.

Victoria, however, felt it no constitutional impropriety to simply adhere to current precedent; giving up her male household officers with or without political connections constituted a sufficient and correct, if not generous, display of royal support. Furthermore, Victoria identified the request with a threat to her remaining prerogative, later telling Melbourne, "I repeated that I maintained I had the power about my ladies, else what power had I left!"[112]

Shocked and dismayed at the conclusion of his initial meetings with the queen, Peel suspended all further proceedings, informing

Victoria that he needed to consult his advisors. Peel returned later that day with Wellington, who Peel hoped could help salvage the situation. Wellington found Victoria just as obdurate as had Peel. The duke had his own argument: the opinions of the ladies did not matter, but the ministry did, in the case of a queen regnant, possess the power to control the appointments of bedchamber ladies, citing the wording of the Civil List Bill, "that the Ladies were instead of the Lords."[113] Victoria reminded Wellington that she had lords *and* ladies; according to the version that filtered down to Greville, Victoria retorted, "No I have Lords besides, and these I give up to you."[114] Victoria informed Peel that she would consider the matter further, but that it was doubtful she would change her mind.

While the May 8 meetings with Peel and Wellington had merely upset her, the May 9 exchanges infuriated her. Already put off by Peel's stiff manner, Victoria railed against his and Wellington's political arguments, believing they were taking advantage of her youth and her sex to brainwash her out of her prerogative. In a note to Melbourne, she reported, "I was calm but very decided, and I think you would have been pleased to see my composure and great firmness. The Queen of England will not submit to such trickery."[115]

Victoria's accusations of deception were political and gendered. While she fully appreciated Peel's political vulnerability, she was unable to comprehend how the presence of Tory bedchamber ladies could alter the fate of a Tory ministry in parliament, remarking, "the ladies his only support! What a sign of weakness!"[116] The Queen also plainly viewed Peel's attempt to assign political significance to women in a male dominant political culture as absurd, remarking sarcastically, "I should like to know if they mean to give the ladies seats in parliament?"[117] Forward thinking as he was, Peel's was in fact the radical interpretation in articulating a political perception of women that had not existed in the past. In Victoria's estimation, Peel exceeded constitutional propriety and violated social convention in his refusal to recognize any difference between the households of male and female kings.

To Victoria, this distinction was crucial. While her ladies were not political, they were dear to her; to part with them would have been a pointless display of royal support at great personal cost to her emotional well being. The personal bolstered the political: Victoria was also unwilling to gamble on the remainder of her prerogative, as she observed to Melbourne, following her second interview with Peel on May 9,

> If it should lead to Peel refusing to undertake the formation of a government, which would be absurd, the Queen will feel satisfied that she has only been defending her own rights, on a point which so nearly concerned her person, and which, if they had succeeded in, would have led to every sort of unfair attempt at power.[118]

By Thursday afternoon, it had occurred to the queen that the Tories might not form a government, allowing the Whigs to return to office. Victoria concluded a lengthy note to Melbourne with the warning, "Keep yourself in readiness, for you may soon be wanted."[119] As Peel had suspended all further proceedings until the queen gave him a definite answer on the ladies, Melbourne scoured operas and dinner parties to gather his former cabinet together for an emergency session.[120]

Meeting on the evening of May 9, the shadow Whig cabinet was keenly aware of the queen's immovable stance. A minor furor arose when it was learned that Peel had requested changes for some, not all, of the queen's bedchamber attendants. But after Melbourne read aloud letters he had received that day from the queen, the shadow cabinet voted to back her in an emotionally charged scene. Bolstered by the legal opinion of former prime minister Lord Grey, the ministers concluded that, in defending the queen's constitutional position, some or all made little difference: even removing one bedchamber lady amounted to an intolerable encroachment on a female king's prerogative. In the reply to Peel that the cabinet drafted for Victoria, the ministers echoed her own personal and political defense of her queenly prerogative:

> The Queen having considered the proposal made to her yesterday by Sir Robert Peel to remove the Ladies of her Bedchamber cannot consent to adopt a course which she conceives to be contrary to usage, and which is repugnant to her feelings.[121]

Peel still possessed his commission to form a government. However, it could only occur according to Victoria's interpretation of current constitutional practice and precedent. Peel did not possess the means to coerce her without launching a challenge upon the ambiguous status of the monarchy within the contemporary political structure. Accordingly, after consulting his advisors, who agreed that the government could not stand without the fullest display of royal support, Peel resigned his commission on Friday, May 10.[122] The next day Victoria recalled the Melbourne ministry to office.

On Monday, May 13, Peel and Whig Minister Lord John Russell offered their respective explanations for the now resolved crisis to an expectant House of Commons. Over the weekend rumors raged through London; as Greville noted, "It was speedily known all over the town that the whole thing was at an end, and nothing could surpass the excitement and amazement that prevailed."[123] Speaking first, Peel recounted the events leading to his resignation to the House of Commons. True to his modernizing administrative nature, Peel argued for flexibility over precedent:

> The policy of these things depends not on what has been done in former times, it mainly depends upon a consideration of the present.[124]

Peel insisted to the Commons that "The Household has been allowed to assume a completely political character," emphasizing his belief that there was no difference in the political value of male or female bedchamber attendants. Peel argued that the accession of a regnant queen had created a novel political sector in the royal household that should be subject to the ministry in power. In his opinion the perceived political influence of bedchamber ladies outweighed the queen's personal relationship with them. Only in a convoluted and indirect fashion did Peel acknowledge the final result of the crisis to the Commons, that the victory lay with the queen's assertion of royal prerogative to resolve the matter. Like Grenville and Grey in the ministerial crisis of 1812, Peel did not possess a mechanism to force the monarch's hand, nor did he have the stomach to go to battle with the queen for the sake of leading a minority government.[125]

The resurrected Whig cabinet was not nearly so overjoyed to be back in office as the queen was to have them. However, Lord John Russell had researched the issues at stake over the weekend, and offered a number of justifications for the queen's refusal. Russell recounted how Melbourne had advised the queen on recent precedent regarding household changes incumbent upon a change of governments, but denied Melbourne had said anything about ladies; Victoria had made up her mind about them all on her own. Russell also challenged Peel's refusal to recognize political differences between male and female kings, as he stressed the uniqueness of the queen's position.

> It will be difficult to find cases exactly suited to that of a Queen regnant, a case which, since the death of Queen Anne, has not occurred in this country.[126]

Russell did find cases, however, describing how in 1710 the wives of dismissed ministers lords Sutherland and Rialton remained Anne's bedchamber ladies. Russell went on to describe the history of politically motivated household changes from the reign of George III and the circumstances of 1812, noting that Grey's and Grenville's demands, which the prince Regent refused, only included the great officers of the household, and "did not apply in any way to the Lords of the bedchamber."[127] While these precedents applied to Victoria's position as king, Russell's final argument drew to attention that she was king and queen at the same time. In 1832, at the time of the Reform bill, "The ladies of Queen Adelaide's household were ladies whose husbands gave their votes constantly in opposition to the King's government."

Yet Russell recounted that, "There was an apprehension that some of the ladies would be removed by Lord Grey, but it was a most groundless alarm, because neither that noble Lord nor his government ever entertained the slightest wish to interfere with the comfort of her majesty."[128]

Russell offered an unambiguous defense of the private domestic sphere of queens. While he did not reiterate Victoria's insistence that her ladies were not political, Russell's defense of her actions rested not only on applicable precedent from Victoria's male and female predecessors, but also upon the personal and emotional consequences for the queen. If it was royal support that Peel yearned for, Russell argued, a Tory government should not alienate the queen by forced changes of her intimate attendants.

Peel himself came to the same conclusion. Although he considered the removal of ladies he considered to be ancillary "Whigs" as necessary for the stability of his projected government, he belatedly came to consider the personal feelings of the queen as a legitimate factor to be considered, and said so in his formal letter of resignation, "Each individual appointment in the household should be entirely acceptable to your majesty's personal feelings."[129]

Peel also learned the hard way to treat the queen as a sovereign in full possession of her prerogative, as he observed shortly after the crisis, "In respect to those appointments in the Household which formed the subject of recent discussion, [the ministerial power] should be restrained by every possible deference to the wishes and every possible consideration for the feelings of the sovereign."[130]

Other Tories were not so charitable, judging the constitutionality of the queen's position along partisan lines that discounted Victoria's understanding of the salient issues at stake during the crisis. Greville wrote that, "I think every minister must have the power of advising the Queen to remove a Lady of her Court, in the same way as he is admitted to have that of removing a man."[131]

But Greville's opinion also contained a healthy dose of paternalistic disapproval, writing, "There is something which shocks one's sense of fitness and propriety in the spectacle of a mere baby of a queen setting herself in opposition to this great man."[132] Victoria in turn was shocked and dismayed that Tory politicians would take advantage of her youth and her gender to prevail upon her an unconstitutional encroachment upon her prerogative.

Conclusion

In 1841, Peel and the Tories won a substantial victory in the general election that did not require an overt show of royal support as deemed necessary in 1839. By this time Victoria had married, and Peel and Prince Albert had already begun a personal correspondence that laid the groundwork for Peel's later rapprochement with the queen. With the change of governments, Victoria once again shed considerable tears over losing Melbourne. However, by this time, Albert had already begun to replace both Melbourne and her bedchamber ladies as a primary source of political counsel and emotional support for the queen.

Nonetheless, the trauma of the Bedchamber Crisis still lingered in 1841. Victoria remained decidedly anti-Tory, while Peel, once bitten and now twice shy, was apprehensive about requiring household changes that extended to female office holders. After a series of behind-the-scenes negotiations between Peel and Albert's private secretary, George Anson, Victoria secured the resignations of ladies Normandy and Bedford, whom Peel considered the most obnoxious of the queen's female attendants, and waived all right to fill the top male posts in the household.[133] Thus, two years following the Bedchamber Crisis, in a situation not nearly so emotionally charged, Victoria freely, though not happily, compromised with Peel as she handed over to him that aspect of her prerogative she had so zealously defended during the Bedchamber Crisis.

Encouraged by her husband, in time Victoria came to appreciate Peel's talents, and later considered him one of the most able of her prime ministers.[134] With the passage of time also came a more mature perspective. Four years before her death in 1897, Victoria reflected on the Bedchamber Crisis to her secretary, Arthur Bigge, remarking,

> Yes I was very hot about it and so were my ladies, as I had been so brought up under Lord Melbourne, but I was very young, only 20, and never should have acted so again—Yes! it was a mistake.[135]

This quote is the only source that included the bedchamber ladies themselves as participants in the Crisis, sharing Victoria's outrage at the attempted invasion of their private domestic sphere. Yet the reflection came from an old, experienced, confident woman who had been Queen for sixty years, after Melbourne, Peel, and her original bedchamber ladies had long departed from her life. Victoria recalled that, in her youthful enthusiasm for her royal office, she had defended the rather corroded gauntlet of royal power that had fallen from the grasp of her predecessors, to prevent further inroads against the royal prerogative.

It is not surprising that Victoria minimized the impact of her political victory resulting from the Bedchamber Crisis; in the long run it ran against the grain of subsequent political development. When she died in 1901, Great Britain had evolved into an unambiguously constitutional monarchy. Over the course of a sixty-four-year reign, Victoria witnessed the final transformation of parliamentary sovereignty that ultimately relegated the monarch to the "dignified" part of the constitution.[136] The mature Victoria skillfully maintained the political "rights" outlined in Walter Bagehot's *English Constitution*, to "consult, encourage, and warn," while, by the end of her reign, Victoria's bedchamber ladies had completely lost the political luster the Tories so vehemently insisted they possessed during the Bedchamber Crisis.

At the end of her life, Victoria herself possessed the hindsight that generations of historians have used to discredit her role in the

Bedchamber Crisis. But assessed in the fluctuating, unstable political context of its time, the Crisis, for Victoria and her contemporaries, demonstrated the complexity gender imposed upon political processes, particularly the relationship between parliament and a female monarch's royal household. By the time the Crisis erupted, Victoria understood her unique position as a female king, and recognized the distinct spheres in which she lived her life as both king and queen in conventional nineteenth-century terms. Thus, Victoria battled not only against Peel's insistence that her ladies played a political function, which she considered ludicrous, but Peel's attempted invasion of the private domestic sphere of queenship that previously had never concerned parliament under her immediate predecessors. Victoria also believed that Peel and Wellington tried to take advantage of her youth and her gender to convince her to consent to a policy she knew was merely a form of political expediency, at great personal cost to her domestic tranquility.

Assessed in its own time, Victoria's position was technically correct: there was no direct precedent for ministerial control over such blatantly nonpolitical figures as bedchamber ladies. There was, however, indirect precedent from the reigns of Victoria's immediate male predecessors. Peel was correct in his assertion that the accession of a female king fundamentally altered the nature of the royal office. Victoria knew this also; the irreconcilable differences of opinion arising during the crisis brought the historical progression of parliamentary supremacy to a momentary halt over the course of four days in May 1839. That all this occurred because a youthful and unmarried female king had successfully exercised political power in the public arena of a male dominant political culture remains as startling today as it did to contemporaries.

Victoria's defense of prerogative to control her domestic sphere provided the context in which she articulated the gendered differences between male and female kingship. Victoria's own conception of her role as a female king compelled her constantly to shuffle between the public and private spheres of kingship and queenship. Before her marriage, Victoria lived her personal life surrounded by women, but throughout her reign, politics was a game she played with men alone; while Melbourne may have been welcome in her private domestic spaces, her ladies were persona non grata in the public spaces where government business was transacted.[137] The Bedchamber Crisis thus provided a momentary glimpse into how female kingship affected the progression of British political development, as contemporaries debated women's political relationship to parliamentary politics sixty years before they were able to hold seats in parliament. At the same time, the Crisis demonstrated how the gender transformations characterizing nineteenth-century British society affected the evolution of the monarchy. Victoria based her refusal to dismiss her ladies on her recognition and acceptance of the socially constructed, distinct public and private spheres for men and women only she, as king and queen at the same time, was able to transgress. Furthermore, Victoria was indignant at Peel's attempt to treat her like a young and inexperienced queen, and used her kingly power to defend the private domestic sphere of queenship.

Victoria herself summed up the entire range of political and gender implications that arose during the Crisis in a letter to Leopold shortly after its conclusion. Powerful emotional motivations were clearly evident, as she reiterated her personal devotion to Melbourne, "that truly inestimable and excellent man" as well as her emotional trauma, "What I have suffered I cannot describe!" Victoria also made it clear to her uncle that the Crisis had demonstrated her ability to be a king and a queen simultaneously, as she stated her firm belief in her constitutional propriety, "Everything fair and just I assented to," and asserted her ability as a young unmarried queen to defend herself and her prerogative in the all-male realm of politics:

> You will easily imagine that I firmly resisted this attack upon my power, from these people who pride themselves upon up holding the prerogative! I acted quite alone, but I have been, and shall be, supported by my country.[138]

Conclusion: Does the Lioness Still Roar?

One of the most striking features of British history has been the adaptability of its monarchy. From William the Conqueror to Elizabeth II, the institution of kingship has survived depositions, abdications, revolutions glorious and otherwise, as well as the paring away of its political power over the last three centuries. Nevertheless, the monarchy has been as integral to the development of English and British national identity as it has to its political evolution.[1] As modern Britain moves closer to political integration with Europe, the monarchy, in all likelihood, will survive this redefinition of its sovereignty, as will the rest of the surviving Western European monarchies.

Today, as in the past, female kingship has formed an integral facet of the historical evolution of British monarchy. This study has endeavored to investigate a number of problems particular to female rulers in English history, and integrate these findings within larger historical explanations of English kingship. To the central question identified in the introduction—did women endure additional handicaps as occupants of the kingly office in comparison to their male counterparts—the answer is a resounding yes. For the next question—did these female rulers devise effective strategies to mitigate contemporary social and legal barriers to female power—the answer here is also in the affirmative. Indeed, if the ultimate goal of all our subjects, from the Empress Matilda to Britain's present queen, Elizabeth II, was recognition of a woman in sole possession of kingly sovereignty, then the historical evolution of British female kingship can be considered a resounding success. But this rather Whiggish conclusion contains a glaring caveat: if we consider whether the achievements of Britain's woman rulers made a contribution to modern feminist consciousness and goals, the answer is "not exactly."

As this study began with an essay on Elizabeth I, so it shall conclude with a brief discussion of the second Elizabeth, the present queen of Great Britain and Northern Ireland. In theory,

Elizabeth II possesses awesome temporal and spiritual sovereign authority, enjoying the titles Defender of the Faith, Supreme governor of the Church, and a host of other designations that British monarchs have carried with them into the modern world. At the time of this writing, as she celebrates fifty-three years as queen; Elizabeth II has been a head of state longer than any individual on the planet. When she ascended the throne in 1952 at the age of twenty-five, the same age as the first Elizabeth upon her accession, there was no question that she would inherit and inhabit the royal office, even in a gloomy postwar Britain ossified by the divisions of class, race, and gender, and dismayed by the dismantlement of Empire. Upon her accession, however, Elizabeth II demonstrated how female kingship retained its status as an indelible part of the constitution; the declarations included in the 1554 Act Concerning Regal Power, though dusty and seemingly moribund, offered a constitutional guarantee to Elizabeth II's right to exercise regal authority, in the same fashion as her noble progenitors, the kings of England.[2]

Nevertheless, as with all of her predecessors as female kings, Elizabeth II was constrained to negotiate a gendered change from male to female kingship. Over the course of her first fifty years as queen, she has herself accommodated and negotiated change within the monarchy, in its relationship with a parliamentary system of government, and its relationship with the mass of its citizens, in her current position as a reluctant media star of global proportions.[3] The gendered problems, which the queen encountered in the early years of her reign, bear a remarkable similarity to the various problems discussed in all the chapters of this study.

Elizabeth II is commonly held to be a conservative public figure in Britain today. From her style-defying fashions to her mechanical wave and smile, the queen embodies the first Elizabeth's motto, *semper eadem*, always the same, as she reflects the continuity of the twentieth-century Windsor kings. Historians have been reluctant to study Elizabeth II, since any scholarly estimate of her reign must remain tentative; her mother lived to be 101 years old, and she is well poised to challenge her great-great-grandmother Victoria's record of sixty-four years on the throne, the longest reign in English history.[4] Throughout her reign, Elizabeth II has recognized and maintained a rigidly gendered distinction between her kingly and queenly functions.[5] Her June 1953 coronation was a globally televised media event, one of the first of its kind, which demonstrated the queen's symbolic assumption of male gendered kingship. In the manner of Mary I, Elizabeth I, Anne, and Victoria, Elizabeth II was crowned in the fashion of a king: anointed, girt with a sword, and touching the spurs, the symbolic vestments of kingly military authority.[6] The newly crowned queen accepted the homage of her subjects, including her husband, Philip Mountbatten, a Greek prince created duke of Edinburgh on his wedding day in 1947.

Philip's status at the time of his wife's accession in 1952 corresponded to George of Denmark's in 1702. Both were European princes with little chance of inheriting a foreign throne, and naturalized British subjects, holding the rank of royal duke. During Anne's coronation in 1702, and Elizabeth II's in 1952, respectively, both princes held the position of highest ranking peer of the realm. Unlike the wives of male kings, who became queens when their husbands became kings, George of Denmark, Albert of Saxe-Coburg-Gotha, and Philip Mountbatten were all denied the kingship enjoyed by the sixteenth-century Philip of Spain and the seventeenth-century William of Orange.

It is moot to discuss what Royal House Anne and George of Denmark's children would have represented, but Philip Mountbatten, like Albert of Saxe-Coburg-Gotha, succeeded in propagating the dynasty through the female line. Soon after her coronation, Elizabeth II, on the advice of her prime minister, Winston Churchill, demonstrated her kingly identification with her male progenitors, George V and George VI, by announcing that her descendants on the throne would continue to bear the name Windsor.[7] Philip was reportedly furious, describing himself as an "amoeba."[8] Nevertheless, despite her married status, Elizabeth II herself has added to the precedents related to female rule, and enjoys recognition of her singular possession of kingly sovereignty. While Anne bestowed high office on her husband, and Albert enjoyed considerable informal influence over Victoria, Philip was reduced to one single function: to further a dynasty that does not bear his name.[9] In this sense, Elizabeth II has completed the process begun in the twelfth century, when the Empress Matilda made her bid for kingly sovereignty within the context of marriage, with the near-total disposal of the male counterpart to female kingship. In this sense, the lioness roars louder than ever.

But Elizabeth II is also a woman who has responded to conventional expectations of her gender. As did Mary I, Anne, and Victoria,

Elizabeth II has tried to create the impression that she is a good wife.[10] In 1958, the queen announced that her and Philip's descendants not in the direct line of succession would bear the name Mountbatten-Windsor, an obvious concession to her husband of symbolic value only. In their domestic life, Elizabeth II has fostered the impression that her husband is supreme in the domestic sphere of their family life. As did Victoria during the Bedchamber Crisis, Elizabeth II moves freely from the public sphere of government to the domestic spaces of her family life. As scholars have conceptualized Elizabeth I as king and queen at the same time, Elizabeth II also inhabits both roles with equal facility.

Elizabeth II performs a definite political role. At the same time she contemplated offering her husband a dynastic concession, she also was deciding the fate of governments.[11] In choosing Harold Macmillan as prime minister over R.A. Butler in 1957, and Alec Douglas-Home over Butler again in 1963, Elizabeth II drew contemporary attention to the political prerogatives of the crown.[12] Similar to Victoria's position as queen, Elizabeth II endeavors to stay above the fray of press criticism and intrusion into her and her family's private life, a development which has maintained a fevered crescendo since 1992; the queen's self proclaimed *annus horribilis*.[13] In 2002, the queen became embroiled in an uproar concerning her role in ending a prosecution against a butler of her former daughter-in-law, the late Diana, Princess of Wales. The queen did not offer testimony under oath, but the indictment was quashed because the queen's word, issued to the media, was considered sufficient evidence.[14] The incident demonstrated the informal power and influence the queen continues to maintain over contemporary British society.

The queen weathered this crisis as she has done in the past. Today, cabinet ministers enjoying access to the queen remark on her political skill and capacity to absorb and converse on the diverse affairs of her government. Elizabeth II guards and exercises her remaining prerogatives in a kingly fashion. Upon her accession in 1952, Elizabeth inherited the Tory government of Winston Churchill. As contemporaries proclaimed a new Elizabethan age, they also drew comparisons between Churchill and Lord Melbourne, as the septuagenarian old politician served as the new queen's unofficial political tutor. Fifty years and nine prime ministers later, the queen is an active part of the political process, meeting with her prime minister weekly, and exercising her constitutional right to advise, consult, and warn her governments. Exactly what occurs during these sessions remains speculation; their study must await full access to the historical record. The queen does not grant interviews, or write books, or reveal anything concerning her interactions with her ministers. She is, nevertheless, a public figure, as all her predecessors had been, opening parliaments, visiting hospitals, and traveling tirelessly around the world as the living representative of Great Britain.[15] However, the British public today has little idea whether the queen actually likes current Prime Minister Tony Blair or not; a clear demonstration of the queen's highly refined royal discretion as a constitutional monarch above the sway of partisan politics.

For Elizabeth II, as for her predecessors, being monarch means being king, but it also means being a queen, her chief identity to her subjects. In the fashion of her mother Elizabeth, the beloved "queen mum," consort of George VI, Elizabeth II has embodied middle class values, in her marriage and family life. Similar to the model described by sixteenth-century theorist John Aylmer in his work, *An Harborowe For Faithful and Trewe Subjects*, the queen, in her capacity as chief magistrate, is not subject to her husband, but in the private sphere of their domestic life, Elizabeth II has endeavored to create the image of wifely submission to her husband. In the manner of Mary I, Anne, and Victoria, Elizabeth II appears to have recognized the sanctity of her own moral reputation within the context of marriage as a particular quality of female kingship. The only female ruler who did not marry, Elizabeth I, is the only one to have endured slanders on her moral reputation as a single woman.[16] In this regard, Elizabeth II has rigidly reproduced Victorian royal precedents concerning morality and the sanctity of marriage, although she has been unsuccessful in transferring her reverence for such middle class ideals to her children.

This leads us back to our original point: the queen is a conservative figure in British society. Within her royal household, Elizabeth II has maintained a rigid gender distinction between court posts held by men and women. The top posts remain in the hands of aristocratic men, while aristocratic women hold the conventionally domestic positions, such as bedchamber ladies. Although there are undoubtedly numerous capable women within the queen's own social class capable of performing the roles of lords chamberlain or steward, Elizabeth II has never been inclined to erase the gendered distinctions between her male and female household officers. Like all her predecessors as female kings, Elizabeth II is an honorary male, with no apparent interest in furthering feminist goals of gender equality for her female subjects.

The Empress Matilda, Mary I, Anne, and Victoria also hold a problematic place in the evolution of women's history. Elizabeth II's conception of her office draws from precedents created by her recent male predecessors, but also from the precedents of female kingship reaching much deeper in British history. Her own reign in fact is yet another consolidation for the concept and structure of female sovereignty, building from Mary I's efforts to create a viable model for female kingship. The present queen's own gendered problems do not have the same political dimension of her predecessors, as she is a constitutional monarch, but they have corollaries in the reigns of Mary I, Anne, and Victoria. Indeed, the queen's approach to kingship is symptomatic of the force of male dominance in contemporary British social and political structures. Like the Elizabeth I of Christopher Haigh, Elizabeth II is widely seen as a conservative, suspicious, high-wire act, outwardly conforming to contemporary gender expectations for women in her endeavor to be king.

Fitting Elizabeth II's achievements in the context of modern feminism is problematic, as are the successes of England's other female kings throughout English history. While these women fought tenaciously for their rights as monarch, they did so for themselves alone, not for other women. But how could they? The female ruler was constantly embroiled in the singular task of constructing a means to exercise authority in the face of gendered ideologies and legalities that normally refused to recognize womanly authority. So, to bolster their own legitimacy, female kings were compelled to distance themselves politically from all other women, while outwardly conforming to normative gender expectations from the societies in which they lived.

All of the preceding chapters support these general conclusions. We have suggested that the twelfth-century Empress Matilda sought kingly power for herself as she constructed a representational strategy reproducing and ultimately transcending the means by which royal women had previously exercised political power. Four centuries later, Mary I achieved what Matilda failed to do, claiming and consolidating her hold on kingly power. While Matilda constructed her sovereignty on the pillars of male gendered kingship, Mary conformed to conventional gender expectations, as she attempted to wield regal power in the guise of a queen, representing herself as her kingdom's dutiful and submissive wife. Our study has suggested that this perception masked Mary's resolve to exercise kingly power, which ultimately served to destabilize her public façade as a conventional woman conforming to normative codes of gendered behavior, as she negotiated the terms of her marriage to Philip of Spain in the first, unmarried year of her reign.

Nevertheless, Mary I created the conceptual model for female kingship in England, which Elizabeth I consolidated over the course of a long forty-five-year reign. The historical force of their combined success became evident during the Glorious Revolution. Although William of Orange's quest for regal power subsumed his wife's hereditary claim, the Bill of Rights and the Act of Settlement recognized the sixteenth century precedents of female rule in their recognition of Anne's hereditary status as heir, despite her married state. Following her 1702 accession, Anne was the true English Deborah, recognized politically as a single woman in the public sphere of politics and government, even though she catered to conventional social expectations in her public perception as a good wife, within the context of her marriage to George of Denmark.

Queen Victoria also recognized and conformed to contemporary forms of gender expectations during the Bedchamber Crisis. The evidence presented in the final chapter demonstrates the sincerity behind Victoria's insistence that her ladies were not political, and had no function in her life as queen except as domestic companions. As did her predecessors, Victoria recognized the crucial difference between her kingly functions, performed in the public sphere of politics and government, and her queenly functions, which outwardly conformed to gendered expectations for women.

As this brief discussion of her reign suggests, Elizabeth II reflects the problems and strategies of Britain's historical procession of female rulers. That Elizabeth II has suffered gendered problems and challenges demonstrates the cleavage between contemporary notions of gender equality and the actual experiences of women in Western societies, especially one with such a high global profile as the present queen. The lack of symmetry between a woman occupant of the royal office and the male gendered office itself persists to this day. English female kings endured a social and legal status radically different from all their female subjects. The 1554 Act Concerning Regal Power declared ruling queens to enjoy the same royal prerogative as male kings. But the act did not absolve female rulers from adherence to the considerable social burden attached to being a woman in their society. Inside this basic contradiction, as the "other" to socially constructed categories of both men and women, the female king has existed, and continues to exist, in what must be an exceedingly lonely social category. No resolution to this dilemma seems likely during Elizabeth II's reign, and it will undoubtedly pass unresolved to her male successors, should the British monarchy endure the twenty-first century and beyond.

Notes

The Lioness Roared: Introduction

1. John Foxe, *The Acts and Monuments of John Foxe*, vol., 6, ed. George Townsend and Stephen Cattley (New York: AMS Press, 1965, orig. pub. 1559), p. 414.
2. Ibid.
3. Historians have not traditionally considered the female ruler, or queen regnant, in the same context as male kings. An early but potent example from the modern era is Agnes Strickland's eight volume *Lives of the Queens of England* (London: Henry Colburn, 1852). Strickland acknowledged the crucial differences between the roles of queens regnant and consort, but her contextual reasoning clearly placed queen regnant outside the context of kingship, which Strickland viewed in male terms characteristic of mid-Victorian gendered social constructs.
4. Studies of European kingship in general do not include analysis of women as kings; for a fairly recent example see Henry A. Myers, *Medieval Kingship* (Chicago: Nelson-Hall, 1982), also *Kings and Kingship in Medieval Europe*, ed. Anne Duggan (London: King's College London Centre for Late Antique and Medieval Studies, 1993). Only recently have scholars begun to interpose the role of women upon the evolution of kingship, see Paul Kleber Monod, *The Power of Kings: Monarchy and Religion in Europe* (New Haven, Conn.: Yale University Press, 1999). While Monod includes discussions of female rulers in his study, they remain "exceptional, each case has to be examined separately," p. 7.
5. Since 1066, six female sovereigns (including Elizabeth II, excluding Mary II) have occupied the English throne, comprising 179 regnal years (in 2005) out of 936.
6. See John W. Houghton, "No Bishop, No Queen: Queens Regnant and the Ordination of Women," *Anglican and Episcopal History*, 67, 1 (1998), pp. 2–25.
7. England experienced the reigns of six boy kings between 1216 and 1553. The fourth of these, Henry VI (1422–1461, 1470–1471), suffered from periodic episodes of acute psychosis during his adult

reign. George III (1760–1820) lapsed into senility and blindness, necessitating the appointment of a regency in 1811. Even so, George III remained king until his death.

8. See Judith L. Richards, "Mary Tudor: Renaissance Queen", *High and Mighty Queens of England: Realities and Representations*, ed. Carole Levin, Jo Eldridge Carney, and Debra Barrett-Graves (New York: Palgrave Macmillan, 2003), p. 36. Richards noted how English contemporaries of Isabel of Castile, queen regnant of Castile from 1469 to 1503, referred to her as a king. In conjunction with her husband, Fernando of Aragon, the pair were referred to as "los reyes" in diplomatic documents sent to England, which were translated as "the kings" since the English could not comprehend, linguistically, a term to describe female kingly power.

9. Historians continue to examine female rule within the context of other forms of female power, see *Medieval Queenship*, ed. John Carmi Parsons (New York: St. Martin's Press, 1993), Lisa Hopkins, *Women Who Would Be Kings: Female Rulers of the Sixteenth Century* (New York: St. Martin's Press, 1991), Dick Harrison, *The Age of Abbesses and Queens: Gender and Political Culture in Medieval Europe* (Lund, Sweden: Nordic Academic Press, 1998), *Queens and Queenship in Medieval England*, ed. Anne Duggan (Woodbridge, Suffolk: Boydell Press, 1997), Antonia Fraser, *The Warrior Queens* (New York: Vintage Books, 1988).

10. Arthur Taylor, *The Glory of Regality: An Historical Treatise of the Anointing and Crowning of the Kings and Queens of England* (London: Payne and Foss, 1820), p. 3.

11. Ibid.

12. England's deposed monarchs include Edward II (1327), Richard II (1399), Henry VI (1461, 1471), Edward IV (1470), Edward V (1483), Richard III (1485), Charles I (1649), and James II (1688), while in 1936 Edward VIII was prevailed upon to abdicate, as were Edward II and Richard II.

13. Gerda Lerner, *The Creation of Feminist Consciousness* (Oxford: Oxford University Press, 1993), p. 15.

14. For a groundbreaking call to arms for the need to integrate women's history within the historical discipline, see Elizabeth Fox Genovese, "Placing Women's History in History," *New Left Review*, 133 (May/June 1982), pp. 5–29.

15. The implications derived from the use of gender as a mode of historical analysis have spread far and wide in the historical discipline, far beyond the scope of this project. It will suffice here to briefly outline a few seminal works that pointed the way: Joan Scott's groundbreaking article, "Gender: A Useful Category of Historical Analysis" appeared in the *American Historical Review*, 91, 5 (December 1986), pp. 1053–1075. In this work, Scott argued that

gender represented the context of power relations between the sexes. Scott has since both modified and expanded her analyses of the usefulness of gender as a category of historical analysis, see *Gender and the Politics of History* (New York: Columbia University Press, 2000). While Scott gets much of the credit for the emergence of gender studies, Elizabeth Fox-Genovese, in her 1982 article. "Placing Women's History in History," delivered a well argued pitch for the introduction of the "gender system as a fundamental category of historical analysis," 6. For further studies on the social construction of gendered hierarchies, see Christine Ward Gailey, "Evolutionary Perspectives on Gender Hierarchy," *Analyzing Gender*, ed. Beth B. Hess and Myra Marx Feree (Newberry Park: Sage Productions, 1987), pp. 32–67. For more specialized studies of English female kingship, see Carole Levin, *The Heart and Stomach of a King* (Philadelphia: University of Pennsylvania Press, 1994), also A.N. Mclaren, *Political Culture in the Reign of Queen Elizabeth* (Cambridge: Cambridge University Press, 1999).

16. See Joan Hoff, "Gender as a Postmodern Category of Paralysis," *Women's History Review*, 3, 2 (1994), pp. 80–99.

17. This theoretical starting point is nicely fleshed out in Bonnie Smith, *The Gender of History* (Cambridge, Mass.: Harvard University Press, 1998).

18. For a survey of the origins of patriarchy in Western culture, see Gerda Lerner, *The Creation of Patriarchy* (Oxford: Oxford University Press, 1986). The ambivalence of historians to utilize the word patriarchy as a descriptive term appears in a number of theoretical works: see Carole Pateman, *The Sexual Contract* (Oxford: Polity Press, 1988), and Judith Bennett, "Feminism and History," *Gender and History* 1 (1989), pp. 259–263.

19. For a recent study of medieval English women's political power, see J.A. Green, "Aristocratic Women in Early Twelfth Century England," *Anglo-Norman Political Culture and the Twelfth Century Renaissance*, ed. C. Warren Hollister (Woodbridge, Suffolk: Boydell Press, 1997), pp. 60–72, and Susan M. Johns, *Noblewomen, Aristocracy and Power* (Manchester: Manchester University Press, 2003). For the standard study of the early-modern aristocracy, see Lawrence Stone, *The Crisis of the Aristocracy, 1558–1641* (Oxford: Clarendon Press, 1965).

20. See Duggan, *Queens and Queenship*, pp. 1–120.

21. For a recent study of the exercise of delegated queenly sovereignty in late-medieval Spain, see Theresa Earenfight, "Maria of Castile, Ruler or Figurehead?" *Mediterranean Studies*, 4 (1994), pp. 45–61.

22. This fundamental problem is identified in Mary Erler and Maryanne Kowalski, "Introduction," *Women and Power in the Middle Ages*, ed. Mary Erler and Maryanne Kowaleski (Athens, Georgia: University of Georgia Press, 1988), pp. 1–4.

23. See Allan G. Johnson, *The Gender Knot: Unraveling Our Patriarchal Legacy* (Philadelphia: Temple University Press, 1997), pp. 5–7.

24. For an explanation for why Mary II is not considered a de jure female ruler, see chapter 4.

25. For an analysis of the means by which male historians through time have dismissed the historical roles of women on the basis of natural womanly deficiency, see Smith, *The Gender of History*, pp. 1–13.

26. For a recent example, see Peter Brimacombe, *All the Queen's Men: The World of Elizabeth I* (New York: St. Martin's Press, 2000). Brimacombe identified Mary I's previously unidentified accomplishment, noting that, "Mary's reign, unsatisfactory though it may have been, had at least been advantageous in a accustoming the English kingdom of a female monarch, an institution which was becoming increasingly prevalent in Europe." A backhanded compliment, but a new perspective all the same, p. 40.

27. See Myers, *Medieval Kingship*, pp. 2–13, Monod, *The Power of Kings*, pp. 6–41, for discussion of the social construct of kingship.

28. See J.L. Laynesmith, *The Last Medieval Queens* (Oxford: Oxford University Press, 2004), p. 5.

29. For a survey of biblical and classical injunctions against women, see Diana Coole, *Women in Political Theory: From Ancient Misogyny to Contemporary Feminism* (New York: Harvester/Wheatsheaf, 1993), pp. 1–37. Scholars who have demonstrated the limits of culturally hegemonic male dominance include Amy Louise Erickson, *Women and Property in Early Modern England* (New York: Routledge, 1993), Merry Wiesner, "Women's Defense of Their Public Role," *Women in the Middle Ages and the Renaissance*, ed. Mary Beth Rose (Syracuse: Syracuse University Press, 1986), pp. 1–22, and Alice Clark, *Working Life of Women in the Seventeenth Century* (New York: Routledge, 1992).

30. Some of the works that identify a dual system of accommodation and resistance to forms of male dominance include Judith Bennett, *Medieval Women in Modern Perspective* (Washington DC: American Historical Association, 2000), also Merry Wiesner, "Women's Defense," pp. 1–22.

31. For further discussion of the social and legal status of medieval and early-modern Englishwomen, see Henrietta Leyser, *Medieval Women: A Social History of Women in England, 450–1500* (London: Weidenfeld and Nicolson, 1995), also Pearl Hogrefe, *Tudor Women* (Ames, Iowa: Iowa University Press, 1975). For studies of women in the larger context of medieval Europe, see *Medieval Women*, ed. Derek Baker (Oxford: Studies in Church History, Subsidia I, 1978), *Medieval Women and the Sources of Medieval History*, ed. J.T. Rosenthal (Athens, Ga.: University of Georgia Press, 1990), S. Shahar, *The Fourth Estate: A History of Women in the Middle Ages* (London: Metheun, 1983).

32. See Michael K. Jones, *The King's Mother: Lady Margaret Beaufort, Countess of Richmond and Derby* (Cambridge: Cambridge University Press, 1992). For a feminist viewpoint of Beaufort, see Karen Lindsey, *Divorced Beheaded Survived: A Feminist Reinterpretation of the Wives of Henry VIII* (Reading, Mass.: Perseus Books, 1995), pp. 3–11.

33. See Jurgen Habermas, *The Structural Transformation of the Public Sphere*, trans. Thomas Burger, Frederick Lawrence (Cambridge, Ma.: M.I.T. Press, 1989, orig. pub. 1962). Although Habermas categorically states that a recognizable public sphere only emerged in England following the Glorious Revolution (1688), he does say that "private" referred to the exclusion from the sphere of the state apparatus, p. 11. In this sense, female kings transcended the private sphere of womanhood upon their accessions.

34. For an influential description of the relationship between female agency and public and private power, see Jo Ann McNamara and Suzanne Wemple, "The Power of Women Through the Family in Medieval Europe, 500–1100," *Clio's Consciousness Raised: New Perspectives on the History of Women*, ed. Mary S. Hartman and Lois Banner (New York: Harper Colophon, 1974), pp. 103–118.

35. For more discussion of the public roles played by elite Anglo-Saxon women, see Christine Fell, *Women in Anglo-Saxon England* (London: Colonnade, 1984).

36. See Leyser, *Medieval Women*, 24.

37. For further discussion of the evolution of feudal inheritance practices, see John Hudson, *Land, Law, Lordship in Anglo-Norman England* (Oxford: Clarendon Press, 1994) and S.F.C. Milsom, "Inheritance by Women in the Twelfth and Early Thirteenth Centuries," *On the Laws and Customs of England*, ed. Morris S. Arnold, Thomas A. Green, Sally A. Scully, and Stephen D. White (Chapel Hill, N.C.: University of North Carolina Press, 1981), pp. 60–89.

38. Jointures and dowers constituted similarly constructed incomes and or property due to a woman upon the death of her husband.

39. For a basic model of female inheritance rights, see Frederick Pollock and Frederic William Maitland, *The History of English Law Before the Time of Edward I*, vol. 2 (Cambridge: Cambridge University Press, 1968, orig. pub. 1898), pp. 420–428. For a survey of early-modern refinements, see Erickson, *Women and Property*.

40. For more on the career of Lucy of Lincoln, Countess of Chester, see *Complete Peerage of England, Scotland, Ireland*, ed. G.E. Cokayne, vol. 7, app. J, pp. 743–746, cited in Marjorie Chibnall, *The Empress Matilda* (Oxford: Blackwell, 1991), p. 92, and Johns, *Noblewomen, Aristocracy and Power*, pp. 55–61. For a study of the status of single women such as widows, see Amy M. Froide, "Marital Status as a

Category of Difference: Single women and Widows in Early
Modern England," *Singlewomen in the European Past: 1250–1800*,
ed. Judith Bennett and Amy M. Froide (Philadelphia: University of
Pennsylvania Press, 1999), pp. 236–269.

41. In the twelfth century, the Empress Matilda transmitted her claim
to the English throne to her son Henry II. Four hundred years later,
Richard, Duke of York, invoked a female inclusive rule of primogeniture as he based his claim on his descent from the Plantagenet
princess, Philippa of Clarence. In turn, both a Lancastrian heiress,
Margaret Beaufort, and a Yorkist heiress, Elizabeth of York,
provided the hereditary claims of the House of Tudor.

42. See Gayle Rubin, "The Traffic in Women: Notes on the 'Political
Economy' of Sex," *Toward an Anthropology of Women*, ed. Rayna R.
Reiter (New York: Monthly Review Press, 1975), pp. 157–210.

43. For an analysis of the origins of this plan, see E. Searle, "Women
and the Legitimization of Succession of the Norman Conquest,"
Anglo-Norman Studies, vol. 3, ed. Marjorie Chibnall (Woodbridge,
Suffolk: Boydell Press, 1980), pp. 159–170.

44. The single exception to this general rule was the accession of John in
1199. John overrode the claims of his nephew, Arthur, Count of
Brittany, the son of John's deceased elder brother Geoffrey, who later
died in John's custody. When John himself died in 1216, his eldest son,
ten-year-old Henry III, succeeded largely because of a lack of royal
adult male challengers. Nevertheless, the precedent of a successful
royal minority set into place the primacy of primogeniture. See
Charles Beem, *The Royal Minorities of Medieval England*, unpublished
M.A. thesis (Flagstaff: Northern Arizona University, 1990).

45. See William Stubbs, *The Constitutional History of England*, 3 vols.
(Oxford: Clarendon Press, 1897) II, p. 552.

46. In December 2004, Labour peer Lord Dubs introduced a private
bill to alter the succession that, among its various clauses, included
a change from cognatic to lineal, or absolute, primogeniture,
which would have allowed males and females to inherit equally.
However, the bill was withdrawn after the Blair government said it
would block the bill's passage.

47. See Lois L. Huneycutt, "Female Succession and the Language of
Power in the Writings of Twelfth Century Churchmen," *Medieval
Queenship*, pp. 190–199.

48. In her otherwise impressive scholarly study of Matilda's career,
Marjorie Chibnall only briefly mentions the impact of contempo-
rary notions of gender on the course of Matilda's career. See
Marjorie Chibnall, *The Empress Matilda*, pp. 97–98.

49. This particular problem was first tackled by William Huse
Dunham Jr., in his article "Regal Power and the Rule of Law: A
Tudor Paradox," *Journal of British Studies*, 3, 2 (May 1964), pp. 34–37.

50. Social scientists will never agree on just what the terms of civil or political society actually mean. For the purposes of this study, we shall refer to "political society" as those male voices through time providing the bulk of the primary sources utilized in this study. Thus, the political society that provides us with commentary for the career of the twelfth-century Empress Matilda is miniscule compared to those existing during the reigns of early-modern female kings. Each chapter shall include a discussion of the specific context of the political society it describes.

51. For a recent discussion of Elizabeth's continuing historical popularity, see Susan Doran, "Elizabeth I: Gender, Power, and Politics," *History Today*, 53, 5 (2003), pp. 29–35.

52. David Starkey, *Elizabeth: Apprenticeship* (London: Chatto and Windus, 2000), p. x.

53. For instance, in his study of Elizabeth's relationship with her courtiers, Neville Williams observed, "there was the significance of her sex, and where many queens found this a matter of weakness Elizabeth made it a source of strength." Like so many other conventional historians, Williams identified the problem, but left it for gender analysis to provide the explanation. *All the Queen's Men: Elizabeth I and Her Courtiers* (London: Cardinal, 1974), p. 14.

54. Perhaps the best example of this phenomenon is J.E. Neale, the most influential of Elizabeth's modern biographers, who recognized and contrasted the gendered restraints upon Elizabeth with an unabashed wonder at her success as monarch. See J.E. Neale, *Queen Elizabeth I* (New York: Anchor Books, 1957, orig. pub. 1937).

55. Susan Bassnett sounded the feminist call to arms for a gendered analysis of Elizabeth I in her work, *Elizabeth I: A Feminist Perspective* (Oxford: Berg, 1988). While Bassnett is often careless in her attention to factual detail, she poses a number of alternative explanations for conventional critiques of Elizabeth's shortcomings as natural feminine deficiency.

56. Among my more recent favorites are: Elizabeth Jenkins, *Elizabeth the Great* (New York: Coward-McKann, 1959), Carolly Erickson, *The First Elizabeth* (New York: Summit Books, 1983), and Anne Somerset, *Elizabeth I* (London: Weidenfeld and Nicolson, 1991).

57. For a recent, edited version of this work, see William Camden, *The History of the Most Renowned and Victorious princess Elizabeth Late Queen of England*, ed. with intro. by Wallace McCaffery (Chicago: University of Chicago Press, 1990).

58. For recent analyses of gender perceptions in Tudor society, see Anthony Fletcher, *Gender, Sex, and Subordination in England* (New Haven, Conn.: Yale University Press, 1995), also Susan Amussen, *An Ordered Society: Gender and Class in Early Modern England* (New York: Columbia University Press, 1988).

59. John Aylmer, later Bishop of London, wrote his work, *An Harborowe For Faithful and Trewe Subjects* (London: 1559) as a rebuttal to John Knox's scathing critique of female rule, *First Blast of the Trumpet Against the Monstrous Regiment of Women* (Geneva: 1558). Aylmer's emphasis on the mixed nature of the English constitution was also incorporated into Sir Thomas Smith's political critique, *De Republica Anglorum*, ed. L. Alston (New York: Harper and Row, 1973, orig. pub. 1584).

60. Writing in the late seventeenth century, Gilbert Burnet, Bishop of Salisbury, considered Elizabeth's success a providential work of God, see *History of the Reformation of the Church of England*, vol. 2 (New York: D. Appleton and Co., 1848, orig. pub. 1665). Elizabeth also faired well in the estimation of Henry St. John, Lord Bolingbroke, see *Remarks on the History of England* (Dublin: G. Faulkner, 1743). Writing later on in the eighteenth century, Henry Hallam displayed no ambivalence in assigning masculine traits as an explanation for Elizabeth's remarkable talents in ruling. See *Constitutional History of England* (Boston: Wells and Lily, 1829). For a discussion of Elizabeth's seventeenth-century historical reputation, see J.P. Kenyon, "Queen Elizabeth and the Historians," *Queen Elizabeth I: Most Politick Princess*, ed. Simon Adams (London: History Today, 1983), pp. 52–55, also D.R. Woolfe, "Two Elizabeths? James I and the Late Queen's Famous Memory," *Canadian Journal of History*, 20 (1985), pp. 167–191.

61. For a number of analyses on nineteenth-century gender formations, see Leonore Davidoff and Catherine Hall, *Family Fortunes: Men and Women of the English Middle Class, 1780–1850* (Chicago: Chicago University Press, 1987), Anna Clark, *The Struggle for the Breeches* (Berkeley: University of California Press, 1995), and John Tosh, *A Man's Place: Masculinity and the Middle Class Home in Victorian England* (New Haven: Yale University Press, 1999).

62. See Rohan Amanda Maitzen, *Gender, Genre, and Victorian Historical Writing* (New York: Garland Publishing, 1998).

63. Strickland, *Queens of England*, V, pp. 620, 712.

64. James Anthony Froude, *The Reign of Elizabeth*, 5 vols. (London: J.M. Dent, 1911).

65. Froude, *Elizabeth*, IV, p. 364.

66. Mandell Creighton, *Queen Elizabeth* (New York: Thom Y. Crowell, 1966, orig. pub. 1899), p. 29.

67. Ibid.

68. Ibid., pp. 27–28, 51, 176.

69. Creighton did not see this as a problem. Instead, it occurred to him right in the middle of his narrative that "Elizabeth discovered the advantages to be gained by combining the parts of the woman and the Queen," p. 51.

70. Neale, *Queen Elizabeth I*, p. 83.
71. Ibid., p. 1.
72. Ibid., p. 83.
73. Ibid., p. 63.
74. Ibid., p. 67.
75. Ibid., pp. 85–101.
76. Ibid., p. 294. Neale here is referring to the 1558 publication, *First Blast of the Trumpet Against the Monstrous Regiment of Women*, by John Knox, a vitriolic indictment of female rule, directed against Mary I of England, and Mary of Guise, Regent of Scotland. Unfortunately for Knox, by the time it was published Elizabeth had ascended her throne, and was annoyed by its assertions.
77. A.L. Rowse, in his *Expansion of Elizabethan England* (New York: St. Martin's Press, 1955), appropriated Creighton's views on the impact of Elizabeth's gender, p. 266.
78. G.R. Elton, *England Under the Tudors* (New York: Barnes and Noble, 1965), p. 262.
79. Ibid. Elton is not the only one to use the highly gendered analogy of a housewife to describe Elizabeth; J.P. Kenyon, in his post-Whig critique of Neale, quoted a mid-seventeenth-century description of Elizabeth, "a sluttish housewife, who swept the house but left the dust behind the door." J.P Kenyon, *Stuart England*, 2nd ed. (London: Penguin, 1978), p. 19.
80. Elton, *England Under the Tudors*, p. 398.
81. Ibid., p. 262.
82. Christopher Haigh, *Elizabeth I* (New York: Longman, 1988), p. 171.
83. Ibid., 172.
84. David Loades has published two major works on Mary I. The first, *The Reign of Mary Tudor*, 2nd ed. (London: Longmans, 1991, orig. pub. 1978) does not contain any specific references to Mary's gendered problems. The second work, *Mary Tudor: A Life* (London: Basil Blackwell, 1989), contains passing references to the impact of Mary's gender on her rule, but no sustained investigation, pp. 1–3, 218.
85. See Alison Heisch, "Queen Elizabeth I and the Persistence of Patriarchy," *Feminist Review*, 4 (1980), pp. 45–75.
86. See Bassnet, p. 5, who wrote, "The great division between Elizabeth and twentieth century readers is time itself. In the four hundred years since her death, perceptions have changed so completely that we can only with great difficulty imagine how the Renaissance mind worked."
87. This line of theoretical reasoning also informs several of the essays in the volume, *Dissing Elizabeth: Negative Representations of Gloriana*, ed. Julia M. Walker (London: Dale University Press, 1998). In particular, see Susan Doran, "Why Did Elizabeth Not Marry?,"

pp. 30–59, and Carole Levin, "We Shall Never Have A Merry World While the Queene Lyveth: Gender, Monarchy, and the Power of Seditious Words," pp. 77–95.

88. See Susan Frye, *Elizabeth I: The Competition for Representation* (Oxford: Oxford University Press, 1993).

89. Constance Jordan also has based much of her study on the interpretation of literary texts as a means to gauge the problems of female rule, see *Renaissance Feminism: Literary Texts and Political Models* (Ithaca: Cornell University Press, 1990).

90. Frye's analysis of the paternalistic pressures Elizabeth faced upon her accession is also discussed in Louis Montrose, "Shaping Fantasies: Figurations of Gendered Power in Elizabethan Culture," *Representing the English Renaissance*, ed. Stephen Greenblatt (Berkeley: University of California Press, 1988), pp. 31–64.

91. Frye, *Elizabeth I*, pp. 26–46.

92. Ibid., pp. 36–48.

93. Sydney Anglo argued persuasively for a contextual and analytical approach in his explanation for the representational power generated by Tudor royal pageantry, see *Spectacle, Pageantry, and Early Tudor Policy*, 2nd ed. (Oxford: Clarendon Press, 1997).

94. Frye, *Elizabeth I*, pp. 26–30.

95. Levin, *Heart and Stomach*, p. 1.

96. Ibid., p. 121.

97. Ibid., p. 68.

98. Ibid.

99. Levin offered a brief discussion of the Act Concerning Regal Power, which prompted this historian to investigate the origin and motivation behind this landmark statute, *Heart and Stomach*, p. 121.

100. The recognition that Elizabeth was king and queen at the same has filtered down to popular historical surveys. For a recent example, see Simon Schama, *A History of Britain: At the Edge of the World, 3000 b.c.–a.d. 1603* (New York: Hyerion, 2000), p. 387.

101. The formidable difficulties Elizabeth encountered in the various marriage negotiations during the first twenty years of her reign are skillfully discussed in Susan Doran, *Monarchy and Matrimony: The Courtships of Elizabeth I* (London and New York: Routledge, 1996).

1   Making a Name for Herself: The Empress Matilda and the Construction of Female Lordship in Twelfth-Century England

1. *Gesta Stephani*, trans. and ed. K.R. Potter (Oxford: Clarendon Press, 1976), pp. 118–119.

2. See Marjorie Chibnall, *The Empress Matilda*, pp. 195–206.

3. For analyses of the gendered roles of medieval women, see *Women and Power in the Middle Ages*, Leyser, *Medieval Women Queens and Queenship in Medieval Europe Medieval Queenship*.

4. Brian fitz Count, vassal of both Henry I and Matilda, recorded his views on female inheritance in letters exchanged with Henry of Blois, Bishop of Winchester and King Stephen's brother. The correspondence was preserved in Richard Bury's fourteenth-century book of letters, and reproduced in H.W.C. Davis, "Henry of Blois and Brian fitz Count," *English Historical Review*, 25, (1910), pp. 297–303. Gilbert Foliot, Abbott of Gloucester, remarked and agreed on fitz Count's assessment of Matilda's legitimate claim to the English throne. See *The Letters and Charters of Gilbert Foliot*, 2nd ed., ed. C.N.L. Brooke (Cambridge: Cambridge University Press, 1967), pp. 60–66.

5. The impact of clerics as "masters of the medium of communication with both contemporaries and with historians who use their texts to study the period" is discussed in M. Bennett, "Military Masculinity in England and Northern France ca. 1050–ca.1225," *Masculinity in Medieval Europe*, ed. D.M. Hadley (London: Longman, 1999), pp. 71–88. See also Lois Huneycutt, "Female Succession and the Language of Power in the Writings of Twelfth-Century Churchmen," *Medieval Queenship*, pp. 189–201.

6. In his commentary on the post-Whig revisionism of Richardson and Sayles's 1963 collaboration, *The Governance of Medieval England*, R.L. Schuyler summed up their contrast with William Stubb's idealized version of a twelfth-century constitution, noting that "the idea of a definite constitution, providing the essentials of government, was not a medieval idea. Important political questions were left to be determined by chance, accident, or the will of god." See "Recent Work of Richardson and Sayles," *Journal of British Studies*, 3, (May 1964), pp. 1–23.

7. William of Malmesbury, *Historia Novella*, trans. K.R. Potter, ed. Edmund King (Oxford: Clarendon Press, 1998).

8. Henry of Huntington, *The Chronicle of Henry of Huntington*, ed. Thomas Forester (London: Henry Bohn, 1853).

9. William of Malmesbury's *Historia Novella* was actually a more detailed version of the final chapters of Malmesbury's larger work, *William of Malmesbury's Chronicle of the Kings of England* (afterward referred to as *Malmesbury*), ed. J.A. Giles (London: Henry Bohn, 1897). Like Henry of Huntington's history, Malmesbury's chronicle reached deep into Anglo-Saxon history to provide a continuous narrative of English history down to his present day.

10. For a discussion of the possible identity of the chronicle's author, see *Gesta Stephani*, pp. xviii–xxxviii.

11. For a discussion of the *Gesta Stephani's* gendered attack on Matilda, see pp. 54–56.

12. The Worcester chroniclers have been identified as the monks Florence, writing up to 1118, and John, continuing the chronicle up to 1140. The entire chronicle is subsumed in *The Chronicle of John of Worcester* (afterward referred to as *John of Worcester*), ed. P. McGurk (Oxford: Clarendon Press, 1998). In her work, *The Empress Matilda*, Chibnall, Matilda's sole twentieth-century scholarly biographer, cited the commentary of the Durham chronicler, see Symeon of Durham, *Symeonis Monachi Opera Omnia*, 2 vols., ed. T. Arnold, RS, 1882–85.

13. Orderic Vitalis, *Historia Ecclesiastica*, vol. 6, ed. Marjorie Chibnall (Oxford: Clarendon Press, 1998). Vitalis also contributed to the *Gesta Normannorum Ducam of William of Jumieges, Orderic Vitalis and Robert of Torigni*, ed. Elisabeth M.C. Van Houts (Oxford: Clarendon Press, 1995). For an analysis of Vitalis's attitudes toward women, see Marjorie Chibnall, "Women in Orderic Vitalis," *Haskin's Society Journal*, 2 (1990), pp. 105–121.

14. Vitalis, *Historia*, pp. 455–473.

15. For a number of analyses of the principal chronicler's political biases, see C. Warren Hollister, *Henry I* (New Haven: Yale University Press, 2001), pp. 3–12, and Edmund King, "Introduction," *The Anarchy of Stephen's Reign*, ed. Edmund King (Oxford: Clarendon Press).

16. The first modern study of Matilda is found in Agnes Strickland, *Lives of the Queens of England*, I. Strickland subsumed Matilda's career in the chapter describing Stephen's queen, Matilda of Boulogne. Betraying her own Victorian notions of proper roles for women, the empress Matilda's "Juno" like efforts to secure her inheritance are contrasted with Queen Matilda's salutary performance as her husband's helpmate, pp. 208–231. Since this time, the vast majority of historical works examining Matilda are found in the context of Stephen's reign. See R.H.C. Davis, *King Stephen*, 3rd ed. (London: Longman, 1990), H.A. Cronne, *The Reign of King Stephen, 1135–1154* (London: Weidenfeld and Nicolson, 1970), and K.J. Stringer, *The Reign of King Stephen* (London: Routledge, 1993). Only two monographs devoted primarily to Matilda appeared in the second half of the twentieth century. The first, Nesta Pain, *Empress Matilda: Uncrowned Queen of England* (London: Weidenfeld and Nicolson, 1978), made the revelatory leap in identifying Matilda as a queen, but the work, while engaging and romantic, is not scholarly. The other, Marjorie Chibnall, *Empress Matilda*, is an impressive work by a renowned editor of primary narrative sources. Chibnall, however, only briefly noted the impact of gender upon Matilda's efforts to gain the English crown, pp. 96–97. Matilda finally gained equal billing with Stephen in Jim Bradbury, *Stephen and Matilda: The Civil War of 1139–1154* (Stroud,

Gloucestershire: Alan Sutton, 1996). Bradbury's work is primarily concerned with military tactics, and does not concentrate on Matilda's representational strategies to gain her inheritance.

17. Mid-twentieth-century Anglo-Norman studies rarely give Matilda's career much space or analysis. See A.L. Poole, *From Domesday Book to Magna Carta 1087–1216* (Oxford: Clarendon Press, 1951), also Frank Barlow, *The Feudal Kingdom of England*, 2nd ed. (London: Longmans, 1961).

18. The major twelfth-century documentary source used in this chapter is the *Regesta Regum Anglo-Normannorum* (afterward referred to as *Regesta*) 3 vols., III, ed. H.A. Cronne and R.H.C. Davis (Oxford: Clarendon Press, 1968). The *Regesta* is a compilation of charters issued during the reign of king Stephen, ca. 1135–1154, including those of the empress Matilda, as well as Stephen's queen Matilda of Boulogne, and the empress's son Henry Plantagenet. Cronne and Davis drew from a wide sweep of manuscript sources; those whose issue dates are uncertain are conjectured.

19. For a recent study of Anglo-Saxon kingship. See Ann Williams, *Kingship and Government in Pre-Conquest England* (New York: St. Martin's Press, 1999).

20. For an influential study of the relationship between the family and political power in the European Middle Ages, see Jo Ann McNamara and Suzanna Wemple, "The Power of Women Through the Family in Medieval Europe," pp. 1–28.

21. Cited in Leyser, *Medieval Women*, p. 13. Alfred the Great of Wessex (871–899) commissioned the *Anglo-Saxon Chronicle* as a vernacular historical source. What is significant about this quote is that Seaxburgh's one-year reign was considered important enough for the chronicler to recall it two hundred years later.

22. The *Anglo-Saxon Chronicle*, trans. and ed. Michael Swanton (London: J.M. Dent, 1997).

23. Pauline Stafford, *Queen Emma and Queen Edith* (Oxford: Blackwell, 1997), pp. 56–57.

24. Pauline Stafford, "The King's Wife in Wessex, 800–1066," *Past and Present*, 91, (May 1981), pp. 3–27.

25. Stafford, *Queen Emma*, pp. 56–65, 164–187.

26. See Janet L. Nelson, "Early Medieval Rites of Queen Making and the Shaping of Medieval Queenship," *Queens and Queenship in Medieval Europe*, pp. 302–313.

27. Ibid.

28. Stafford, *Queen Emma*, pp.165–187, 192–247.

29. For a larger discussion of the *Encomium Emmae* and the *Vita Edwardi Regis*, see Stafford, "The King's Wife," p. 5, notes 15 and 16.

30. See Christine Fell, *Women in Anglo-Saxon England*, pp. 160–164.

31. Pauline Stafford, "Emma: The Powers of the Queen," pp. 3–26, Mary Strol, "Maria Regina: Papal Symbol," pp. 173–203, *Queens and Queenship in Medieval Europe*.

32. For a study of this particular dimension of Anglo-Saxon queenship, see Stafford, "The King's Wife," pp. 3–27.

33. Stafford, *Queen Emma*, pp. 7–8, 93–94.

34. See H.G. Richardson and G.O. Sayles, *The Governance of Mediaeval England: From the Conquest to Magna Carta* (Edinburgh: Edinburgh University Press, 1963), p. 139.

35. Stafford, *Queen Emma*, p. 187.

36. Richardson and Sayles, *The Governance*, pp. 25–27.

37. For a still useful study, see F.M. Stenton, *The First Century of English Feudalism, 1066–1166* (Oxford: Clarendon Press, 1932).

38. See E. Searle, "Women and the legitimization of Succession at the Norman Conquest," *Anglo-Norman Studies*, 3 (1981 for 1980), pp. 159–170.

39. Robert Bartlett, *England Under the Norman and Angevin Kings* (Oxford: Clarendon Press, 2000), pp. 127–129.

40. See W.M. Aird, 'Frustrated Masculinity', The Relationship between William the Conqueror and his Eldest Son,". *Masculinity in Medieval Europe*, pp. 39–55.

41. *Gesta Normanorum Ducam*, p. 277.

42. In his work *Land, Law, Lordship in Anglo-Norman England*, John Hudson noted a peculiar rise in the numbers of heiresses to feudal tenancies in the eleventh century, p. 111. For a classic discussion of the origins of the primacy of primogeniture, see Frederick Pollock, and Frederick William Maitland, *The History of English Law Before the Time of Edward I*, I, pp. 262–278, 292–294.

43. Percy Ernst Schramm, *A History of the English Coronation*, trans. Leopold G. Wickham Legg (Oxford: Clarendon Press, 1937) p. 152. Also see C. Warren Hollister, "Anglo-Norman Succession Debate of 1126: Prelude to Stephen's Anarchy," *Journal of Medieval History*, I (April 1975), pp. 19–42.

44. See W.L. Warren, *Henry II* (Berkeley: University of California Press, 1973), p. 10.

45. For a discussion of the dynastic importance of this marriage, see E. Searle, "Women and the Legitimization of Succession of the Norman Conquest," pp. 159–170.

46. In describing the reasoning for why Henry I first designated his daughter Matilda as his heir, William of Malmesbury emphasized the importance of her combined Anglo-Saxon and Norman blood-lines. See *Malmesbury*, p. 482.

47. Robert of Torigny recalled that Hugh Capet associated his son Robert in his kingship, see *Gesta Normannorum Ducam*, p. 245.

48. See Bartlett, *England*, p. 9.

49. The Salic law prescribed royal inheritance through the male line only. For a detailed study of the succession patterns of Capetian France, see A.W. Lewis, *Royal Succession in Capetian France: Studies on Familial Order and the State* (Cambridge Mass.: Harvard University Press, 1981).

50. Contemporaries differ on the date of when these first oaths were given: William of Malmesbury dated the oaths at Christmas, 1127, while John of Worcester dated them in April 1128. See *Malmesbury*, pp. 482, 483, *John of Worcester*, pp. 176–177.

51. Malmesbury stated, "if he himself [Henry I] died without a male heir, they [the nobles of England] would immediately and without hesitation accept his daughter Matilda, formerly empress, as their lady." *Historia Novella*, pp. 6–7.

52. Malmesbury, *Historia Novella*, p. 9.

53. Fulk relinquished his county of Anjou to his son Geoffrey not only to give his son noble status prior to his marriage, but also because Fulk was affianced to Melisende, the royal heiress of the Crusader Kingdom of Jerusalem. Although Fulk intended to rule Jerusalem as king in right of his wife, Melisende successfully forced her husband to share sovereignty with her, as her father, Baldwin II, had intended. See Bernard Hamilton, "Women in the Crusader States: The Queens of Jerusalem, 1100–1190," *Medieval Women*, ed. Derek Baker, pp. 143–174, also Sarah Lambert, "Queen or Consort? Rulership and Politics in the Latin East, 1118–1128," *Queens and Queenship in Medieval Europe*, pp. 153–169.

54. This is the view generally held by some Anglo-Norman scholars, see Warren, *Henry II*, pp. 7–12, Bartlett, pp. 9, 145. Other scholars have minimized the extent of Angevin–Norman hostility, see Hollister, *Henry I*, pp. 323–325, Chibnall, *Empress Matilda*, p. 55. It is significant to note that it took Geoffrey Plantagenet eight years to subdue Normandy, ostensibly in his son's right, while he played no part in Matilda's efforts to gain her English inheritance.

55. Henry I's justiciar, Roger, Bishop of Salisbury, complained to Malmesbury that "no one had been involved in arranging that marriage, or had been aware that it would take place, except Robert, earl of Gloucester, Brian fitz Count, and the bishop of Lisiuex." Malmesbury, *Historia Novella*, p. 11.

56. William of Malmesbury observed that "I myself have often heard Roger, Bishop of Salisbury, saying that he was released from the oath he had taken to the empress, because he had sworn only on condition that the king should not give his daughter in marriage to anyone outside the kingdom without consulting himself and the other chief men" Malmesbury, *Historia Novella*, pp. 10–11.

57. See *Gesta Normannorum Ducam*, pp. 240–241.

58. Chibnall disputes the assertion of Hildebert of Lavarin's modern biographer, and conjectures that Hildebert's letter to Matilda dated from 1127, while she was still in England prior to her second marriage. Peter von Moos, in *Hildebert von Lavardin 1056–1133* (Stuttgart: Pariser Historiche Studien 3, 1965), pp. 365–367, dated the letter 1129. Chibnall conjectured that Matilda was on good terms with her father in 1129, following her separation from Geoffrey Plantagenet.

59. See Huntington, *Henry of Huntington*, p. 258.

60. Malmesbury, *Historia Novella*, pp. 19–21.

61. For an analysis of the intersection of love and status within the context of aristocratic marriage in the twelfth century, see John Gillingham, "Love, Marriage and Politics in the Twelfth Century," *Forum for Modern Language Studies*, 25 (1989), pp. 292–303.

62. Chibnall cited the Durham chronicler as stating that there was agreement in England that Geoffrey Plantagenet should succeed Henry I, and the Le Mans chronicler, who indicated Geoffrey's aspirations for England and Normandy, *The Empress Matilda*, p. 57, ns. 53, 54.

63. Vitalis, *Historia*, p. 445.

64. One high profile example of this process was Henry I's bestowal in marriage of Matilda, heiress of Miles Crispin, to Brian fitz Count, which brought Brian his late father-in-law's honor of Wallingford, see Chibnall, *Empress Matilda*, pp. 12–13.

65. See Judith A. Green, *The Government of England Under Henry I* (Cambridge: Cambridge University Press, 1986), pp. 247–248.

66. For further discussions of this process, see Hudson, *Land, Law, Lordship,* pp. 111–112, Milsom, "Inheritance by Women in the Twelfth and Early Thirteenth Centuries," *On the Laws and Customs of England*, ed. Morris S. Arnold, Thomas A. Green, Sally A. Saully, and Stephen D. White (Chapel Hill, N.C.: University of North Carolina Press, 1981), pp. 60–89. This process is also analogous to Gail Rubin's anthropological model. See "The Traffic in Women: Notes on the 'Political Economy' of Sex," *Towards an Anthropology of Women*, ed. Rayna R. Reiter (New York: Monthly Review Press, 1975), pp. 157–210.

67. Karl Leyser has offered provocative circumstantial evidence that the Emperor Henry V, Matilda's first husband, may have considered himself Henry I's heir, see "The Anglo-Norman Succession, 1120–1125," *Anglo-Norman Studies*, vol. 13, ed. Marjorie Chibnall (Woodridge, Suffolk: Boydell Press, 1991), pp. 234–235.

68. Malmesbury, *Historia Novella*, pp. 7–9, John of Worcester, pp. 176–179.

69. The 1131 oath, given at a great council in Northampton, is mentioned by Malmesbury, *Historia Novella*, pp. 17–20; the same

council Henry of Huntington reported had decided to repatriate Matilda back to her husband in Anjou, p. 258. A further oath in 1135, to Matilda and her eldest son, was reported long after the fact, during Henry II's reign, by Roger de Hovedon, see *The Annals of Roger de Hovedon*, I, ed. Henry T. Riley (London: Henry Bohn, 1853), p. 224. J.H. Round disputed the authenticity of both the 1131 and the 1135 oaths. See *Geoffrey de Mandeville* (New York: Burt Franklin, 1960, orig. pub. 1892), p. 31, n.2.

70. In contrast, Geoffrey's father Fulk was involved in the government of Jerusalem following his marriage to Melisende, but before the death of his father-in-law. Orderic Vitalis wrote that "His aging father in law offered him the crown; but the younger man declined to wear it in his lifetime, though he exercised authority undisturbed as his son in law and heir throughout the realm during the remaining year of the old king's life," pp. 390–391.

71. See Charlotte Newman, *The Anglo-Norman Nobility in the Reign of Henry I* (Philadelphia: University of Pennsylvania Press, 1988), p. 19.

72. Malmesbury reported that "After deliberating long and deeply on this matter, he . . . bound the nobles of all England . . . [to] accept his daughter Matilda . . . as their lady." Malmesbury, *Historia Novella*, pp. 6, 7.

73. Ibid.

74. C. Warren Hollister has argued that the choice of Geoffrey for Matilda's second husband centered on his ability to counter the threat posed by William Clito, son of Henry I's elder brother Robert Curthose, who considered himself a legitimate claimant to the Anglo-Norman Empire. Clito's cause was aided by the efforts of Louis VI of France, who helped him gain the county of Flanders in March 1127, three months after Matilda's designation as Henry I's heir. Thus the Anglo-Norman–Angevin alliance was just one more shift in the balance of power in northern France between the dukes of Normandy and the Capetian kings of France at this time. However, as Hollister has argued, Clito's untimely death in July 1128, one month after Matilda and Geoffrey's marriage, removed the main justification for the choice of Geoffrey as Matilda's husband. See Hollister, *Henry I*, pp. 317–325.

75. See Bradbury, *Stephen and Matilda*, p. 10, Hollister, *Henry I*, pp. 323–325.

76. See *Regesta*. The editors indicate in their introductory essay the problem of providing exact dates for a number of Matilda's surviving charters. By cross-referencing narrative descriptions of Matilda's movements with the locations where the charters were issued, Cronne and Davis conjecture the dates assigned. Given this, one charter bearing the style *imperatrix regum Anglie filia*, confirming Angers Abbey's possession of various English churches, could be dated as early as 1133, p. 7, n.20.

77. While Matilda was crowned Queen of the Romans at Mainz, July 25, 1110, she never received an imperial coronation from the pope. See Karl Leyser, *Medieval Germany and its Neighbors* (London: Hambledon Press, 1982), pp. 197–200.

78. *Gesta Normannorum Ducam*, p. 243.

79. K. Leyser, "Anglo-Norman Succession," p. 229.

80. For a larger discussion of Matilda's experience as Holy Roman Empress, see Chibnall, *Empress Matilda*, pp. 18–44.

81. *Malmesbury*, p. 481.

82. See P. Marchegay and A. Salmon, *Chroniques des Comtes d'Anjou*, vol. 1 (Paris: 1856–71), p. xv, n. 1, cited in Chibnall, *Empress Matilda*, 70.

83. See Hudson, *Land, Law, Lordship*, p. 111.

84. This is the verdict of C. Warren Hollister, see *Henry I*, pp. 323–325.

85. Bernard F. Reilly, *The Kingdom of Leon-Castilla Under Queen Uracca* (Princeton: Princeton University Press, 1982). See also Bernard Hamilton, "Women in the Crusader States: The Queens of Jerusalem 1100–90," *Medieval Women*, ed. Baker, pp. 143–174, and Sarah Lambert, "Queen or Consort: Rulership and Politics in the Latin East 1118–1128," *Queens and Queenship in Medieval Europe*, pp. 153–169.

86. The *Gesta Stephani* reported that Robert of Gloucester "was advised, as the story went, to claim the throne on his father's death, deterred by sounder advise he by no means assented, saying it was fairer to yield it to his sister's son, to whom it more justly belonged." pp. 12–13.

87. On Edith-Matilda's regencies, see *Regesta Regum Anglo-Normannorum*, II, ed. C. Johnson and H.A. Cronne (Oxford: Clarendon Press, 1968), pp. 971, 1000–1001, 1190, 1198.

88. *John of Worcester*, p. 167, Malmesbury, *Historia Novella*, pp. 6, 7.

89. *Malmesbury*, p. 489, Vitalis, *Historia*, pp. 445.

90. The exchange of arguments concerning female inheritance between Brian fitz Count and Henry of Blois, Bishop of Winchester, from Richard of Bury's fourteenth-century book of letters, were reproduced by H.W.C. Davis, "Henry of Blois and Brian fitz Count," pp. 297–303.

91. See *The Letters and Charters of Gilbert Foliot*, pp. 60–66, n.26.

92. See above n. 90.

93. *Malmesbury*, p. 483.

94. Vitalis, *Historia*, p. 445.

95. Ibid.

96. Warren, *Henry I*, p. 17.

97. In Marjorie Chibnall's otherwise impressive biography, the reasons why Matilda did not bolt for England are not discussed. Instead, Chibnall simply asserted that "Matilda, together with Geoffrey of Anjou, acted as quickly as possible to assert her rights where they were most likely to be accepted," p. 66. Similarly, Jim Bradbury

noted that "Matilda made no attempt to come to England, and made no overt claim to the throne. It does not appear as if she had seen herself as her father's heir, or had been planning to take over the kingdom and the duchy," p. 13.

98. Matilda's third son, William, was born in July 1536.

99. *Gesta Normannorum Ducam*, pp. 264–265.

100. *Malmesbury*, p. 490, Vitalis, *Historia*, p. 455.

101. Chibnall has argued that Matilda and Geoffrey concentrated their efforts on those regions in Normandy where her rights were most likely to be accepted, but does not contemplate what may have happened if Matilda had immediately bolted for London, *Empress Matilda*, p. 66.

102. *Malmesbury*, p. 518. Malmesbury described Henry of Blois's justification for the accession of his brother Stephen; "Therefore, as it seemed long to wait for a sovereign who delayed coming to England, for she [Matilda] resided in Normandy, we provided for the peace of the country, and my brother was allowed to reign."

103. See William Stubbs, *The Constitutional History of England*, I, pp. 551–552, Richardson/Sayles, pp. 136–155, Pauline Stafford, "Emma: The Powers of the Queen," *Queens and Queenship in Medieval Europe*, p. 22.

104. Schramm, *English Coronation*, pp. 20–29.

105. Vitalis, *Historia*, p. 455, *Gesta Normannorum Ducam*, pp. 264–265.

106. Orderic Vitalis reported that soon after Henry I's death, Geoffrey of Anjou sent Matilda into Normandy to take possession of castles that formed part of her dowry. However, a year and a half later, in May 1137, Geoffrey invaded Normandy himself, "acting as his wife's stipendiary commander," pp. 454, 455, 482, 483.

107. Robert of Torigny described the near-fatal complications arising from Matilda's second pregnancy. See *Gesta Normannorum Ducam*, pp. 246, 247.

108. *Gesta Stephani*, pp. 11–13.

109. The *Gesta Stephani* implied that Matilda's failure to claim her inheritance justified Stephen's accession, since there was "no one at hand who could take the king's place and put an end to the great dangers threatening the kingdom except Stephen, who . . . had been brought to them by providence," pp. 6, 7. For a discussion of the role the Londoners played in Stephen's accession see M. McKisack, "London and the Succession to the Crown During the Middle Ages," *Studies In Medieval History: Presented to Frederick Maurice Powicke*, ed. R.W. Hunt, W.A. Pantin, and R.W. Southern (Oxford: Clarendon Press, 1948), pp. 76–89.

110. John of Worcester called Stephen's elevation an election, *John of Worcester*, p. 215.

111. *Gesta Stephani*, pp. 11–13.

112. Henrietta Leyser, *Medieval Women*, p. 82.
113. Orderic Vitalis simply observed that "When Stephen, count of Boulogne, heard of his uncle's death he crossed at once to England, and after being accepted by William, archbishop of Canterbury, and the other bishops and magnates he ascended the royal throne," pp. 454, 455. Malmesbury made no mention of Matilda other than that she delayed her journey to England, but simply recounted the steps Stephen took to gain the throne, *Historia Novella*, pp. 26–29.
114. See Schuyler, "Recent Work of Richardson and Sayles," p. 13.
115. Chibnall, *Empress Matilda*, p. 64.
116. *Regesta*, III, p. xxxii.
117. Ibid., p. xxix.
118. Huntington, *Henry of Huntington*, p. 272.
119. Orderic Vitalis may have been offended that Matilda engaged in such activities during the holy season of Lent, pp. 513–515.
120. Much of what occurred at the papal curia is dicussed in a letter from Gilbert Foliot, Abbott of Gloucester, to Brian fitz Count, see *The Letters and Charters of Gilbert Foliot*, pp. 60–66, n.26.
121. See John of Salisbury, *Historia Pontificalis*, ed. Marjorie Chibnall (Oxford: Clarendon Press, 1986). Political philosopher John of Salisbury, was a contemporary of Matilda's son Henry II. In the *Historia Pontificalis*, Salisbury recounted Matilda's and Stephen's efforts in 1138 to sway the papal curia, p. 84.
122. Contemporaries and subsequent historians alike have offered a variety of explanations for why Stephen granted Matilda a safe-conduct to join her half-brother in Gloucester, see *Gesta Stephani*, 88, Huntington, *Henry of Huntington*, p. 272, *Malmesbury*, p. 506. Vitalis does not say why Stephen did it, but noted "In granting this license the king showed himself either very guileless or foolish, and prudent men must deplore his lack of regard for both his own safety and the security of the kingdom," p. 535.
123. *Regesta*, n. 20, n. 368, n. 391, n.597, n. 628, n. 697, n. 794. All of these charters, bearing the style *imperatrix* and *Henrici regis filia*, were issued between September 1139 and April 1141.
124. Chibnall found it difficult to accept that Matilda was functioning in England without Geoffrey Plantagenet's participation and approval. In the face of a decided lack of documentary evidence, Chibnall remarked that "his [Geoffrey's] assent to any grant involving lands on both sides of the Channel was clearly necessary; and it is hard to believe that there was no discussion about whether he should be associated with his wife in grants in England." Chibnall, *Empress Matilda*, p. 106.
125. *Gesta Stephani*, pp. 85, 87, 97.
126. Ibid., p. 115.

127. Sarah Lambert drew a similar conclusion in her analysis of the narrative sources that describe the careers of the Latin Kingdom of Jerusalem's ruling queens, see Lambert, pp. 153–169.
128. All of the contemporary narrative sources describe the "anarchy." Orderic Vitalis took Stephen to task for his failure to snuff out Matilda's challenge and the resultant "rapine and slaughter and the devastation of their country" pp. 534–535.
129. *Gesta Stephani*, p. 117, *John of Worcester*, pp. 293–295, Huntington, *Henry of Huntington*, p. 381.
130. *Gesta Stephani*, pp. 118–119, *John of Worcester*, pp. 293–295.
131. Matilda's charters confirm that after April 7 or 8, 1141, Matilda incorporated the style *domina Anglorum* following her usual *imperatrix* and *Henrici regis filia*, see *Regesta*, III, p. xxix. A number of Matilda's charters are difficult to date exactly, and the dates the editors assign are often a matter of conjecture. However, as late as March 30, 1141, in a charter informing the Barons of the Exchequer of a grant made to the canons of Oxford, she still styled herself *imperatrix* and *Henrici regis filia*, n. 628.
132. Matilda's first reference as *domina Anglorum* in her charters occurred in early April 1141. See *Regesta*, III, p. xxix.
133. Stubbs, *Constitutional History*, I, p. 368, Schramm, *English Coronation*, p. 57.
134. See Walter de Gray Birch, *A Fasciculus of the Charters of Mathildis Empress of the Romans, and an Account of her Great Seal* (reprinted from the *Journal of the British Archaeological Association*) (London: 1875), p. 381.
135. See Susan M. Johns, *Noblewomen, Aristocracy and Power* (Manchester: Manchester University Press, 2003), pp. 122–151.
136. Ibid.
137. Arthur Taylor, *The Glory of Regality: An Historical Treatise of the Anointing and Crowning of the Kings and Queens of England* (London: 1820), p. 9.
138. See *Regesta*, n. 76, Queen Matilda is simply styled *Matildis Anglorum Regina* But she also occasionally added *Boloniemsium comitissa* (countess of Boulogne) to her style, n.24. As Queen Matilda was the heir of Count Eustace III of Boulogne, Stephen ruled Boulogne as count in right of his wife.
139. It is interesting to note that Matilda's granddaughter-in-law, Constance, the female heir of Conan, Count of Brittany, often attested charters and grants as Countess of Brittany, despite her successive marriages to Geoffrey Plantagenet, and Ranulf II, Count of Chester, emphasizing her Breton patrimony as she downplayed her status as a wife. See Johns, *Noblewomen,* p. 138.
140. See Schramm, *English Coronation*, p. 57.

141. See Schramm, *English Coronation*, p. 57.
142. Pauline Stafford includes a discussion of the evolution of the term *domina* as a signifier of female power, see *Queen Emma*, pp. 58–59.
143. Both J.H. Round and A.L. Poole argued that Matilda's title "Lady of the English" described an intermediate stage between recognition of the possession of kingly authority and coronation. See Round, *Geoffrey de Mandeville*, pp. 70–75, and A.L. Poole, *From Domesday Book*, p. 3, n.1. See also Birch, *A Fasiculus*, p. 383.
144. Vitalis, *Historia*, p. 547.
145. Ibid., p. 549.
146. *John of Worcester*, p. 295. Henry of Huntington reported that "The whole English nation now acknowledged her as their sovereign," p. 280.
147. *Gesta Stephani*, p. 115.
148. *Malmesbury*, p. 517. Malmesbury claims to have been personally present at these proceedings.
149. Robert of Torigny considered Matilda's piety above and beyond the conventional religiosity usually displayed by aristocratic women, see *Gesta Normannorum Ducam*, pp. 244–245. For a more detailed discussion of Matilda's efforts to construct the image of a pious woman, see Chibnall, *Empress Matilda*, pp. 177–194.
150. The *Gesta Stephani* asserted that the Bishop of Winchester secretly opposed Matilda, and was only playing for time, p. 119.
151. The most detailed description of Matilda's investment as Lady of the English was Malmesbury's, who was personally present, *Historia Novella*, pp. 88–89.
152. Schramm considered Matilda's Winchester election, principally by clerics, "legal anarchy," *English Coronation,* p. 157.
153. *Regesta*, III, n. 343.
154. Ibid. nos. 275, 343. Chibnall has reservations concerning the authenticity of some of these charters, see Chibnall, *Empress Matilda*, pp. 102, n.47, pp. 103–104, n. 53.
155. See Birch, *A Fasciculus*, p. 379.
156. *Regesta*, III, p. xxix, also Birch, *A Fasciculus*, p. 383.
157. Chibnall, *Empress Matilda*, p. 63.
158. Malmesbury makes no mention of Matilda's sudden assumption of arrogance, *Malmesbury*, pp. 520–521.
159. *Gesta Stephani*, 119.
160. See Huntington, *Henry of Huntington*, p. 280, *John of Worcester*, p. 297. Writing during the reign of Henry II, Roger de Hovedon served to perpetuate further the condemnation of Matilda's behavior, writing, "However, she soon became elated to an intolerable degree of pride, because her affairs, after their uncertain state, had thus prospered in warfare," p. 244.

161. S. Bernard, *Bernardi Opera*, vol. 8, ed. J. Leclercq, C.H. Talbot, and H.M. Rochais (Rome: 1957–1977), pp. 297–298 (ep. 354), quoted in Chibnall, *Empress Matilda*, p. 97.

162. *Gesta Stephani*, p. 121.

163. Ibid., p. 123.

164. Ibid.

165. *Historia Novella*, pp. 97–99.

166. Ibid.

167. Huntington, *Henry of Huntington*, p. 280.

168. *John of Worcester*, p. 297.

169. *Gesta Stephani*, pp. 120–123.

170. Ibid.

171. *Historia Novella*, pp. 99–101.

172. *Gesta Stephani*, pp. 126–127.

173. *John of Worcester*, p. 299.

174. *Gesta Stephani*, p. 135.

175. See *Malmesbury*, pp. 522, 524, for the most detailed description of the rout of Winchester, also Huntington, *Henry of Huntington*, pp. 280–281. Other contemporaries expressed amazement that Matilda, in her flight from Winchester, rode her horse in the manner of a man, *John of Worcester*, p. 301.

176. *Gesta Stephani*, p. 135.

177. Graeme J. White countered the long held notion that Henry II's succession to Stephen was inevitable. See "The End of Stephen's Reign," *History*, 75 (February 1990), pp. 3–22.

178. *Regesta*, III, n. 794. In a charter sealed at Falaise, June 10, 1148, Matilda is simply styled *imperatrix Henrici regis filia.*

179. *Regesta*, III, n. 635.

180. See A.L. Poole, "Henry Plantagenet's Early Visits to England," *English Historical Review*, 47 (1910), pp. 447–450.

181. *Regesta*, III, n.43. In this charter issued in 1144 at Devizes, Matilda and Henry granted Geoffrey Ridel his inheritance in England and Normandy.

182. The *Regesta* includes a grant dated October 1147, issued by Geoffrey Plantagenet, which mentioned the consent of Matilda, when she was still in England, III, no. 599. Chibnall has argued that the grant must have been misdated, and was really in the year 1148, to bolster her assertion that in 1148 Matilda resided with her husband and children in Rouen, *Empress Matilda*, p. 153.

183. See Chibnall, *Empress Matilda*, pp. 151–176.

184. Matilda had recommended against Becket's appointment as Archbishop of Canterbury, but was overruled. Commenting on the letters Becket's adherents forwarded to her, Matilda wrote to her son, asking his intentions, and remarking, "when I know his

wishes I consider that any efforts of mine can accomplish anything, I will do all in my power to bring about peace between him
and the church," *Materials for the History of Thomas Becket*, V,
ed. J.C. Roberston, (London: 1872), pp. 144–151, cited in Chibnall,
Empress Matilda, p. 169.

2   Her Kingdom's Wife: Mary I and the Gendering of Regal Power

1. "Announcing the Accession of Queen Mary I," London, July 1553
   19, *Tudor Royal Proclamations*, 1553–1587, vol. 2, ed. P.L. Hughes and
   J.F. Larkin (New Haven: Yale University Press, 1969), p. 3, n. 388.
2. See John Foxe, *The Actes and Monuments of John Foxe*, VI, ed.
   George Town send (New York: AMS Press, 1965), p. 414.
3. See Ernst Kantorwicz, *The King's Two Bodies: A Study in Medieval
   Theology* (Princeton: Princeton University Press, 1957), and Marie
   Axton, *The Queen's Two Bodies: Drama and the Elizabethan Succession*
   (London: Royal Historical Society, 1977).
4. Mary was the target of a number of religiously motivated attacks
   against female rule. The most famous of these works, John Knox's
   First Blast of the Trumpet Against the Monstrous Regiment of Women
   (Genera: 1558), drew upon scripture and classical authority to
   demonstrate why the accession of a female ruler was a violation of
   the divinely ordained subjugation of women to men. Similarly, in
   his work *How Superior Powers Ought to be Obeyed of their Subjects,
   and Wherein They May Lawfully by god's word be Disobeyed and
   Resisted* (Geneva: 1558), Christopher Goodman pointed to the fact
   that women were not allowed magistracies of any kind in
   England, and concluded that it was a grave error to allow one to
   assume the supreme magistracy of a kingdom. Other works that
   attacked Mary because of her Catholicism include Anthony
   Gilby's, *Admonition to England and Scotland to Call them to
   Repentance* (Geneva: 1558), and Thomas Becon's *Humble
   Supplication Unto God for the Restoring of Hys Holye Woorde unto the
   Church of England* (Geneva: 1558). For a discussion of these works,
   see Constance Jordan, *Renaissance Feminism*, pp. 117–118, and
   "Women's Rule in Sixteenth Century Thought," *Renaissance
   Quarterly*, 40, (Autumn 1987), pp. 436–443. Also Patricia Ann Lee,
   "A Bodye Politique to Governe: Aylmer, Knox, and the Debate on
   Queenship," *Historian*, 52 (February 1990), pp. 242–262.
5. See above note. 1.
6. Barbara J. Harris, *English Aristocratic Women 1450–1550* (Oxford:
   Oxford University Press, 2002), pp. 1–26.

7. See James Anthony Froude, *History of England*, V (London: Longmans, Green, and Co., 1893). Froude erected the first modern model of Mary's mediocrity as monarch. While G.R. Elton did much to challenge and modify the findings of the first generation of modern Tudor-era scholars, he adopted the conventional interpretation of Mary I's reign, see his *Reform and Reformation* (London: Edward Arnold, 1977), p. 376, while John Guy, in his *Tudor England* (Oxford: Oxford University Press, 1988), summed up a century of historical interpretation, declaring that "despite the efforts of modern historiography to boost her reputation, Mary I will never appear creative," p. 226. For a concise analysis of the evolution of Marian historiography, see David Loades, "The Reign of Mary Tudor: Historiography and Research" *Albion* 21 (1989), pp. 547–558.

8. At the dawn of the Whig era, during the exclusion crisis of the early 1680s, Mary I's role as a "popish prince" gained new relevance as a warning to the succession of James II, see [anonymous] "Memoirs of Mary's Days,' wherein the Church of England, and all the Inhabitants, may plainly see (if God hath not suffered them to be infatuated) as in a glass, the sad Effects which follow a Popish successor enjoying the Crown of England,' " *Harleian Miscellany*, ed. William Oldys and Thomas Park, 6 vols (London: 1808), I, pp. 212–215.

9. Mary I has been the subject of a number of popular biographies of the twentieth century; H.F.H. Prescott, *Mary Tudor* (London: Eyre and Spottiswoode, 1952), Jasper Ridley, *The Life and Times of Mary Tudor* (London: Weidenfeld and Nicolson, 1973), Milton Waldman *The Lady Mary: A Biography of Mary Tudor* (New York: Scribner, 1972), and Carolly Erickson, *Bloody Mary* (New York: St. Martin's Press, 1978).

10. David Loades posed the first substantial challenge to conventional Marian historiography in a pair of m onographs, see *The Reign of Mary Tudor*, and *Mary Tudor: A Life*. In these works, Loades stressed the efforts of Mary's government to resolve the formidable economic and administrative problems inherited from Edward VI's minority government. In the second work, *A Life*, Loades identified and briefly discussed the gendered obstacles Mary faced in establishing her authority, pp. 1–8. More recent works have centered on the history of parliament during her reign, as Mary sought statutory sanction for her religious changes. See Jennifer Loach, *Crown and Parliament in the Reign of Mary Tudor* (Oxford: Oxford University Press, 1986), Michael Graves, *Early Tudor Parliaments* (London: Longman, 1990), and Robert Tittler, *The Reign of Mary I* (London: Longman, 1991).

11. This process was first begun by Paula Louise Scalingi, in her article "The Sceptre or the Distaff: The Question of Female Sovereignty, 1516–1607," *Historian*, 41 (November 1978), pp. 59–75. In this work, Scalingi called for debate on the emergence of gynecocracy, noting that too little attention has been paid to the issue of women's government in sixteenth-century historical studies. Twelve years later, Elizabeth Russell met this challenge in her article "Mary Tudor and Mr. Jorkins," *Bulletin of the Institute of Historical Research*, 152 (October 1990), pp. 263–276, suggesting that Mary consciously utilized her perceived political weaknesses as a strategy to override opposition to both her religious changes and her projected marriage to Philip of Spain. While Scalingi and Russell imply the impact of gender on Mary's efforts to stabilize her rule, Mary w as subject to a more full blown gender analysis in a pair of articles by Judith L. Richards, "Mary Tudor as a 'Sole Quene'?: Gendering Tudor Monarchy," *The Historical Journal*, 40, 4 (1997), pp. 895–924, and "To Promote a Woman to Beare Rule: Talking of Queens in Mid-Tudor England," *Sixteenth Century Journal*, 28 (1997), pp. 101–121. In these works, Richards challenged the assumption that the works of John Knox and Christopher Goodman defined contemporary attitudes toward female rule (see note 1) as she noted the permeability of socially constructed gender roles in Tudor England. However, Richards also noted the gendered complexity of Mary's efforts to construct a female royal persona and contract a foreign marriage.

12. The one exception to this rule was the accession of John in 1199. John overrode the claims of his elder brother's son, Arthur of Brittany. See Dominica Legge, "William Marshall and Arthur of Brittany," *Bulletin of the Institute of Historical Research*, 55 (May 1982), pp. 18–24. The subsequent ascendancy of primogeniture as the primary means to determine the succession resulted in a series of six royal minorities from 1216 to 1553. It is more than a bit ironic that the last of the royal minors, Edward VI, was succeeded by the first queen regnant.

13. William Stubbs, *The Constitutional History of England*, II (Oxford: Clarendon Press, 1897), p. 126, F.M. Powicke, *King Henry III and the Lord Edward: The Community of the Realm in the Thirteenth Century*, 2 vols. (Oxford: Clarendon Press, 1947) II, pp. 732–733, 788. For a recent analysis of the fourteenth-century succession, see Michael Bennett, "Edward III's Entail of the Succession," *English Historical Review* 113, 452 (June 1998), pp. 580–609.

14. Richard II was the son of Edward, Prince of Wales, "The Black Prince," the eldest son of Edward III.

15. *Letters and Papers Illustrative of the Wars of the English in France During the Reign of Henry VI*, ed. J. Stevenson (2 vols. Rolls Series, 1861–64) II, p. 770.

16. See Mortimer Levine, *Tudor Dynastic Problems, 1460–1571* (London: George Allen and Unwin, 1973), p. 129.

17. In the mid–fifteenth century, Sir John Fortescue, Chief Justice of the Bench under Henry VI, wrote a treatise, "*De Titulo Edwardi Comitis Marchiae*," attacking the Yorkist claim to the throne. Fortescue cited scripture and classical authorities, such as Aristotle, to refute the right of women to inherit thrones, in effect recognizing an English form of Salic law. In his political theory, Fortescue anticipated John Knox's a century earlier. However, once Edward IV became king, Fortescue modified his position to allow for female transmission of royal inheritance. See *The Life and Works of Sir John Fortescue (Lord Chief Justice Under Henry VI)*, ed. Thomas Fortescue and Lord Clermot (London: 1869), pp. 78–81, 193, 254–258.

18. The Beauforts were the illegitimate children of John of Gaunt and Katherine Swynford. When Gaunt subsequently married Swynford, Richard II legitimized their children by letters patent. Henry IV reconfirmed their legitimacy, with the added codicil that they may not inherit the crown. Nevertheless, the Beauforts served as a cadet branch of the Lancastrian Royal House until their male line was extinguished during the Wars of the Roses.

19. In 1525, Cardinal Wolsey outfitted Mary with a household and council and sent her to Wales, as the formal head of marcher administration. Even so, her father did not create her "Princess of Wales." See W.R.B. Robinson, "Princess Mary's Itinerary in the Marches of Wales 1525–27: A Provisional Record, *Historical Research*, 71, 175 (1998), pp. 233–252.

20. Charles was the eldest son of Juana "*La Loca*," Queen of Castile, eldest surviving sister of Catherine of Aragon, and Philip, "The Handsome," of Burgundy, son of Holy Roman Emperor Maximilian I.

21. From a Garter manuscript, Sir. H. Nares Collection, folio MS, p. 22, cited in Strickland, *Lives of the Queens of England*, III, 514, n. 4.

22. Henry VIII's elder sister Margaret Tudor married James IV of Scotland in 1503.

23. *Letters and Papers, Foreign and Domestic, of the Reign of Henry VIII*, vol. 4, ed. John S. Brewer, James Gairdner and Robert H. Brodie (London: 1875), pp. 600, 767. For a brief analysis of the marriage negotiations between Mary and James V of Scotland, see Levine, *Tudor Dynastic Problems*, pp. 51–53.

24. For a discussion of the relationship between Mary's marriage negotiations and English continental policy, see Loades, *Mary Tudor: A Life*, pp. 21–29.

25. Edward Hall, *Hall's Chronicle*, ed. Henry Ellis (London: 1809), pp. 754–756.

26. In August 1537, the privy council recommended that Henry's daughters be married, but nothing apparently came of this

proposal, see *State Papers of Henry VIII*, vol. 1 (London: 1830), pp. 545–546. In 1542, negotiations for a marriage between Mary and a son of Francis I of France fell through because Henry VIII would not allow her to be declared legitimate, while in 1545–46, after Mary had been restored to the succession by statute, marriage negotiations with the Hapsburgs, as well as a Protestant nephew of the elector Palatine came to nothing. For an analysis of these negotiations, see J.J. Scarisbrick, *Henry VIII* (Berkeley: University of California Press, 1968), pp. 434, 460, 469.

27. *Statutes of the Realm*, vol. 3, Anno 35, Henrici VIII, c. I. For an analysis of the Act's marriage qualifications, see Levine, *Tudor Dynastic Problems*, pp. 74–75, and Stanford E. Lehmberg, *The Later Parliaments of Henry VIII* (Cambridge: Cambridge University Press, 1978), pp. 24, 193–194.

28. The fact that Mary took a husband after becoming queen formed the theoretical base of the Dudley conspiracy of 1555, as the conspirators claimed that Mary had vacated her right to the throne by not consulting the surviving Edwardian councilors for their approval on her marriage, thus violating the terms of Henry VIII's will! See Mortimer Levine, *The Early Elizabethan Succession Question* (Stanford: Stanford University Press, 1966), p. 153.

29. See Levine, *Tudor Dynastic Problems*, pp. 74–75.

30. Judith Richards briefly also discussed the gendered complexities surrounding the marriage of a queen regnant, see *Mary Tudor as Sole Quene*, p. 96.

31. Prior to the plot to topple Protector Somerset in October, 1549, Mary was approached by conservative and Catholic magnates for support, which she refused to extend, while the Imperial ambassador reported a rumor that she was to be made regent. See *Calendar of State Papers, Spanish* (15 vols.) (afterword referred to as *Cal. St. Pap., Span.*) IX, ed. Royall Tyler (London: 1914), p. 459.

32. See Retha Warnicke, *Women of the English Renaissance and Reformation* (Westport, Conn.: Greenwood Press, 1983), pp. 54–55.

33. See David Starkey, *Elizabeth I: Apprenticeship*, pp. 94–104. Starkey's analysis emphasized Elizabeth's and Mary's positions as powerful independent female magnates during their brother's reign.

34. Mary's and Elizabeth's ability to play a quasi-public political role during their brother's reign is consistent with Pearl Hogrete's analysis of the permeability of gendered roles for sixteenth-century English women, see *Tudor Women: Commoners and Queens*, pp. xii–xiii, 9–10.

35. John Foxe recounted in detail Mary's opposition to the religious changes of her brother's government, VI, pp. 7, 1–22.

36. Imperial ambassador Scheyfve reported one of these visits, during Christmas 1550, to Mary of Hungary, Charles V's regent in the Netherlands, see *Cal. St. Pap., Span*, IX, pp. 410–411.

37. Edward VI conducted a sustained effort in his correspondence with Mary to induce her to abandon her Catholicism, pp. 308, 323–324, also Foxe, *Actes and Monuments*, pp. 11–12.
38. Jane Grey was the granddaughter of Mary Tudor, younger sister of Henry VIII. The Third Act of Succession also gave statutory force to Henry's will, which named his younger sisters heirs to succeed failing his own children. The will ignored the descendants of Henry's elder sister Margaret, who married James IV of Scotland.
39. The question of who was the primary instigator of the attempt to disinherit Mary—Edward VI or Northumberland—is, like the princes in the tower, a largely unsolvable historical controversy. This historian will simply ask the reader to consider how possible it was for Northumberland to manipulate, against his will, an extremely intelligent fifteen-year-old king who knew he was dying. For a larger analysis of this historiographical debate, see Charles Beem, "The Minority of Edward VI," *The Royal Minorities of Medieval England*, pp. 263–267.
40. For a study of Edward VI's attempt to alter the succession, see W.K. Jordan, *Edward VI: The Threshold of Power* (Cambridge, Mass.: Belknap Press, 1970), pp. 515–517.
41. *Literary Remains of Edward VI*, pp. 571–572.
42. See William Huse Dunham, Jr., "Regal Power and the Rule of Law," pp. 24–56.
43. See Loades, *Mary Tudor, A Life*, pp. 182–183.
44. See Alison Weir, *The Children of Henry VIII* (New York: Ballantine, 1996), pp. 167–168.
45. See Robert Tittler, Susan L. Battley, "The Local Community and the Crown in 1553: The Accession of Mary Tudor Revisited," *Bulletin of the Institute of Historical Research* 57, 136 (1984), pp. 131–149. In this article, Tittler and Battley challenged the conventional dictum that the entire realm supported Mary's candidacy based upon statutory and dynastic principles.
46. Mary's first royal proclamation, announcing her accession, was issued July 19, 1553 in London, see *Tudor Royal Proclamations*, II, p. 3.
47. For a contemporary account from a Catholic, East Anglian point of view, see Robert Wingfield, "Vitae Mariae Angliae," *Camden Miscellany*, 4th series, vol. 29 (London: Royal Historical society, 1984), pp. 181–301.
48. Recent historiographical assessments suggest a more powerful conservative religiosity present in Edwardian/Marian England than identified in the Whig tradition. See Jennifer Loach, "Conservatism and Consent in Parliament," *The Mid-Tudor Polity*, ed. Robert Tittler and Jennifer Loach (London: Macmillan, 1980), pp. 12–19.
49. *Cal. St. Pap., Span.*, XI, p. 130.

50. Charles Wrioethesley, Windsor herald, wrote a concise summary of Mary's accession. See *A Chronicle of England During the Reigns of the Tudors*, ed. William Douglas Hamilton (London: Camden Society, 1877), pp. 87–89.

51. *Cal. St. Pap., Span.*, vol. XI, p. 73.

52. Ibid.

53. Wingfield, "Vitae Mariae Angliae," p. 260.

54. By 1542, when Mary was 26, she was convinced she would never marry while her father lived. See *Letters and Papers of Henry VIII*, XVII, pp. 220–221.

55. For a discussion of women's status as their male kinsmen's wards, which prevailed in sixteenth-century English aristocratic and gentry social practice, see Warnicke, *Women*, pp. 7–9, Hogrete, *Tudor Women*, pp. 10–24.

56. *Tudor Royal Proclamations*, II, p. 3, n. 388. Mary's use of the term sovereign lady echoed that of sovereign lord used by kings. As in the use of the term queen, which changed in meaning upon Mary's accession, so the usage of the term lady was analogous to the empress Matilda's sovereign title *domina Anglorum*.

57. This situation was remedied by Mary's first parliament, October 1553, which repealed those portions of the First Act of Succession relating to her parent's marriage, see *Statutes of the Realm*, IV, I Mary, st. 2, cap. I.

58. Henry Machyn, *The Diary of Henry Machyn*, ed. John Gough Nichols (London: Camden Society, 1848), p. 35. Chronicler Charles Wrioethesley also observed upon Mary's accession, "the people were so joyful, both man, woman, and childe," p. 89.

59. See Susan Amussen, *An Ordered Society*, pp. 1–7. Merry Wiesner has further argued that early-modern women who wished to assume male gendered economic and social roles did not seek to overturn patriarchy, but to create mitigating circumstances that allowed the occasional woman to fulfill such a role. See *"Women's Defense of Their Public Role,"* pp. 1–28.

60. A number of contemporary descriptions exist for Mary's October 1553 coronation. See *The Chronicle of Queen Jane and the first Two years of Mary*, ed. John Gough Nichols (London: Camden Society, 1850), pp. 28–31, also Wingfield, "Vitae Mariae Angliae," pp. 275–277, John Stow, *Annales, or a Generall Chronicle of England* (London: 1631), p. 617, and Machyn, *The Diary*, pp. 45–47. For a foreign account, see *Cal. St. Pap., Span.*, XI, pp. 261–262.

61. See Laynesmith, *Medieval Queens*, pp. 82–110.

62. A number of contemporaries drew attention to Mary's creation of knights of the bath. See Machyn, *The Diary*, p. 45, and Wingfield, "Vitae Mariae Angliae," p. 275.

63. Wingfield, "Vitae Mariae Angliae," p. 265.

64. See Glyn Redworth, " 'Matters Impertinent to Women': Male and Female Monarchy Under Philip and Mary," *English Historical Review* (June 1997), pp. 596–613, 599.

65. Helen Hackett, *Virgin Mother, Maiden Queen* (New York: St. Marin's Press, 1995), pp. 34–37.

66. Simon Renard related the coronation ritual to Prince Philip, describing the ritual surrounding the creation of Knights of the Bath, which required the monarch's presence in front of naked men, remarking that "the Queen being a woman, the ceremony was performed for her by the Earl of Arundel, her Great Master of the Household." *Cal. St. Pap., Span.*, XI, p. 262.

67. Antonio de Guaras, *The Accession of Queen Mary*, ed. Richard Garnett (London: Lawrence and Bullen, 1892), p. 121.

68. Contemporary narrative sources describing Mary's coronation are unanimous in their insistence that the ceremony was a traditional one in its rituals and outward forms, see *The Chronicle of Queen Jane*, p. 30, Stow, p. 617, and Wingfield, "Vitae Mariae Angliae," p. 276.

69. Contemporary accounts vary widely on what kind of attire Mary wore for her coronation. The interpretation followed here reflects Judith L. Richard's assessment. See "Mary Tudor as Sole Queen," p. 901.

70. See Laynesmith, *The last Medieval Queens*, pp. 92–94.

71. Following Elizabeth I's reign, and her own identification as her kingdom's wife, James I reversed the gender identity of his kingdom, as he identified himself as England's husband. See A.N. McLaren, "The Quest for King: Gender, Marriage, and Succession in Elizabethan England," *Journal of British Studies*, 41 (July 2002), pp. 259–290.

72. For studies of sixteenth-century gender perceptions, see Anthony Fletcher, *Gender, Sex, and Subordination in England*, pp. xv–xix.

73. John Foxe described Mary's devotion to the "popish religion." See *Actes and Monuments*, VI, pp. 390–391.

74. Catherine was serving as regent when the Earl of Surrey defeated the Scots at Flodden Field, September 9, 1513. Catherine sent the bloody shirt of James IV of Scotland to Henry in France. The standard account of Catherine's life remains Garrett Mattingley, *Catherine of Aragon* (Boston: Little Brown, 1941). For more recent analyses of Catherine's tenure as queen, see Karen Lindsey, *Divorced Beheaded Survived*, pp. 1–50, and David Starkey, *The Six Wives of Henry VIII* (New York: Harper Collins, 2003), pp. 11–248.

75. Wingfield, "Vitae Mariae Angliae," p. 271. Following her accession, only Northumberland and his closest aides were executed, as Mary initially spared Jane Grey, and forgave a number of her brother's former councilors. While Mary easily forgave political treason, her animus toward the leading Protestant clerics, notably Archbishop

Cranmer, is primarily responsible for Mary's popular reputation as "bloody." For a study on why Mary was considered bloody, see David Loades, "Why Queen Mary was Bloody," *Christian History*, 14 (1995), pp. 4–8.

76. The envoy of Philip II of Spain in London, Count Feria, wrote that "She (Elizabeth) seems to me incomparably more feared than her sister, and gives her orders and has her way as absolutely as her father did," cited in J.E. Neale, *Elizabeth I*, p. 67.

77. Imperial ambassador Simon Renard voiced these concerns to the Bishop of Arras, September 9, 1553, *Cal. St. Pap.*, XI, p. 228.

78. See Russell, "Mary Tudor and Mr. Jorkins," pp. 263–276. The best study on Renard's and Noailles's diplomatic machinations remains E. Harris Harbison, *Rival Ambassadors at the Court of Queen Mary* (Freeport, N.Y.: Books for Libraries Press, 1970, orig. pub. 1940). Although Harbison offered a detailed analysis of the ambassador's motivations, he assigned Mary herself little agency concerning her role and influence upon the marriage negotiations.

79. Catherine of Aragon requested the Spaniard humanist, Juan Luis Vives, to write a work especially for the edification of her daughter, *The Instruction of a Christian Woman*, which emphasized women's divine subjection to men, as it heralded chastity as a woman's primary virtue. See *Vives and the Renascence Education of Women*, ed. Foster Watson (London: Edward Arnold, 1912).

80. Carole Levin has suggested that Mary's image as a chaste and devout woman bolstered her attempt to adapt the mystical attributes of kingship to the female gender, in particular, touching for scrofula, the king's evil, a ritual Elizabeth continued to perform. See Levin, *The Heart and Stomach of a King*, p. 24.

81. William, Lord Paget was Renard's probable source for the inner workings of the queen and her privy council; Paget later likened Mary's government to a "republic" in a letter to the emperor, November 14, 1555, *Cal. St. Pap., Span.*, XIII, p. 88. Later theoretical discussions of female rulership published during Elizabeth's reign stressed the "mixed" nature of the English constitution as a built in restraint on feminine political inadequacy. See John Aylmer, *A Harborowe For Faithful and Trewe Subjects*, h 3, and Sir Thomas Smith, *De Republica Anglorum*, pp. 78–88.

82. Letter from the Ambassadors in England to the emperor, September 30, 1553, *Cal. St. Pap, Span.*, XI, p. 259.

83. In November 1555, Paget advised the emperor, following the marriage of Mary and Philip, that "the Queen's gentle character and inexperience in governing, would be that the king (Philip) should take over the task himself with the assistance of the best qualified Englishmen in Council." *Cal. St. Pap., Span.*, XIII, p. 88.

84. Letter from the ambassadors in England to the emperor, August 2, 1553, *Cal. St. Pap., Span.*, XI, p. 132.

85. In her first interview with the imperial ambassadors, July 29, 1553, Mary "declared she had never thought of marrying before she was Queen, and called God to witness that as a private individual she would never have desired it, but preferred to end her days in chastity." *Cal. St. Pap., Span.*, XI, p. 132. Three months later, following Mary's interview with a parliamentary delegation which attempted to sway her from a foreign match, Simon Renard reported that Mary still insisted that marriage "was contrary to her own inclination," p. 364.

86. Mary's Yorkist cousin, Reginald Pole, appeared to be the only notable to suggest that Mary abstain from marriage, and rule as a virgin queen, see *England Under the Reigns of Edward VI and Mary*, II, ed. Patrick Fraser Tytler (London: Richard Bentley, 1839), p. 232.

87. Protestant chronicler Richard Grafton, writing in the first decade of Elizabeth I's reign, observed that "the subjects of Englande were most desirous thereof" that Mary marry Courtenay. Richard Grafton, *Grafton's Chronicle: a Chronicle of the History of England* (London: 1569), p. 1327.

88. *Cal. St. Pap., Span.*, IX, pp. 73–73.

89. *Cal. St. Pap., Span.*, XI, p. 131.

90. John Fox, *Fox's Book of Martyrs*, 3 vols. (London: George Virtue, 1851), II, p. 1001.

91. Elizabeth Russell first suggested the inconsistencies of Renard's opinion of Mary's political abilities, see "Mary Tudor and Mr. Jorkins," pp. 274–275.

92. The emperor to Prince Philip, January 21, 1554, *Cal. St. Pap., Span.*, XII, p. 36.

93. Grafton, p. 1330.

94. [Miles Hogherde], *Certayne Questions Demanded and Asked By the Noble Realme of Englande of her True Natural Chyldren and Subjectes of the same*, (London, 1555), p. 1–8.

95. Writing in November 1555, Paget informed the emperor that "England, which had always been a monarchy, was now governed by a crowd that it was much more like a republic." *Cal. St. Pap., Span.*, XIII, p. 88.

96. *Cal. St. Pap., Span.*, XI, p. 312.

97. Simon Renard to the emperor, November 17, 1553, *Cal. St. Pap., Span.*, XI, p. 312. While this evidence is obviously hearsay, the initial printed volumes of the *Journal of the House of Commons* lack detailed descriptions of parliamentary debates for Mary's reign.

98. Parliament's gendered encroachment on the issue of the marriage of a ruling queen illustrates a crucial difference between

contemporary perceptions of sixteenth-century male and female rulership; for a recent analysis of male politician's perceived rights to counsel Elizabeth I, see A.N. Mclaren, *Political Culture in the Reign of Elizabeth I*, pp. 2–11, also Louis Montrose, "Shaping Fantasies: Figurations of Gendered Power in Elizabethan Culture," pp. 31–64.

99. Paget's central role in the marriage negotiations is emphasized in Samuel Rhea Gammon, *Statesman and Schemer: William, First Lord Paget, Tudor Minister* (Hamden, Conn: Archon Books), 1973.

100. *Cal. St. Pap., Span.*, XI, p. 290.

101. See introduction, note 59.

102. Renard to Emperor, Novomber 29, 1553, *Cal. St. Pap., Span.*, XI, p. 399.

103. Ambassadors in England to the emperor, January 7, 1554, *Cal. St. Pap., Span.*, XII, p. 11. In his work *The Instruction of a Christian Woman*, Vives wrote "it becometh not a maid to talk, where her father and mother be in communication about her marriage," *Vives*, p. 109.

104. Ambassadors in England to the emperor, January 12, 1554, *Cal. St. Pap., Span.*, XII, p. 12.

105. *Cal. St. Pap., Span.*, XI, p. 178.

106. Ibid., p. 247.

107. Ibid., XII, pp. 2–4.

108. Ibid.

109. *Statutes of the Realm*, I Marie, sess. 3, cap. II, pp. 222–224.

110. *Letters and Papers of Henry VIII*, I, pt. 2 (London: 1920), p. 1277, n. 2958.

111. Ibid., XIV, pt. 2 (London: 1895), p. 108, n. 286.

112. See J.J. Scarisbrick, *Henry VIII*, pp. 433–35.

113. Simon Renard to the emperor, December 8, 1553, *Cal. St. Pap., Span.*, XI, p. 415.

114. *Cal. St. Pap. Span.*, XII, pp. 4–6.

115. Philip never came to terms with the limitations imposed by the marriage treaty. Writing in October 1555, a year and three months after the marriage, Venetian ambassador Frederico Badoer wrote to the Doge and Senate, "I have been told on good authority that the King of England has written to the Queen his consort, that he is most anxious to gratify her wish for his return, but that he cannot adapt himself to it, having to reside there in a form unbecoming his dignity, which requires him to take part in the affairs of the realm." *Calendar of State Papers, Venetian*, I, pt. 1, ed. Rowdon Brown (London: Longman, 1877), p. 212.

116. See Elizabeth Lehfeldt, "Ruling Sexuality: The Political Legitimacy of Isabel of Castile," *Renaissance Quarterly* 53, 1 (Spring 2000), pp. 31–56.

117. For a recent study of the controversies surrounding the reign of Juana of Castile, see Bethany Aram, "Juana 'The Mad's' Signature: The Problem of Invoking Royal Authority, 1505–1507," *Sixteenth Century Journal*, 29 (Summer 1998), pp. 331–358.

118. See Daniel R. Doyle, "The Sinews of Hapsburg Governance in the Sixteenth Century: Mary of Hungary and Political Patronage," *Sixteenth Century Journal* 31, 2 (2000), pp. 349–360.

119. *The Chronicle of Queen Jane*, p. 35.

120. Ibid.

121. Ambassadors in England to the emperor, January 27, 1554, *Cal. St. Pap., Span.*, XII, p. 51.

122. Quoted from *The Chronicle of Queen Jane*, p. 43. Also see John Proctor, *The History of Wyates Rebellion* (London: 1554). David Loades has argued that the threat of Spanish domination was Wyatt's primary motivation. See *Mary Tudor: A Life*, p. 212.

123. *Cal. St. Pap., Span.*, XII, 65.

124. Foxe, *Actes*, VI, p. 414.

125. Ibid.

126. Ibid.

127. Jennifer Loach wondered why such a "curious act was passed in Mary's second, and not her first session of Parliament." See *Crown and Parliament in the Reign of Mary Tudor*, pp. 217–218.

128. See Froude, *History of England*, V, pp. 386–387. Froude discussed what he called the "Act for the Queen's authority," suggesting that one of its main impulses was policing powers. A.F. Pollard simply assumed that the act "gave once and for all a statutory quetus to the doubts, which troubled many a generation of Englishmen, whether a woman could reign in England or not" *The Political History of England, 1547–1603* (London: Longman, Green, and Co., 1910). Later twentieth-century scholars have depended on William Fleetwood's 1575 Treatise, *Itineratum ad Windsor*, for an explanation for the motivation behind the passage of the act. In a 1964 article, William Huse Dunham Jr. accepted the historical veracity of the treatise in his interpretation of Mary as a "parliamentary" monarch, see "Regal Power and the Rule of law: A Tudor Paradox," pp. 24–56. Mortimer Levine also accepted the treatise uncritically in his explanation for the act's passage, see *Tudor Dynastic Problems*, p. 90. Rhetorician Dennis Moore cast doubts on the authenticity of the conversations described in the treatise, see "Recorder Fleetwood and the Tudor Queenship Controversy," *Ambiguous Realities: Women in the Middle Ages and the Renaissance*, ed. Carole Levin and Jeanie Watson (Detroit: Wayne University Press, 1987), pp. 235–251, while historian J.D. Alsop argued for the essential veracity of Fleetwood's narrative, see "The Act for the

Queen's Regal Power," *Parliamentary History*, 13, 3 (1994), pp. 261–276. Other scholars insist that the doubts raised by common law lawyers concerning the possible alienation of royal prerogative by a ruling queen's marriage was the primary impetus for the act's passage, see David Loades, "Philip II and the Government of England," p. 177.

129. *Journals of the House of Commons*, I, 1547–1628 (London: 1803), p. 33.
130. *Cal. St. Pap., Span.*, XII, pp. 15–16.
131. David Loades, "Philip II and the Government of England," p. 177.
132. *Cal. St. Pap., Span.*, XII, p. 15.
133. Ibid., p. 220.
134. William Fleetwood, "Itineratum ad Windsor" (afterward referred to as "Itineratum"). Several manuscript versions exist: *A*, Oxford, Bodelian Library, Tanner MS. 84, fols. 202–217v, *B*, British Library, Harleian MS 6234, fols. 10–25, *C*, British Library, Harleian ms. 168, fols. 1–8v. My thanks to Dennis Moore for his unpublished edited version, which draws from all three manuscript versions. The following citations follow the Harleian MS 6234 version.
135. "Itineratum," p. 21.
136. "Itineratum," p. 22. In his article "The Act For the Queen's Power, 1554," J.D. Alsop suggested that the "chancellor of the dukedome of Mediolanum" was in fact Simon Renard, pp. 267–68. While intriguing, this interpretation contradicts Renard's efforts to secure ratification and consummation of the marriage.
137. Renard reported to the emperor that the marriage treaty was "passed by all members present, without any opposition or difficulty," *Cal. St. Pap., Span.*, XII, p. 215, as did the Venetian ambassador, Giacomo Soranzo, reporting back to the Senate, see *Calendar of State Papers, Venetian* (afterword referred to as *cal. St. Pap., Ven.*), V, ed. Rowdon Brown (London: Longman, 1873), p. 561.
138. Renard reported to the emperor on March 8 that "trustworthy and catholic men were going to be called to help Parliament not make trouble." *Cal. St. Pap., Span.*, XII, p. 141.
139. *Cal. St. Pap., Ven.*, V, p. 561.
140. "Itineratum," pp. 20–21.
141. Ibid.
142. Ibid.
143. Ibid.
144. Ibid.
145. *Statutes*, I. Mary st. 3 cap I, 222.
146. See Hogherde, *Certayne Questions*, pp. 1–8.
147. "The Marriage of Queen Mary and King Philip," *The Chronicle of Queen Jane*, appendix 9, pp. 167–172.

148. John Elder, *The Copie of a Letter Sent into Scotlande of the Arrival and landing of the most illustre Prince Philippe, Prince of Spain, to the moste excellente Princes Marye Quene of Englande* (London: 1554), p. 6.

149. Ibid., p. 17.

150. On July 27, 1554, Mary issued a proclamation authorizing the use of the style Philip and Mary for all subsequent enactments of their joint reign. *Rymer's Feodera*, 20 vols, ed. Thomas Rymer and Robert Sanderson (London: 1727–35), VI (May 1509–July 1586), p. 31.

151. David Loades has argued that Mary retained significant autonomy as queen following her marriage to Philip, see "Philip II and the government of England," pp. 177–194. Glyn Redworth has challenged this interpretation in his article, " 'Matters Impertinent to Women," pp. 597–613. Both historians offer intriguing evidence to support their assertions, which suggests that a gender analysis of Philip and Mary's political marriage is long overdue.

152. Although Elizabeth never married, Mary and Philip's marriage treaty served as a blueprint for her possible marriage to the duke of Anjou, see "Calendar of the Manuscripts of the Most Hon. Marquis of Salisbury," *Reports of the Historical Manuscripts Commission*, IX, pt. 2, pp. 243, 288–293, 543–544. For a revisionist analysis of the historical legacy of Mary and Philip's marriage, see Susan Doran, *Monarchy and Matrimony: The Courtship of Elizabeth I* (London and New York: Routledge, 1996), pp. 8–9, 81.

153. Hackett, *Virgin Mother*. Hackett's main argument is that the cult of Elizabeth replaced that of the Virgin Mary, a process that wide segments of her subjects participated in, in the creation of a particularly protestant iconography.

154. Levin, *The Heart and Stomach of a King*, pp. 16, 24–26, and Doran, *Monarchy and Matrimony*, pp. 7–8.

3 "I Am Her Majesty's Subject": Queen Anne, Prince George of Denmark, and the Transformation of the English Male Consort

1. Stuart J. Reid, *John and Sarah Duke and Duchess of Marlborough: Based Upon Unpublished Letters and Documents of Blenheim Palace* (London: John Murray, 1915), p. 106. This anecdote is also cited in Agnes Strickland, *The Lives of the Queens of England*, VIII, p. 157. Strickland noted "This is one of those floating anecdotes which may be almost considered oral; it is, however, printed in the antiquary Hutton's visit to London, being a tour through Westminster-abbey, the Tower, &c., published in the Freemason's Magazine, 1792 to 1795."

2. Portions of this chapter first appeared in my article, "I Am Her Majesty's Subject: Prince George of Denmark and the Transformation of the English Male Consort," *Canadian Journal of History*, 39 (December 2004), pp. 457–487, and are reprinted with the kind permission of the journal.

3. Out of forty-one English kings since the Norman Conquest, only thirteen were married upon their accessions: William the Conqueror (1066), Henry II (1154), Edward II (1307), Edward III (1327), Henry IV (1399), James I (1603), James II (1685), George I (1714), George II (1727), George IV (1820), William IV (1837), Edward VII (1901), and George VI (1936). Of the female kings of England, only Anne (1702) and Elizabeth II (1952) were married upon their accessions. Both of their husbands, Prince George of Denmark and Prince Philip of Greece, held the informal position of consort.

4. Post-Whig assessments of the Glorious Revolution fail to include the demise of the male consort as one of the consequences of the Revolution settlement. See Robert J. Frankle, "The Formulation of the Declaration of Rights," *Historical Journal*, 5, 3 (June 1974) pp. 265–279, J.R. Jones *The Revolution of 1688 in England* (New York: W.W.Norton and co., 1972), Henry Horwitz, *Parliament, Policy, and Politics in the Reign of William III* (Manchester: Manchester University Press, 1977), Lois G. Schwoerer, *The Declaration of Rights 1689* (Baltimore: Johns Hopkins University Press, 1981), and Evelyn Cruickshank, *The Glorious Revolution* (New York: Palgrave Macmillan, 2000). Recent scholarship has stressed the importance of the Anglo-Dutch relationship, and makes no mention of George of Denmark. See *The World of William and Mary: Anglo-Dutch Perspectives On the Revolution of 1688–89*, ed. Dale Hoak and Mordechai Feingold (Stanford: Stanford University Press, 1996). Also, Jonathan Israel, "The Dutch Role in the Glorious Revolution," *The Anglo-Dutch Moment: Essays on the Glorious Revolution and its World Impact*, ed. Jonathan Israel (Cambridge: Cambridge University Press, 1991.

5. See Anthony Fletcher, *Gender, Sex, and Subordination in England*, pp. i–xv. In his introduction, Fletcher identified a system of structural patriarchy at work in early-modern England, which denied women access to the public sphere of politics. At the same time, reflecting Judith Bennett's deconstruction of the term patriarchy, Fletcher defined patriarchy as "an unstable historical construct," constantly under pressure amid the social and political changes of the early-modern period. Within this dynamic process, Fletcher argues that "the essence of gender scheme is overlap," allowing men and women to negotiate and transgress the boundaries between socially constructed gender roles. Within Fletcher's model,

Mary II and Anne present a striking contrast in attitudes toward their positions as royal heiresses.

6. "And that the sole and full exercise of the regal power be only in and executed by the said Prince of Orange in the names of the said Prince and Princess during their joynt lives," *Statutes of the Realm*, vol. 6 (London: 1819), William and Mary, sess. 2, chap. 2, p. 143.

7. Mary II, *Memoirs of Mary, Queen of England, (1689–1693)*, ed. R. Doebner (London: David Nutt, 1886). Doebner edited Mary II's political journal, one of its kind in the history of female kingship. Mary's observations over the course of her short reign display a wifely concern for her husband's political problems, as well as her domestic contentment with her consort-like role. For a recent analysis of Mary II's reputation as a model of domestic virtue, see Lois Schwoerer, "Images of Queen Mary II, 1689–1695," *Renaissance Quarterly* 42, 4 (Winter 1989), pp. 717–48, and Rachel Weil, *Political Passions: Gender, The Family, and Political Argument in England 1680–1714* (Manchester: Manchester University Press, 1999) pp. 113–116.

8. Robert Filmer, *Patriarcha, Or the Natural Power of Kings* (London: 1680).

9. For analyses of seventeenth-century patriarchal theory, see James Daly, *Sir Robert Filmer and English Political Thought* (Toronto: University of Toronto Press, 1979), and Elizabeth Ezell, *The Patriarch's Wife: Literary Evidence and the History of the Family* (Chapel Hill: University of North Carolina Press, 1987).

10. John Locke, *Second Treatise on Civil Government (an essay Concerning the True Original, Extent and end of civil government), and A Letter Concerning Toleration*, ed. J.W. Gough (New York: Macmillan, 1956). For an analysis of the patriarchal qualities of Locke's contract theory, see Carole Pateman, *The Sexual Contract* (Oxford: Polity, Basil Blackwell), pp. 34, 93–95.

11. For a recent study of the Glorious Revolution's succession dilemma, see Howard Nenner, *The Right To Be King: The Succession to the Crown of England, 1603–1702* (Chapel Hill: University of North Carolina Press, 1995), pp. 149–249.

12. See Agnes Strickland, *Lives of the Queens of England*, VIII, pp. 142–143. Writing in the 1850s, Strickland observed that "The law by which prince George of Denmark was excluded from ascending the British throne has hitherto eluded our search, and it seems passing strange that a lawless precedent should be followed." Historians since have not considered the question of why George did not become king, or have simply stated that George's exclusion was unconstitutional. See William Coxe, *Memoirs of John, Duke of Marlborough* (London: Longman, Hurst, Rees, Orme, and Brown, 1818) p. 155, M.R. Hopkinson, *Anne of England* (New York: Macmillan, 1934), p. 173, David Green, *Queen Anne* (London: Collins,

1970), p. 94. In his work, *Queen Anne* (London: Routledge and Kegan Paul, 1980), Edward Gregg considered George's ill health the primary reason why he was not elevated to the royal dignity, p. 80.

13. For a succinct recent assessment of Anne's historiographical evolution, see Richard Wilkinson, "Queen Anne," History Review, 31 (September 1998), pp. 39–45.

14. Richard Lodge, *The Political History of England, 1660–1702* (London: Longmans, Green, and Co., 1910). In this work, the first survey able to take full advantage of the cataloguing, editing, and publication of British historical sources in the nineteenth century, Lodge observed "Prince George was a nonentity in English affairs," p. 232. Fifty-seven years later, in what remains a still standard political study, Geoffrey Holmes assigns very little agency to prince George, remarking that on the only occasion when Anne turned to her husband for political support, she did so only because of her estrangement from Godolphin, Harley, and both of the Marlboroughs. *See British Politics in the Age of Queen Anne* (London: Macmillan, 1967), p. 212.

15. Of all the historical figures associated with Anne's life and career, Sarah Churchill, Duchess of Marlborough remains the most fascinating. David Green, in a pair of back-to-back monographs, *Sarah, Duchess of Marlborough* (Collins: London, 1967), and *Queen Anne* (1970), assigned Anne increased historical agency in his detailed studies of two strong-willed women. For a more recent study of Sarah's political influence, see Frances Harris, *A Passion for Government* (Oxford: Clarendon Press, 1991).

16. This process started with George Macaulay Trevelyan's multivolume *The Reign of Queen Anne* (London: Longman's Green and Co., 1930–34). Trevelyan's analysis constitutes the final phase of Whig Stuart historiography, as he recognized Anne as an active historical agent: "She did not leave affairs to her favorites or even wholly to her Ministers. In order to do what she thought right in Church and State, she slaved at many details of government. II, p. 169. While a number of popular or literary treatments of Anne's reign appeared over the later twentieth century, Gregg's definitive 1980 biography, *Queen Anne*, demonstrated the complexity of Anne's role as monarch amid the political turbulence of the early eighteenth century. Gregg's analysis dispelled the myth of Anne's political dependence upon the Duke and Duchess of Marlborough and Sidney Godolphin, and demonstrated her resolve to reconcile the party divisions of Tory and Whig, which plagued her entire reign. More recently, in his work on court ritual, R.O. Bucholz has demonstrated an additional context to monarchical political power, see "Nothing But Ceremony: Queen Anne and the Limitations of

Notes ♦ 221

Court Ritual," *Journal of British Studies*, 30 (1991), pp. 288–323, "Queen Anne: Victim of Her Virtues?" *Queenship in Britain: 1660–1837*. ed. Clarissa Campbell Orr (Manchester: Manchester University Press, 2002), pp. 94–129, and *The Augustan Court: Queen Anne and the Decline of Court Culture* (Stanford: Stanford University Press, 1993). Bucholz summed up the evolution of Anne's historical image, remarking that "For it is only in recent years that the traditional Whig picture of Anne as well intentioned but weak, dull, and easily led has begun to be seriously questioned," p. 68.

17. John Tosh articulated an argument for the relevance of incorporating the study of masculinity in gender analysis, see "What Should Historians do with Masculinity? Reflections on Nineteenth Century Britain," *History Workshop Journal*, 38 (Autumn 1994), pp. 179–202. Further studies of early-modern masculinity include Philip Carter, *Men and the Emergence of Polite Society, Britain, 1660–1800* (London: Longman, 2001), Elizabeth Foyster, *Manhood in Early Modern England* (London: Longman, 1999), and Tim Hitchcock and Michele Cohen, "Introduction," *English Masculinities 1660–1800*, ed. Tim Hitchcock and Michele Cohen (London: Longman, 1999).

18. This was one of the major tenets of the Whig interpretation of the seventeenth century. See J.P. Kenyon, *Stuart England*, pp. 1–56. For a more recent analysis of this phenomenon see Levin, *The Heart and Stomach of a King*, pp. 91–120, and Mclaren, "The Quest For A King," pp. 269–290.

19. For a discussion of the evolution of Elizabeth I's seventeenth-century historical reputation, see J.P. Kenyon, "Queen Elizabeth and the Historians," pp. 52–55, D.R. Woolfe, "Two Elizabeths? James I and the Late Queen's Famous Memory," pp. 167–191, and the "Conclusion" in Christopher Haigh's *Elizabeth I*, pp. 164–174.

20. As Henry VIII's line ended with Elizabeth I's death, James I based his accession on his lineal descent from Henry VII, through his great-grandmother Margaret Tudor, eldest daughter of Henry VII, the Tudor progenitor.

21. For a recent study of the evolution of conceptual kingship over the course of Elizabeth I's reign, see McLaren, "The Quest For a King," pp. 259–290.

22. See John Aylmer, *An Harborowe For Faithful and Trewe Subjects*. Aylmer's work was a rebuttal to John Knox's *First Blast of the Trumpet Against the Monstrous Regiment of Women*, the most voracious of sixteenth-century tracts attacking female rule. For a discussion of these works, see Jordan, "Women's Rule in Sixteenth Century British Thought," pp. 436–443, and Lee, "A Bodye politique to Govern: Aylmer, Knox, and the Debate on Queenship," pp. 242–262.

23. James VI and I, *The True Law of Free Monarchies and The Basilikon Doron*, ed. Daniel Fischlin and Mark Fortier (Toronto: Center For Reformation and Renaissance Studies, 1996), passim.

24. See *King James VI and I: Political Writings*, ed. Johann P. Summerville (Cambridge: Cambridge University Press, 1994), pp. 132–137.

25. Quoted in Kenyon, "Queen Elizabeth and the Historians," p. 52.

26. See Nenner, *The Right to Be King*, pp. 36–37.

27. See note 18.

28. The classic study of these historical process remains Edward Hyde, the first earl of Clarendon, *The History of the Rebellion and Civil Wars in England* (Oxford: Clarendon Press, 1888, orig. pub. 1702–04).

29. For a recent study, see Ronald Hutton, *Charles the Second, King of England, Scotland, and Ireland* (Oxford: Clarendon Press, 1989).

30. Both Mary and Anne Stuart received training in languages, some history, but more importantly singing, dancing, and painting. See Nellie M. Waterson, *Mary II Queen of England 1689–1694* (Durham N.C.: Duke University Press, 1928), pp. 3–9, also Henri and Barbara Van der Zee, *William and Mary* (New York: Alfred A. Knopf, 1973), pp. 57–58.

31. See Starkey, *Elizabeth: Apprenticeship*, pp. 97–104.

32. See Mark Kishlansky, *A Monarchy Transformed* (New York: Penguin, 1997), pp. 316–317. Although Kishlansky offered a humorous characterization of Anne's proclivity for gambling, his overall analysis is post-Whig, arguing for Anne's historical agency in the face of bitter, post–Glorious Revolution partisan politics.

33. See Gila Curtis, *The Life and Times of Queen Anne* (London: Weidenfeld and Nicolson, 1972), p. 28.

34. *The Cambridge History of English Literature*, vol. 9, ed. A.A. Ward and A.R. Walker (New York: G. Putnam, 1908), p. 449.

35. William of Orange's mother was Mary Stuart, daughter of Charles I of England, which placed him in the English line of succession, after his wife and her sister Anne.

36. Gilbert Burnet, *Bishop Burnet's History of his Own Time*, 5 vols. (Oxford, Oxford University Press, 1833 , orig. pub. 1724–34) II, p. 132. Burnet, Bishop of Salisbury, was both an historian and contemporary commentator. Decidedly Whig in political outlook, Burnet enjoyed favor under William III, but Anne despised him. Nonetheless, Burnet generally commented favorably on George of Denmark in his *History*, without the political bias he leveled toward Anne. For a recent assessment of Burnet's *History*, see Philip Hicks, *Neoclassical History and English Culture* (London: Macmillan, 1996), pp. 126–131.

37. "Marriage Treaty of Mary and William." The treaty outlined Mary's freedom to worship Anglican in Holland, assigned her a considerable

dower, and required the King of England's advice and consent for the marriages of any children resulting from the marriage. British Library, Sloane add. mss. 38329, f. 23.

38. See Stephen Baxter, *William III and the Defence of European Liberty, 1650–1702* (Westport Conn.: Greenwood Press, 1966). Baxter's work remains the most comprehensive analysis of William's continental and English careers.

39. David Ogg remarked that, following Anne's marriage to George, "William could no longer claim to be the sole exponent in the family of virtue and Protestantism." *England in the Reign of Charles II* (Oxford: Oxford University Press, 1956), p. 651. See also Baxter, *William III*, pp. 187–188.

40. In a letter from the earl of Sutherland to the earl of Rochester, May 3, 1683, Sutherland remarked that "it [the marriage] ought to have been communicated to the council—that is to say, it ought to have been prevented." British Museum add. MS 17017, f. 130.

41. Burnet, *History*, II, p. 391.

42. See J.P. Kenyon, *Robert Spencer, Earl of Sutherland, 1641–1702* (London: Longmans, Green, and Co., 1958), p. 87. In a letter to the Earl of Conway, May 26, 1683, Francis Gywn recounted the swift coordination of the marriage treaty and the arrival of Prince George in England, printed in the *Calendar of State Papers, Domestic Series, Charles II, January–June, 1683*, ed. F.H. Blackburne Daniell (London, 1933) p. 296.

43. "Ratification of the Marriage Treaty between Anne Stuart and Prince George of Denmark," Public Records Office, SP-108–547.

44. Sunderland's underhanded role in the marriage arrangements is described in a series of letters included in British Library add. MS. 17017, ff. 129, 130, 135.

45. See Green, *Queen Anne*, p. 34.

46. John *Macky, Memoirs of the Secret Services of John Macky, esq., During the Reigns of King William, Queen Anne, and George I* (London: 1733), b2. Macky, a spy in the service of William III and his successors, published a volume of pen portraits of the leading political figures of his day, including Prince George of Denmark. Macky's description of George, while not exactly malicious, clearly labeled him as a jolly nonentity, reflecting Macky's awareness of George's transgression of socially constructed norms of masculinity.

47. William's belief that his marriage carried a vested interest in the English crown was made explicit in his Declaration of 1688, which stated, "And since our dearest and most entirely beloved consort the Princess, and likewise ourselves, have so great an interest in this matter and such a right, as all the world k nows, to the succession of the crown," William III, *The Declaration of His Highness William Henry, By the Grace of God, Prince of Orange, &c. Of the*

Reasons inducing him to appear in Arms in the kingdom of England, for preserving of the Protestant religion, and for restoring the Laws and Liberties of England, Scotland, and Ireland (London: 1688).

48. Historical Manuscripts Commission, *Calendar of the Manuscripts of the Marquess of Ormonde*, K.P., New Series, VII (London: 1912), p. 22.

49. During the negotiations for George and Anne's marriage, the French ambassador Barillon wrote to Louis XIV, reporting that the Danish attempted to have William of Orange displaced in the English succession. See Baxter, *William III*, p. 187.

50. Writing in 1710, one observer remarked that "For the security of the Protestant interest and religion, our Queen was happily marry'd to his royal highness, Prince George of Denmark," William Cockburn, *An Essay Upon the Propitious and Glorious Reign of Our Gracious Sovereign Anne* (London: 1710) p. 10.

51. Macky, Memoirs, b3. In his brief pen portrait of George, Macky described him as "a great lover of the High Church of England, the nearer it comes to Lutheranism."

52. Writing at the time of Anne's marriage to George, the Marquess of Ormonde acknowledged that the marriage "is a French match and contrived to carry that interest." Yet Ormonde also insisted that "None of them can deny but that it is time that the lady should be married, and that it is fit she should have a Protestant, and where to find one so readily, they that mislike this match cannot tell," *Calendar of the Manuscripts of the Marquess of Ormonde*, VII, p. 22.

53. For a recent study of the exclusion crisis, see Mark Knights, *Politics and Opinion in Crisis* (Cambridge: Cambridge University Press, 1994). Still useful is R. Jones, *The First Whigs: The Politics of the Exclusion Crisis, 1678–83* (New York: Greenwood, 1985, orig. pub. 1961).

54. Cockburn, *An Essay*, p. 13. Cockburn's essay, published two years after George's death in 1708, recounted his bravery in the service of his brother, the king of Denmark.

55. *Calendar of State Papers, Domestic Series–Charles II, 1683*, p. 244.

56. John Evelyn, *The Diary of John Evelyn*, vol. 3, intro. and notes by Austin Dobson (London: Macmillan, 1906), p. 107. John Evelyn (1620–1706), a royalist supporter of Charles II who enjoyed royal patronage during the Restoration, kept a lively diary from 1640 until his death, recording his impressions of the major figures of his day, including this brief mention of Prince George.

57. Burnet, *History*, V, p. 351. Burnet observed that George, "knew more than he could well express, for he spake acquired languages ill and ungracefully."

58. Burnet, *History*, III, p. 49.

59. *Reports of the Historical Manuscripts Commission*, IX, part 2 (London: 1884), p. 458.

60. Macky, *Memoirs*, b2.

61. [Anonymous], *The History of the Life and Reign of her late Majesty Queen Anne* (London: 1740), p. 276. In this popular history published twenty-six years after Anne's death, her marriage still enjoyed a popular reputation as a happy one.

62. See Foyster, *Manhood*, p. 2.

63. [Anonymous], *The Present State of Matrimony* (London: 1749), p. 3.

64. Ibid.

65. In a letter to the earl of Albemarle, March 1, 1697/98, Matthew Prior commented on George's conjugal fidelity, "the (French) dauphin he dismissed—much like prince George, except that the one only makes love to the princess, and the other every girl at the opera without distinction." *Reports of the Royal Manuscripts Commission, Calendar of the Manuscripts of the Earl of Bath*, III (Prior papers) (London: 1908), p. 195. See also M.R. Hopkinson, Anne of England (New York: Macmillan, 1934), pp. 89–91.

66. Macky, *Memoirs*, b3.

67. Reid, *John and Sarah*, p. 141.

68. This recognition implicit upon Mary I's accession in 1554, was made explicit upon Elizabeth I's in 1558. See William Camden, *The History of the Most Renowned and Victorious Princess Elizabeth Late Queen of England*, p. 18. Legal opinions incorporating recognition of the theory of the king's two bodies date from the reigns of Mary I and Elizabeth I. This theory provided a theoretical bolster to the authority of female kings. See Kantorwicz, *The King's Two Bodies*, and Axton, *The Queen's Two Bodies*.

69. Anne's need for a male proxy in the public spaces of government mirrored the restrictions placed on women of property in their own public dealings. See Mary Louise Erickson, *Women and Property in Early Modern England*, pp. 1–113, also Susan Moller Okin, "Patriarchy and Married Women's Property in England: Questions on Some Current views," *Eighteenth Century Studies*, 17 (Winter 1983/84) pp. 121–138, for a background on propertied women's status under the Stuarts.

70. *The Correspondence of Henry Hyde, Earl of Clarendon, and his Brother Laurence Hyde, Earl of Rochester*, II, ed. Samuel Weller Singer (London: Henry Colburn, 1828), pp. 314–315.

71. Narcissus Luttrell, *A Brief Historical Relation of State Affairs From September 1678 to April 1714*, 5 vols (Oxford: Oxford University Press, 1857) II, p. 51. Luttrell's political diary briefly recorded many of Prince George's public appearances and political tasks from 1683 until his death in 1708.

72. Luttrell, *State Affairs*, I, pp. 287, 312.

73. See *Historical Manuscripts Commission, Calendar of the Manuscripts of the Marquess of Ormonde, K.P.*, new series, VII (London: 1912), pp. 264–265.

74. *The Order of the Installation of Prince George of Denmark, Charles, Duke of Somerset, and George, Duke of Northumberland. Knights and Companions of the Most Noble Order of the Garter* (London: 1684).

75. In her political journal, Mary of Orange clearly stated her total identification with a conventional social women's role, accepting of a secondary, domestic role within her marriage. See Mary II, *Memoirs*, pp. 11, 20, 23.

76. In an often quoted letter from Anne to Sarah Churchill in 1692, Anne clearly looked forward to her own "sunshine day" when she would inherit the throne. In this letter, as in many others between the two, Anne referred to Sarah as "Mrs. Freeman," and herself as "Mrs. Morley," so they could correspond as social equals, while the men of the cockpit, Marlborough, Prince George, and later Sidney Godolphin, were referred to as "Mr. Freeman," "Mr. Morley," and "Mr. Montgomery," respectively. See *The Letters and Diplomatic Instructions of Queen Anne*, ed. Beatrice Curtis Brown (New York: Funk and Wagnalls, 1935), pp. 60–61.

77. Luttrell, *State Affairs*, I, pp. 328, 330.

78. On July 2, 1685, James II gave his "Regement of foote" to George of Denmark, see *Historical Manuscripts Commission, Report on the Manuscripts of the Duke of Buccleuch and Queensbury, K.G., K.T.*, II, part 1 (London: 1903) p. 82. For an analysis of the military aspects of James II's reign, see J.R. Western, *Monarchy and Revolution: The English State in the 1680s* (Totowa, N.J.: Rowman and Littlefield, 1972), pp. 142–143.

79. Kenyon, *Robert Spencer*, p. 171.

80. See above n. 46.

81. See Lois G. Schwoerer, "Women and the Glorious Revolution," *Albion*, 18, 2 (Summer 1986) pp. 195–218. In his declaration to the convention parliament, William reiterated his suspicion that "the pretended prince of Wales was *not* born by the Queen—many both doubted of the Queen's bigness and the birth of the child," *Journal of the House of Commons*, X (December 26, 1688–October 26 1693), p. 4.

82. For a contemporary account of James II's desertion, see *The History of the Desertion, or an Account of all public affairs in England, From the beginning of September 1688 to the Twelfth of February following. With an Answer to a Piece call'd the Desertion discussed In a letter to a Country Gentlemen* (London: 1689).

83. From the Earl of Clarendon's diary, November 26, 1688, cited in Thomas Babington Macaulay, *The History of England From the Reign of James II*, 3 vols (New York: American Book Exchange, 1880) II, p. 81.

84. Ibid.

85. See Nenner, pp. 147–249.

86. Ibid. See also Henry Horwitz, *Parliament, Policy, and Politics in the Reign of William III* (Manchester: Manchester University Press, 1977), pp. 1–49.

87. *The Parliamentary History of England*, V, 1688–1702 (London: Hansard, 1809), p. 101.

88. For a recent analysis of William's matrimonial claims to the English crown, see Nenner, pp. 178–181.

89. See Ogg, 227.

90. *Parliamentary History*, V, p. 63.

91. "And that the sole and full exercise of the regal power be only in and executed by the said Prince of Orange in the names of the said Prince and Princess during their joynt lives," *Statutes of the Realm*, VI (London: 1819), William and Mary, sess. 2, chap. 2, p. 143. For a contemporary explanation for why regal power was reserved for William alone, see "The Reasons for Crowning the Prince and Princess of Orange King and Queen Jointly, and for placing the executive Power in the Prince alone" (London: 1689), *Harleian Miscellany*, VI, pp. 606–607.

92. For an analysis of Whig perceptions of William as an elected monarch, see Tony Claydon, "William III's Declaration of Reason and the Glorious Revolution," *Historical Journal*, 39 (1996) pp. 87–108. For contemporary tracts that explicitly labeled William and Mary's elevation as an election, see "Political Remarks on the Life and Reign of William III" (ca. 1702), *Harleian Miscellany*, III, pp. 350–360, and "Reasons For Crowning the Prince and Princess Jointly," p. 606.

93. Mary II, *Memoirs*, p. 11.

94. During William's and Mary's coronation, Mary was crowned in the fashion of a queen consort; according to Strickland, 'neither girt with the sword, nor assumed the spurs or armilla, like the two queens regnant, her predecessors, Mary I and Elizabeth I" VII, p. 25.

95. Roger Morrice, "The Ent'ring Book. Being an Historical Register of Occurances from April 1677 to April 1691," vol. 2, *Dr. Williams Library*, MS 31 Q, 393. Cited in Nenner, p. 162.

96. For a further discussion of the gendered aspects of Mary II's role as queen, see Weil, *Political Passions*, pp. 110–116.

97. [anonymous], *The History of the Life and Reign of her Late Majesty Queen Anne*, p. 19.

98. Gilbert Burnet, *An Inquiry into the Present State of Affairs: and in particular, Whether We Owe Allegiance to the King in these Circumstances? And whether we are bound to Treat with Him, and call him back again, or not?* (London: 1689), p. 10.

99. "Reasons for crowning the Prince and Princess of Orange jointly, and for placing the Executive Power in the Prince alone," *Harleian Miscellany* (London: 1689) VI, pp. 606–607.

100. Burnet, *History*, V, p. 7.
101. *Clarendon Correspondence*, II, p. 189.
102. For a medical reconstruction of Anne's efforts to further the protestant succession and its devastating effects on her health, see H.E. Emson, "For the Want of an Heir: The Obstetrical History of Queen Anne," *British Medical Journal*, 304 (May 1992), pp. 66–67.
103. Luttrell, *State Affairs*, III, p. 55.
104. *Statutes of the Realm*, VI, I Willliam and Mary, sess. 2, private, "For the naturalizing of the most noble Prince George of Denmark, and settling his precedence," p. 155. See also Luttrell, *State Affairs*, I, p. 519.
105. Luttrell, *State Affairs*, I, p. 590.
106. George of Denmark was an avid horseracing fan. See John Ashton, *Social Life in Queen Anne's Reign* (London: Chatto and Windus, 1919), p. 229.
107. See Horwitz, *Parliament, Policy, and Politics*, p. 67. Horwitz speculated on William's attitude towards George, writing "From the onset of the reign, the King had found his Danish brother-in-law an encumbrance."
108. Abel Boyer, *The History of Queen Anne* (London: 1735), p. 6.
109. One contemporary account only mentioned George's participation in William's Irish campaign in the context of a "person of quality" accompanying the king. See Samuel Mulleneaux, *A Journal of the Three months Royal Campaign of His Majesty in Ireland, together with a true and Perfect Diary of the siege of Limerick* (London: 1690), p. 7. One recent study of the Irish campaign also offered no details for George's actions, see Richard Doherty, *The Williamite War in Ireland, 1688–1691* (London: Four Courts Press, 1998). Prince George's regiment was disbanded for its allegedly catholic composition. See J.R. Western, *Monarchy and Revolution*, p. 143.
110. Mary II recorded in her journal her belief that the impetus for George to go to sea lay with her sister Anne. See Mary II, *Memoirs*, p. 38.
111. Anne's quest for a parliamentary subsidy was the occasion for a rather dramatic confrontation between her and her sister, Queen Mary. When asked, Anne replied sheepishly that it was her friends in the Commons that had initiated the request, to which Queen Mary replied, "Pray, what friends have you but the King and me?" See Sarah Churchill, Duchess of Marlborough, *An Account of the Conduct of the Dowager Duchess of Marlborough* (London: 1742), p. 29.
112. Macaulay, III, pp. 86–87.
113. Churchill, *Conduct*, p. 86.
114. Churchill, *Conduct*, p. 39.

115. This episode is also described in Luttrell's political diary, *State Affairs*, II, p. 225.
116. Mary II considered her sister the prime motivator for Prince George's decision to go to sea, to bolster her political affinity, see Mary II, *Memoirs*, p. 38.
117. Churchill, *Conduct*, p. 103.
118. Luttrell, *State Affairs*, II, p. 365.
119. Ibid., p. 391.
120. See *Journal of the House of Commons*, XI, pp. 566–567.
121. Luttrell, *State Affairs*, II, pp. 133,150.
122. References to George's attendance in William's privy councils are found in *Historical Manuscripts Commission, Reports on the Manuscripts of the Duke of Buccleuch and Queensbury*, II, pp. 260–300.
123. Luttrell recorded that, "following Mary's death [the] Prince of Denmark was yesterday to console the King, but his majestie being asleep did not see him." *State Affairs*, III, p. 419.
124. Sarah Churchill mentioned one other occasion of William's ill usage of George: "Prince George, following the death of his brother the King of Denmark, found means to get my Lord Albemarle to ask the King's leave that the Prince might be admitted in his mourning, to wish his majesty joy. The answer was, that the king would not see him, unless he came in colors; and the Prince was persuaded to comply, though he did it with great uneasiness." Churchill, *Conduct*, p. 114.
125. Gregg, *Queen Anne*, p. 98.
126. Letter from T. Brydges to Baron Leibnitz (Hanoverian ambassador to England), January 4, 1695, *State Papers and Correspondence Illustrative of the Social and Political State of Europe, From the Revolution to the Accession of the House of Hanover*, ed. John Kemble (London: John W. Parker, 1857), p. 164.
127. See Horwitz, *Parliament*, p. 205.
128. Ibid., p. 153.
129. Ibid.
130. See Baxter, *William III*, pp. 373–374, also Horwitz, *Parliament*, p. 260.
131. See *Historical Manuscripts Commission*, Fourteenth Report, appendix, part 4, The Manuscripts of Lord Kenyon (London: 1894), p. 422.
132. Van der Zee, *William and Mary*, p. 444.
133. Quoted in Trevelyan, *The Reign*, II, p. 169.
134. See William Coxe, *Memoirs of John, Duke of Marlborough* (London: Longman, Hurst, Rees, Orme, and Brown, 1818), p. 78.
135. See Van der Zee, *William and Mary*, p. 457, Horwitz, *Parliament*, p. 268.
136. The Jacobites were those extreme Tories who only recognized the legitimacy of an indefeasible royal succession, so named for their

support of James Stuart, the son of James II and Mary of Modena, and half-brother to Mary II and Anne. James was known as the Old Pretender, while his son Charles, "Bonnie Prince Charlie," was known as the Young Pretender. As in the supposed catholic threat, the Jacobite threat was more apparent than real; though Anne was rumoured to have favored the succession of her brother, Anne placed no obstacles in the way of the smooth succession of the Elector of Hanover. The Jacobites continue to fascinate historians: see Bruce Lenman, *The Jacobite Cause* (Glasgow: R. Drew in assciation with the National Trust of Scotland, 1986), Jeremy Block and Eveline Cruickshanks, *The Jacobite Challenge* (Edinburgh: J. Donald; Atlantic Highlands, 1988), and Murray Pitock, *Jacobitism* (New York: St. Martin's Press, 1998).

137. See *Sources of English Constitutional History*, 2 vols., ed. Carl Stephenson and George Marcham (New York: Harper and Row, 1972), II, pp. 610–612.

138. Ibid. Following Anne in the line of succession was Sophia, electress dowager of Hanover, granddaughter of James I and the nearest Protestant heir. Because of the eventuality of a series of women monarchs, the Act of Settlement bore a striking similarity to Mary I and Philip of Spain's marriage treaty, in its articles barring foreigners from foreign office or inducing England to go to war in defense of lands not attached to the crown.

139. Ibid.

140. As a member of the House of Lords, George of Denmark took no steps into insinuate himself in Act of Settlement, or to oppose the prohibitions against foreign councilors and office holders also included in the statute.

141. For a recent analysis of the shift in perception from "estate" to "office," see J.R. Jones, "The Revolution in Context," *Liberty Secured: Britain Before and After 1688*, ed. J.R. Jones (Stanford: Stanford University Press, 1992), pp. 11–52.

142. For a contemporary example of Anne's perception as an autonomous and sovereign monarch, see Joseph Gander, *The Glory of her Sacred majesty Queen Anne in the Royal Navy and her Absolute Sovereignty as Empress of the Sea; Asserted and Vindicated* (London: 1703).

143. John Sharp, Archbishop of York, *A Sermon Preached at the Coronation of Queen Anne* (London: 1702).

144. Ibid.

145. Sir Thomas Craig, *The Right of Succession to the Kingdom of England in Two Books*, trans. James Gatherer (London: 1703), p. 83. Craig originally wrote the work in Latin prior to James I's 1603 English accession, to bolster James's legitimacy through female descent.

Gatherer's 1703 translation was a timely bolster to Anne's position as a married monarch.

146. Cockburn, *An Essay*, pp. 12–13.

147. See note 1.

148. Thomas Lediard, *The Life of John, Duke of Marlborough*, 2 vols. (London: 1743), II p. 137. Lediard remarked that, of a plan to elevate George to the royal dignity, "nothing of that nature, as I have already observed, being proposed, or so much hinted at, either in the Queen's speech or otherwise, by any member of either House."

149. See Coxe, *Memoirs*, p. 155.

150. Lediard, II, p. 136.

151. Winston Churchill, *Marlborough: His Life and Times*, 5 vols. (London: George C. Harrapond, 1933–38), II, p. 36.

152. An alleged Tory plot to make George a king was mentioned in a letter to Robert Harley, Speaker of the House of Commons, September 1702, cited in Holmes, p. 90, and Lediard, II, p. 136.

153. Burnet, *History*, V, p. 55.

154. *A Letter to a Member of Parliament in Reference to his Royal Highness Prince George of Denmark*, British Library, misc. 85/1865 ca. 19 (100).

155. Ibid.

156. *Statutes of the Realm*, vol. VIII (London: 1831) 1 Anne, sess. 2, cap.2, "An Act for Enabling Her Majesty to Settle a Revenue for Supporting the Dignity of His Royal Highness Prince George."

157. *Calendar of State Papers, Domestic, Anne, vol. 1, 1702–1703*, ed. Robert Pentland McNaffy (London: 1916), pp. 85, 466.

158. George was often reported to be ill. See Luttrell, *State Affairs*, III, p. 488, 502, 5, 201, 230. *Marlborough–Godolphin Correspondence*, ed. Henry L. Snyder (Oxford: Clarendon, 1975), pp. 737, 1124, *Historical Manuscripts Commission*, Twelfth Report, Appendix, part 3, The Manuscripts of the Earl Cowper, III (London: 1889), p. 283.

159. Letter from Robert Molesworth to his wife, November 5, 1702. "The Manuscripts of the Hon. Frederick Lindley Wood, M.L.S. Clemonts, esq., and S. Philip Unwin, esq.," *Historical Manuscripts Commission, Reports on the Manuscripts in Various Collections*, VII, p. 226.

160. Sir Jonathan Trelawny, *A Sermon Preach'd Before the Queen and Both Houses of Parliament at the Cathedral Church of St. Pauls*, November 12, 1702 (London: 1702).

161. Coxe, *Memoirs*, p. 113.

162. *The Marlborough–Godolphin Correspondence*, p. 103.

163. In 1708, N. Tate, poet laureate to Queen Anne, composed a largely fictitious poem lauding Prince George's contributions to British naval victories in his official capacity as Lord High

Admiral. See N. Tate, *A Congratulatory Poem to his Royal Highness Prince George of Denmark Upon the Glorious Successes at Sea* (London: 1708).

164. *Marlborough–Godolphin Correspondence*, pp. 208, 296.

165. Much evidence attests that George went to the office regularly, see Luttrell, *State Affairs*, vol. 5, pp. 179, 183, British Library, Sloane add. 5440, f. 125, 128, add 5443, f. 215, 221, 223, Huntington Library hm 774, f. 3, 18–19, 23–24, 4041, *Manuscripts of the House of Lords,1702–1704* (London, 1910), 124, 228, 504, 511, 512, 535, 1704–1706, 8, 109, 112, 119–30, 133, 135, 142, 150,160, 375, 1706–1708, 100, 108, 115, 195, 203, 207, 225 , 361, 369, 418, 419, 525, 1708–1710, 33, 34, 64–70, 207, 210, 211, 212, 213, 216.

166. A.S. Turberville, The House of Lords in the XVIII Century (Westport, Conn.: Greenwood Press, 1970), p. 53.

167. Sir David Brewster, *Memoirs of the Life, Writings, and Discoveries of Sir Isaac Newton* (New York and London: Johnson reprint, 1965, reprinted from the Edinburgh edition of 1855) pp. 209–210, 219.

168. "Autobiography of Dr. George Clark" *Historical Manuscripts Commission, Reports of Manuscripts of F.W. Leybourne-Popham*, Esq. (London: 1899), p. 282.

169. Burnet, *History*, V, p. 392.

170. Letter from Lord Raby to Baron Leibnitz, January 17, 1708 (179), *State Papers and Correspondence Illustrative of the Social and Political State of Europe*, p. 464.

171. Marlborough wrote to his Duchess, "The prince would not hear of George Churchill's resignation." *Marlborough–Godolphin Correspondence*, p. 1035.

172. See Jonathan Swift, "Memoirs Relating To that Change Which Happened in the Queen's Ministry in the Year 1710," ed. Herbert Davis and Irvin Ehrenpreis. *The Prose Works of Jonathan Swift: Political Tracts, 1713–1719*, 8 vols. (Oxford: 1954) I, pp. 112–13. According to Swift, "The Prince, thus intimated by [George] Churchill, reported to the Queen, that Marlborough would quit if Godolphin was turned out, so Harley was turned out."

173. *The Marlborough–Godolphin Correspondence*, p. 999.

174. *The Marlborough–Godolphin Correspondence*, p. 1045. George Macaulay Trevelyan, the last historian to consider George of Denmark's political worth, "Prince George the Dane was too stupid or too shrewd to govern her (Anne's) political action." *England Under Queen Anne- Blenheim*, p. 177.

175. In 1707, Parliament passed a regency act, "An Act For the Security of her Majesty's Person and Government and the Succession to the Crown of Great Britain in the Protestant Line," to govern in the interim between Anne's death and the arrival in Britain of the Hanoverian claimant. As Lord High Admiral, George was

appointed to this council. *English Historical Documents*, ed. David C. Douglas (New York: Oxford University Press, 1953), pp. 138–142.

176. See *The Diary of Sir David Hamilton*, ed. Philip Roberts (Oxford: Clarendon Press, 1975), p. 4. Anne's physician, Hamilton remarked, "I shall pass by the trouble which the Prince's death caused her, because of the happiness of her marry'd state, and her inward concern of mind, which follow's his death are so well known."

177. Boyer, *The History*, p. 357.

178. Cockburn, *An Essay*, p. 13.

179. Lord Melbourne, Queen Victoria's first prime minister, considered George of Denmark "a very stupid fellow," as he recounted to Victoria the story of James II and "*est-il possible?*" ed. Viscount Esher *The Training of a Sovereign* (Anne, Queen of Greet Britain, 1819–1901. New York: Longmans, Green, and Co., 1912) (afterwards referred to as Diaries), p. 129.

180. See Robert Rhodes James, "Prince Albert: The First Constitutional Monarch?" *Proceedings of the Royal Institution of Great Britain*, 64 (1992), pp. 5–21.

181. Sir Charles Cotteril, *The Whole Life and Glorious Actions of Prince George of Denmark* (London: 1708), p. 8.

4. "What Power Have I Left?" Queen Victoria's Bedchamber Crisis Revisited

1. Royal Archives, Windsor, (afterward referred to as RA), RA VIC/C1/27, Queen Victoria to Viscount Melbourne, May 9, 1839.

2. Explanations for the Bedchamber Crisis in political histories are usually frustratingly brief. See E.L. Woodward, *The Age of Reform* (Oxford: Clarendon, 1939), p. 105, who betrayed a decided lack of historical interest, writing "It is difficult to assign responsibility for this absurd business." For most political historians and scholarly biographers, the queen's emotional dependence on Melbourne and her lack of political understanding were her primary motivations. In his work *Peel and the Conservative Party* (Hamden, Conn.: Archon Books, 1964), p. 424, G. Kitson Clark offered a charitable if patronizing summation to his analysis: "She had some excuses and reason on her side, and in palliation of all it must be remembered that she was only nineteen." In a similar vein, Cecil Woodham-Smith wrote "The simple truth in this case is that the queen could not endure the thought of parting with Melbourne, who is everything to her." *Queen Victoria: From her Birth to the Death of the Prince Consort* (New York: Alfred A. Knopf, 1972), p. 174. See also Elizabeth Longford, *Queen Victoria: Born to Succeed*, (New York: Harper and Row, 1964), Norman Gash, *Sir Robert Peel* (London: Longman, 1972),

pp. 222–225, Dorothy Marshall, *Lord Melbourne* (London: Weidenfeld and Nicolson, 1979), p. 144.

3. See *The Nineteenth Century Constitution*, ed. A. J. Hanham (Cambridge: Cambridge University Press, 1969). In the introduction, Hanham wrote, "Queen Victoria made it virtually impossible for Peel to form a government by refusing to change the Whig ladies of her household—a matter of minor importance," p. 29. Similarly, G.H.L. Le May observed that "The Bedchamber Crisis was much less a constitutional landmark than a contest of personalities." *The Victorian Constitution* (London: Duckworth, 1979), p. 43.

4. Charles Greville, *Greville Memoirs, vol. 4*, ed. Henry Reeve (London: Longmans, 1896), p. 166. The brackets are Greville's.

5. Lytton Strachey, *Queen Victoria* (New York: Blue Ribbon Press, 1921), p. 115.

6. See Richard Francis Spall, Jr., "The Bedchamber Crisis and the Hastings Scandal," *Canadian Journal of History*, 22 (April 1987), pp. 19–39. Spall's examination of the press war surrounding the Flora Hastings affair, in which one of the Duchess of Kent's ladies was falsely accused of pregnancy, argued that accusations of immorality leveled at Victoria's chief ladies extended into and affected the Bedchamber Crisis itself. See also Karen Chase and Michael Levenson, " 'I Never Saw A Man So Frightened': The Young Queen and the Parliamentary Bedchamber," *Remaking Queen Victoria*, ed. Margaret Homans and Adrienne Munich (Cambridge: Cambridge University Press, 1997), pp. 200–218. Chase and Levenson, for the first time, subject the Bedchamber Crisis to a gender analysis, calling attention to the contested male and female spaces that constituted the obviously gendered aspects of the Crisis. While both of these studies demonstrate the complexity of the Bedchamber Crisis, they are not concerned with the Crisis's place or significance in modern British political evolution, or its relationship to the reigns of other female rulers. In her own work on Victoria's relationship with the evolution of nineteenth-century British culture, Margaret Homans offered a brief gender analysis of the Bedchamber Crisis. Homans identified Victoria's insistence that the bedchamber constituted a private female sphere distinct from public politics. See Margaret Homans, *Royal Representations: Queen Victoria and British Culture* (Chicago: University of Chicago Press, 1998), pp. 14–15.

7. See Stanley Weintraub, *Queen Victoria: An Intimate Memoir* (New York: Truman Talley Books, 1987), p. 123. Weintraub saw no gendered distinctions between male and female household officers, discounting Victoria's assertion that bedchamber ladies were her "own affair," as he stated, "By custom, however, they were not, and court appointments reflected the power balance in parliament."

8. It should be noted that the edited and published editions of the queen's letters and journals are not complete. Victoria's youngest daughter Beatrice edited her journals after her death, on her instructions, and destroyed the originals. However, for the period of 1837 to February 1840 there exist typed copies of the original journal, which are known as the Esher volumes. Nevertheless, Victoria's surviving letters and journal entries from May 1839 still offer a comprehensive body of evidence used to formulate the interpretation offered here.

9. For discussion of women's status in Medieval and early modern England, see Henrietta Leyser, *Medieval Women*.

10. Barbara J. Harris, "Women and Politics in Early Tudor England," *Historical Journal* 33, 2 (1990), pp. 259–281.

11. For a discussion of the Medieval evolution of the royal household, see Chris Given-Wilson, *The Royal Household and the King's Affinity: Service, Politics and Finance in England, 1360–1413* (New Haven: Yale University Press, 1986).

12. See David Loades, *The Tudor Court* (Totowa N.J.: Barnes and Noble, 1987), pp. 32–36, 54–59, and Pam Wright, "A Change in Direction: The Ramifications of a Female Household, 1558–1603," *The English Court: From the Wars of the Roses to the Civil War*, ed. David Starkey (London and New York: Longman, 1987), pp. 147–160.

13. *Statutes of the Realm*, 1 Marie, sess. 1 caps. 1 and 2. Following her marriage to Philip of Spain in July 1554, Mary continued to formally hold the powers and prerogatives of kingship, as outlined in the Act Concerning Regal Power and the marriage treaty. As a de facto king consort, Philip received a separate royal household.

14. Mary I's bedchamber ladies lent their support to the queen's own determination to marry Philip of Spain, see *Calendar of State Papers, Spanish*, XI, pp. 252, 289, 328, XII, p. 180.

15. Quoted in Carolly Erickson, *The First Elizabeth* (New York: Summit Books, 1983), p. 350.

16. Neil Cuddy, "The Revival of the Entourage: the Bedchamber of James I, 1603–1625," *The English Court*, pp. 173–225.

17. For a recent analysis of the gendered aspects of Mary II's role as queen, see Weil, *Political Passions*, pp. 110–116.

18. See John Christopher Sainty and R.O. Bucholz, *Officers of the Royal Household, vol. 1* (London: University of London, Institute of Historical Research, 1997). The second of these works provides a complete listing of household officers from the reigns of Charles II to William IV, two years before Victoria's accession.

19. Both Sarah Churchill and Jonathan Swift contributed to the perception that Anne was led by the nose by her bedchamber ladies, see Churchill, *Account*, and Jonathan Swift, *The Last Four Years of the*

Queen (London: 1758). The extent of the political influence of Anne's bedchamber ladies remains hotly contested among historians. See Holmes, *British Politics in the Age of Anne*, pp. 210–217, Bucholz, "Nothing But Ceremony," pp. 288–323, and Frances Harris, "The Honorable Sisterhood: Queen Anne's Maid of Honor," *The British Library Journal*, 19, 2 (1993), pp. 181–198.

20. See Anne Somerset, *Ladies In Waiting* (New York: Alfred A. Knopf, 1984), p. 192.

21. Ibid., pp. 193–195.

22. The Duchess of Somerset replaced the Duchess of Marlborough as Groom of the stole on January 24, 1711. See Sainty and Bucholz, *Officers of the Royal Household*, p. 7.

23. Victoria was the last of the English Hanoverian monarchs, George I (1714–1727), George II (1727–1760), George III (1760–1820), George IV (1820–1830), and William IV (1830–1837).

24. Still useful are Basil Williams, *The Whig Supremacy* (Oxford: Clarendon Press, 1939), Archibald Foord, *His Majesty's Opposition* (Oxford: Clarendon Press, 1964), and Lewis Bernstein Namier, *The Structure of Politics at the Accession of George III*, (London: Macmillan, 1957). For an example of recent eighteenth-century revisionism, see Linda Colley, *In Defiance of Oligarchy* (Cambridge: Cambridge University Press, 1982), and *Britons: Forging the Nation, 1707–1837* (New Haven: Yale University Press, 1992). Other surveys have combined social, economic, and religious factors with political analysis: see Paul Langford, *A Polite and Commercial People: England 1727–1783* (Oxford: Oxford University Press, 1984) and J.C.D. Clark, *English Society 1688–1832* (Cambridge: Cambridge University Press, 1985).

25. Archibald Foord, "The Waning of the Influence of the Crown," *English Historical Review*, 62 (October 1947), pp. 484–507. For a more recent survey of the evolution of parliament, see B.W. Hill, *British Parliamentary Parties 1742–1832* (London: Allen and Unwin, 1985).

26. See E. Neville Williams, *The Eighteenth-Century Constitution, 1688–1815* (Cambridge: Cambridge University Press, 1970), pp. 67–135.

27. See J.H. Plumb, *England in the Eighteenth Century* (Harmonsworth, Middlesex: Penguin, 1950), p. 138, and John Cannon, *The Fox-North Coalition* (Cambridge: Cambridge University Press, 1969), pp. 1–64.

28. RA/VIC/QVJ/1839 (E) (afterward referred to as *Journal*), May 16, 1837, p. 223.

29. Ibid.

30. In a draft of a letter to Peel, Tory peer Lord Shrewsbury noted the similarities between the 1812 failure of a proposed ministry to require household changes and the Bedchamber Crisis. See

Sir Robert Peel: From His Private Papers, ed. Charles Stuart Parker (London: John Murrary, 1899), p. 406.

31. *Journal*, May 16, 1839, p. 223.

32. RA/VIC/C43/20, letter from Melbourne to the queen, May 9, 1839. In this letter, Melbourne outlined to the queen the recent precedents relating to household changes, emphasizing the point "no part of the household was removed except those that were in parliament."

33. See A.W. Purdue, "Queen Adelaide: Malign Influence or Consort Maligned?" *Queenship in Britain*, pp. 265–283.

34. See Philip Ziegler, *William IV* (London: Collins, 1971), pp. 149–157. Ziegler quoted a letter from Whig prime minister Lord Grey, from the Lieven–Grey correspondence in the Howick MSS, which stated, "Queen Adelaide does needlework, talks a good deal, but never about politics," p. 156.

35. For more discussion of the concept and ideology of separate spheres for men and women in Victorian society, see Leonore Davidoff and Catherine Hall, *Family Fortunes* (Chicago: University of Chicago Press, 1987), pp. 357–396. Davidoff and Hall's analysis of separate spheres ideology has been subject to critical analysis; see Amanda Vickery, "Golden Age to Separate Spheres? A Review of the Categories and Chronology of English Women's History," *Historical Journal* 36, 2 (June 1993), pp. 383–414. For an analysis of the male role that emerged in the private and domestic space of the family and home, see John Tosh, *A Man's Place: Masculinity and the Middle-Class Home in Victorian England* (New Haven: Yale University Press, 1999).

36. Feminist historians make this concept explicit. See Homans, *Royal Representations*, pp. xx.

37. Dorothy Thompson, *Queen Victoria: Gender and Power* (London: Virago, 1990), p. 23. Thompson quoted a contemporary observation that "Coming after a an imbecile, a profligate, and a buffoon, as the three kings that preceded her have been described, she had much in her favor." For a still useful and entertaining study of Victoria's immediate predecessors, see Roger Fulford, *The Wicked Uncles* (London: Duckworth, 1933).

38. For a comprehensive work on visual representations of Victoria, see Helmut and Alison Gernsheim, *Victoria R* (New York: G.N. Putnam's Sons, 1959).

39. C.R. Sanders, "Carlyle's Pen Portraits of Queen Victoria and Prince Albert," *Carlyle: Past and Present*, ed. K.J. Fielding and Rodger L. Tarr (New York: Barnes and Noble, 1976), p. 216.

40. Victoria's father, the Duke of Kent, the fourth son of George III, died on January 23, 1820, eight months after Victoria's birth.

41. Letter from Lord Palmerston to Sir Frederick Lamb, cited in C.K. Webster, "The Accession of Queen Victoria," *History*, 22 (June 1937), p. 22.

42. For descriptions of Victoria's education, see Dormer Creston, *The Youthful Queen Victoria* (New York: G. P. Putnam and Sons, 1954), Monica Charlot, *Victoria the Young Queen* (Oxford: Basil Blackwell, 1991), Webster, "The Accession," 17, and Woodham-Smith, *Queen Victoria*, pp. 87–138.

43. See Lynne Vallone, *Becoming Victoria* (New Haven and London: Yale University Press, 2001), pp. 62–72. Vallone's work emphasized the political nature of Victoria's education, and the Duchess of Kent's efforts to win support for the curriculum she provided for Victoria.

44. See James, "Prince Albert: The First Constitutional Monarch?", pp. 5–21.

45. By the time of his 1830 accession, William IV was 65 years old. Although he produced a bumper crop of illegitimate children earlier in his life, William IV and his youthful wife, Queen Adelaide, failed to produce living heirs, making Victoria, the daughter of William's younger brother, the Duke of Kent, heir presumptive.

46. Letter from Leopold to Victoria, 1834, *The Letters of Queen Victoria*, I (afterward referred to as *Letters*), ed. Viscount Esher and Christopher Benson (London: John Murray, 1908), p. 48.

47. Victoria to Leopold, October 1834, *Letters*, p. 49.

48. Leopold to Victoria, June 1837, *Letters*, p. 106.

49. See Le May, pp. 54–60. Also, for an analysis of the political prerogative of late-twentieth-century monarchy, see Lord Simon of Glaisdale, "The Influence and Power of the Monarchy in the United Kingdom Monarchy," *Current* (September 1982), pp. 56–60.

50. In 1880, more than forty years following the Bedchamber Crisis, Liberal prime minister William Gladstone feared Victoria might dismiss his government. See Frank Hardie, *The Political Influence of Queen Victoria* (London: Frank Cass, 1963), p. 172.

51. Walter Bagehot, *The English Constitution* (Ithiaca, N.Y.: Cornell University Press, 1966, orig. pub. 1867), p. 168.

52. *Letters*, p. 134.

53. *Letters*, p. 91.

54. RA/VIC/Z 493/27, letter from Victoria to Leopold, October 1834, recounting the fifteen-year-old Victoria's delight in "making tables of the Kings and Queens," adding that she had "lately finished one of English sovereigns *and their consorts* (emphasis is mine)

55. *Journal*, December 15, 1838, p. 194

56. See Ernst Kantorwicz, *The King's Two Bodies*, also Marie Axton *The Queen's Two Bodies*.

57. See Vallone, p. 120

58. Victoria's conversations with Melbourne concerning her female predecessors were often light and amusing, but also revealing in the gendered differences between male and female monarchs that

arose during these discussions. See *Diaries*, pp. 129, 223, 227–228, 230, 266, 292, 295–296, 302, *Letters*, p. 50.

59. *Diaries*, p. 295.

60. *Diaries*, pp. 266–67. Victoria's attitude toward Elizabeth I reflects a conventional nineteenth-century attitude toward a queen who disdained wifely domesticity, see Maitzen, *Gender, Genre, and Victorian Historical Writing*, pp. 161–197.

61. See Vallone, *Becoming Victoria*, p. 120.

62. *Diaries*, p. 302.

63. *Letters*, p. 50.

64. *Diaries*, p. 129. The statement "my heart is entirely English" was first made by Elizabeth I upon her own accession, later co-opted by Anne for hers.

65. *Diaries*, p. 298.

66. *Diaries*, p. 309.

67. *Diaries*, p. 273.

68. While British women had to wait until 1918 to vote or stand for parliamentary seats, in the second half of the nineteenth century women began to obtain the right to vote for candidates offices in local and municipal government and administration.

69. During a discussion with the queen concerning Henry VIII's mistresses, Melbourne remarked, "it was always more the woman's fault than the man's." *Diaries*, p. 228.

70. *Diaries*, pp. 287–88.

71. Quoted in Gernsheim, *Victoria R*, p. 162.

72. See Anna Clark, *The Struggle For the Breeches* (Berkeley: University of California Press, 1997), Sonya O. Rose, *Limited Livelihood: Gender and Class in Nineteenth-Century England* (Berkeley: University of California Press, 1992), Frank Prochaska, *Women and Philanthropy in Nineteenth Century England* (Oxford, Oxford University Press, 1981), and Vickers, "Golden Age to Separate Spheres?," pp. 383–414.

73. *Girlhood of Victoria: A Selection From Her Majesty's Diaries*, ed. Viscount Esher (New York: Longman, Grenn, and Co., 1912) pp. 103–104.

74. Cited in Longford, *Queen Victoria*, p. 170.

75. See W.M. Torres, *Memoirs of Lord Melbourne* (London: Ward, Locke and Co., 1890), p. 438. Melbourne noted that Victoria "was disposed to think that the establishment of a queen consort would be sufficient for her."

76. Letter from Lord Liverpool to Sir Robert Peel, May 20, 1839. Liverpool reminded Peel that "when her majesty's female household was first formed, upon her accession, it was the wish of her uncle, King Leopold, which also was acquiesced in by her majesty, that persons of all parties should compose it, and certainly it is but

fair and just for me to say that no objection was made by Lord Melbourne in several instances to appointments or offers of appointments to persons of adverse politics to himself." Parker, ed., *Peel*, p. 402.

77. See Webster, "The Accession," pp. 26–27.
78. Greville, *Greville Memoirs*, p. 169.
79. See Michael Brock, *The Great Reform Act* (London: Hutchinson, 1973).
80. See Davidoff and Hall, *Family Fortunes*, pp. 150–153, also Anna Clark, "Queen Caroline and the Sexual Politics of Popular culture" *Representations* v. 31 (summer 1990) pp. 47–68.
81. Lord Brougham, *Recollections of a Long life* (New York: AMS Press, 1968, orig. pub. 1910), p. 194.
82. See above note 58.
83. Greville, *Greville Memoirs*, p. 169.
84. See L.G. Mitchell, *Lord Melbourne* (Oxford: Oxford University Press, 1997), p. 232.
85. Brougham, *Recollections*, p. 193.
86. Greville, *Greville Memories*, pp. 160–61, *Journal*, May 7, 1839, p. 164
87. *Journal*, May 7, 1839, p. 163.
88. Greville, *Greville Memories*, p. 161.
89. The standard study of Peel remains Gash. Recent studies have attempted to qualify Gash's analysis of Peel as the central figure of the first half of the nineteenth century, see Ian Newbould, "Sir Robert Peel and the Conservative Party, 1832–1841: A Study in Failure?", *English Historical Review*, 98 (July 1983), pp. 529–538, Donald Read, *Peel and the Victorians* (Oxford: Basil Blackwell, 1987), and T.A. Jenkins, *Sir Robert Peel* (New York: St. Martin's Press, 1999)
90. Parker, ed., *Peel*, p. 393.
91. RA/VIC/C 1/27, Queen Victoria to Lord Melbourne, May 9, 1839
92. See Spall, "The Bedchamber Crisis," pp. 19–39.
93. *Letters*, p. 196.
94. *Journal*, May 7, 1839, p. 168.
95. *Hansard's Parliamentary Series*, 3rd series, 2 Victoriae, 15th April–5th June 1839, May 14, 1839, col. 1015, Melbourne's address to the House of Lords.
96. *Journal*, May 8, 1839, p. 174.
97. Ibid, p. 177.
98. Ibid.
99. Parker, ed., *Peel*, p. 389.
100. See Mitchell, *Lord Melbourne*.
101. *Diaries*, p. 227.
102. Peel's familial relations are intermittently discussed in Gash. For a brief discussion of Peel's relationship with his daughter Julia, see Gash, *Sir Robert Peel*, pp. 179–180.

103. For a detailed study of emergent male domesticity in the private sphere of the middle class family, see Tosh, *A Man's Place*.
104. RA/VIC/C1/29, Victoria to Melbourne, May 9, 1839.
105. Peel recapitulated his conversation to Victoria in the letter he sent to her on May 10, the day he resigned his commission to form a government. See Wellington Papers (University of Southampton), mss. 2/58/162.
106. *Journal*, May 9, 1839, p. 180.
107. Ibid.
108. For the queen's version of this meeting, see *Journal*, May 9, 1839, p. 181. For Peel's, see *Hansard*, cols. 979–991.
109. *Journal*, May 9, 1839, 184.
110. Ibid.
111. Ibid.
112. *Journal*, May 11, 1839, 192.
113. RA/VIC/C1/27, Victoria to Melbourne, May 9, 1839.
114. Greville, *Greville Memoirs*, 162.
115. RA/VIC/C1/29, Victoria to Melbourne, May 9, 1939.
116. *Journal*, May 9, 1839, 182.
117. RA/VIC/C1/27, Victoria to Melbourne, May 9, 1939.
118. Ibid.
119. RA/VIC/C1/29.
120. See Woodham-Smith, *Queen Victoria*, pp. 176–177.
121. RA/VIC/C 1/28, Victoria to Peel, May 9, 1839.
122. A copy of Peel's letter to Victoria is in the Wellington MSS, 2/58/162.
123. Greville, *Greville Memoirs*, 163.
124. *Hansard*, col. 989.
125. Parker, ed. *Peel*, p. 4. 6.
126. *Hansard*, col. 997.
127. *Hansard*, col. 998.
128. *Hansard*, col. 999.
129. Wellington MSS. 2/58/162.
130. Parker, ed. *Peel*, p. 427.
131. Greville, *Greville Memoirs*, p. 168.
132. Ibid., p. 169.
133. For a succinct narrative of these events, see Woodham-Smith, *Queen Victoria*, p. 236.
134. One unconventional and amusing indicator of Peel's place in British history was his inclusion in the photographic montage that adorned the cover of the Beatles 1967 album *Sgt. Pepper's Lonely Hearts Club Band*, the only British prime minister accorded this recognition.
135. RA/VIC/L 17/58.
136. Bagehot, *English Constitution*, p. 168.

137. Later in her reign, the one exception the mature Victoria made to the exclusion of women from formal political functions were her daughters, some of whom married German monarchs, while her youngest daughter Beatrice served as an unofficial private secretary with access to government documents. See E.F. Benson, *Queen Victoria's Daughters* (New York and London: D. Appleton-Century Company, 1938), and Jerrold Packard, *Victoria's Daughters* (New York: St. Martin's Griffin, 1998).
138. RA/VIC/Y 89/37, Victoria to Leopold, May 14, 1839.

Conclusion: Does the Lioness Still Roar?

1. Scholars are generally reticent to discuss the impact of monarchy on the creation of English and British national identity in any comprehensive fashion. This leaves royal biographers and journalists as the main purveyors of such analysis. For a thoughtful introduction into this concept, see Philip Ziegler, *Crown and People* (New York: Alfred A. Knopf, 1978).
2. Both statutes remain part of the constitution. As one recent constitutional scholar has noted, the British constitution is unwritten and uncodified. See Vernon Bogdanor, *The Monarchy and the Constitution* (Oxford: Clarendon Press, 1995).
3. See A.N. Wilson, *The Rise and Fall of the House of Windsor* (New York: W.W. Norton and Co., 1993). Wilson brings a journalistic tone to this discussion of Elizabeth II's transition to a media monarch. While Wilson barely hides his republican sympathies, he gives noticeable credit to Elizabeth II personally as monarch, as he derides both her family as well as Margaret Thatcher.
4. Like her namesake Elizabeth I, Elizabeth II has generated a number of popular biographies. But any assessment of her political role must await the availability of her private papers. In the meantime, for the best scholarly analysis of Elizabeth II's career, see Ben Pimlott, *The Queen: A Biography of Elizabeth II* (London: HarperCollins, 1996).
5. See Sarah Bradford, *Elizabeth* (New York: Farrar, Straus and Giroux, 1996). Bradford's popular biography includes a brief discussion of the queen's gendered approach to her office, pp. 247–285.
6. For an account of Elizabeth II's coronation, see C. Frost, *Coronation June 2, 1953* (London: Arthur Hacker Ltd., 1978).
7. In 1917, in an effort to distance the crown from its undeniable German heritage, George V changed the name of the royal house from Saxe-Coburg-Gotha to Windsor, prompting Kaisar Wilhelm II to request a production of "the Merry wives of Saxe-Coburg-Gotha." The origins of the Queen's declaration in council,

April 10, 1952, that the royal house would remain Windsor, resulted from Dowager Queen Mary of Teck's hearing of the boast of Earl Louis of Mountbatten that the House of Mountbatten now reigned. Queen Mary informed Churchill, who reportedly persuaded the queen to recognize the continuity of the royal line through her. See Pimlott, pp. 183–186. Philip's protest was especially ironic, since Mountbatten was an anglicization of his mother's family name, Battenburg. See E.H. Cookridge, *From Battenburg to Mountbatten* (London: Arthur Baker, Ltd., 1966).

8. See John Parker, *Prince Philip: A Critical Biography* (London: Sidgwick and Jackson, 1990), pp. 149–158.

9. For the most recent scholarly study of the life and career of Albert of Saxe-Coburg-Gotha, see Robert Rhodes James, *Prince Albert: a Biography* (New York: Alfred A. Knopf, 1983).

10. For an early study of Queen Elizabeth II's married life, see H. Cathcart, *The Married Life of the Queen* (London: W.H. Allen, 1970). A more recent study is C. Higham and R. Mosesely, *Elizabeth and Philip: The Untold Story* (London: Sidgwick and Jackson, 1991). Both of these works are popular biographies, reflecting a social interest in the queen and Philip's highly public marriage.

11. For a succinct discussion of the queen's current prerogative powers, see Glaisdale, "The Influence and Power of the Monarchy in the United Kingdom Monarchy," pp. 56–60.

12. See Bogdanor, *The Monarchy*, pp. 84–112.

13. The "horrible" events of 1992 included the break up of the marriages of the queen's two sons, Charles, Prince of Wales, and Andrew, Duke of York, and a fire at her favorite residence, Windsor Castle.

14. *The New York Times*, 11/2/02, v. 152, p. A1.

15. For a study of the modern evolution of the monarch's philanthropic role, see Frank Prochaska, *Royal Bounty: The Making of a Welfare Monarchy* (New Haven: Yale University Press, 1995).

16. Victoria did endure gossip concerning the nature of her relationship with her Scottish servant John Brown during the early years of her long widowhood; however, during the course of her marriage to Prince Albert, she created a public image of domestic tranquility and fidelity. See Thompson, *Queen Victoria: Gender and Power*, pp. 30–61.

BIBLIOGRAPHY

Archival Sources

British Library, London: Harleian Mss. 168, ff. 1–8v, Mss. 6234, ff. 10–25, Sloane add. Mss. 17017, ff. 129, 130, 135, 5431, f. 1, 5440, ff. 125,128, 5443, ff. 215, 221, 223, 38329, f. 21, Misc. 85/1865 c.19 (100).
U.K. Public Records Office: Kew, SP-108–547.
Royal Archives, Windsor: RA/VIC/Y89/37, RA/VIC/C1/27, C1/28, C1/29, RA/VIC/Y65/48, RA/VIC/Y89/37, RA/VIC/C43/20, C43/34, RA/VIC/QJV/.
University of Southampton: Wellington Papers, 2/58/162.

Printed Primary Sources

Acts of the Privy Council of England, ed. John R. Dasent, 32 vols., London: 1890–1907.
The Anglo-Saxon Chronicle, trans. and ed. Michael Swanton, London: J.M. Dent, 1997.
The Annals of Roger de Hovedon, ed. Henry T. Riley, London: Henry Bohn, 1853.
Aylmer, John. *An Harborowe for Faithful and Trewe Subjects*, London: 1559.
Becon, Thomas. *Humble Supplication for the Restoringe of Hys Holy Woorde Unto the Church of England*, Geneva: 1558.
Bernard, St. *Bernardi Opera*, vol. 8, ed. J. Leclercq, C.H. Talbot and H.M. Rochais, Rome: 1957–77.
Boyer, Abel. *The History of Queen Anne*, London: 1735.
Brougham, Lord. *Recollections of a Long Life*, New York: AMS Press, 1968 (orig. pub. 1910).
Burnet, Gilbert. *An Inquiry into the Present State of Affairs: And in Particular, Whether We Owe Allegiance to the King in These Circumstances? And Whether We are Bound to Treat with Him, and Call him Back, or Not?* London: 1689.
———. *Bishop Burnet's History of His Own Time*, 5 vols., Oxford: Oxford University Press, 1833 (orig. pub. 1724).
Calendar of State Papers, Domestic, Anne I, 1702–1703, ed. Robert Petland, London: 1916.

Calendar of State Papers, Domestic, Charles II, January–June, 1683, ed. F.H. Blackburne Daniell, London: 1933.

Calendar of State Papers, Spanish, vols. 9–13, ed. Royall Tyler, London: 1912–1949.

Calendar of State Papers, Venetian, vols. 5–6, ed. Rowdon Brown, London: 1873–1877.

The Cambridge History of English Literature, vol. 9, ed. A.A. Ward and A.R. Walker, New York: G. Putnam, 1908.

Camden, William. *The History of the Most Renowned and Victorious Princess Elizabeth, Late Queen of England*, ed. with intro by Wallace McCaffery, Chicago: Chicago University Press, 1990.

Carlyle Past and Present, ed. K.J. Fielding and Rodger L. Tarr, New York: Barnes and Noble, 1976.

Certain Questions Demanded and Asked by the Noble Realme of Englande of Her True Natural Children and Subjectes of the Same, attributed to Miles Hogherde, London: 1555.

The Chronicle of Henry of Huntington, ed. Thomas Forester, London: Henry Bohn, 1853.

The Chronicle of John of Worcester, vol. 3, trans. and ed. P. Mcgurk, Oxford: Clarendon Press, 1998.

The Chronicle of Queen Jane and of Two Years of Mary, ed. John Gough Nichols London: Camden Society, 1850.

Churchill, Sarah, Duchess of Marlborough. *An Account of the Conduct of the Dowager Duchess of Marlborough*, London: 1742.

Cobbett's Parliamentary History of England, Vol. I, 1066–1625, ed. William Cobbett, London: Hansard T. Curson, 1806.

Cockburn, William. *An Essay Upon the Propitious and Glorious Reign of Our Gracious Sovereign Anne*, London: 1710.

The Correspondence of Henry Hyde, Earl of Clarendon, and His Brother Lawrence Hyde, Earl of Rochester, vol. 2, ed. Samuel Weller Singer, London: Henry Colburn, 1828.

Cotteril, Charles. *The Whole Life and Glorious Actions of Prince George of Denmark*, London: 1708.

Craig, Sir Thomas. *The Right of Succession to the Kingdom of England*, trans. James Gatherer, London: 1703.

De Guaras, Antonio. *The Accession of Queen Mary*, ed. Richard Garnett, London: Lawrence and Bullen, 1892.

Dekker, Thomas. *The Famous History of Sir Thomas Wyat*, London: 1607.

The Diary of Sir David Hamilton, ed. Philip Roberts, Oxford: Clarendon Press, 1975.

Elder, John. *The Copie of a Letter Sent into Scotlande of the Arrival and Landing of the Most Illutre Prince Philippe, Prince of Spain, to the Moste Excellente Princes Marye Quene of Englande*, London: 1554.

England Under the Reigns of Edward VI and Mary, vol. 2, ed. Patrick Fraser Tytler, London: Richard Bentley, 1839.

English Historical Documents, ed. David C. Douglas, New York: Oxford University Press, 1953.

Esher, Viscount, ed. *Girlhood of Queen Victoria: A Selection From Her Majesty's Diaries*, New York: John Murray, 1912.

———. ed. *The Training of a Sovereign . . . Being Her Diaries, 1832–1840*, London: John Murray, 1914.

Esher, Viscount, and Arthur Christopher Benson, eds. *The Letters of Queen Victoria*, vol. 1, London: John Murray, 1908.

Evelyn, John. *The Diary of John Evelyn*, vol. 4, intro. and notes by Austin Dobson, London: Macmillan, 1906.

Filmer, Robert. *Patriarcha, or the Natural Power of Kings*, London: 1680.

Fortescue, John. *The Life and Works of Sir John Fortescue, (Lord Chief Justice Under Henry VI)*, ed. Thomas Fortescue, Lord Clermot, London: 1869.

Foxe, John. *The Acts and Monuments of John Foxe*, vol. 6, ed. George Townsend and Stephen Cattley, New York: AMS Press, 1965 (orig. pub. 1559).

Gesta Normanorum Ducam of William Jumieges, Oderic Vitalis, and Robert of Torigni, vol. 2, books v–viii, ed. Elisabeth M.C. van Houts, Oxford: Clarendon Press, 1995.

Gesta Stephani, ed. K.R. Potter, Oxford: Clarendon Press, 1976.

Gilby, Anthony. *Admonition to England and Scotland to Call Them to Repentance*, Geneva: 1558.

Goodman, Christopher. *How Superior Powers Ought to be Obeyed of Their Subjects, and Wherein They May By God's Word be Disobeyed and Resisted*, Geneva: 1558.

Grafton, Richard. *Grafton's Chronicle: A Chronicle of the History of England*, London: 1569.

Greville, Charles. *The Greville Memoirs*, vol. 4, ed. Henry Reeve, London: Longmans, 1896.

Hall, Edward. *Hall's Chronicle*, ed. Henry Ellis, London: 1809.

Hansard's Parliamentary Series, third series, 2 Victoriae 1839, xlvii, 15th April–5th June, 1839.

Harleian Miscellany, 6 vols., ed. William Oldys and Thomas Park, London: 1808–1810.

Henry of Huntington. *The Chronicle of Henry of Huntington*, ed. Thomas Forester, London: Henry Bohn, 1853.

History of the Desertion, or An Account of All public Affairs in England, From the Beginning of September 1688 to the Twelfth of February following. With an Answer to a Piece Call's the Desertion Discussed In a Letter to a Country Gentleman, London: 1689.

[Anonymous], *The History of the Life and Reign of Her Late Majesty Queen Anne*, London: 1740.

Hovedon, Roger de. *The Annals of Roger de Hovedon*, vol. 1, ed. Henry T. Riley, London: Henry Bohn, 1853.

Hyde, Edward, Earl of Clarendon. *The History of the Rebellion and Civil Wars in England*, Oxford: Clarendon Press, 1888 (orig. pub. 1702–04).

James VI and I. *The True Law of Free Monarchies and the Basilikon Doron*, ed. Daniel Fischlin and Mark Fortier, Toronto: Center for Reformation and Renaissance Studies, 1996.

———. *King James VI and I: Political Writings*, ed. Johann P. Summerville, Cambridge: Cambridge University Press, 1994.

John and Sarah, Duke and Duchess of Marlborough, Based on Unpublished Letters and Documents at Blenheim Palace, ed. Stuart Reid, London: John Murray, 1915.

John of Salisbury. *Historia Pontificalis*, trans. and ed. Marjorie Chibnall, Oxford: Clarendon Press, 1986.

Journals of the House of Commons, vol. 1, 1547–1628, London: 1803, vol. 10, Dec 26 1688–Oct. 26 1693,

Knox, John. *First Blast of the Trumpet Against the Monstrous Regiment of Women*, Geneva: 1558.

Lediard, Thomas. *The Life of John, Duke of Marlborough*, vol. 1, London: 1743.

Leslie, John. *A Defence of the honour of Marie Quene of Scotland*, London: 1569.

The Letters and Charters of Gilbert Foliot, second edition., ed. N. Brooke, Dom Adrian Morey, and C.N.L. Brooks, Cambridge: Cambridge University Press, 1967.

The Letters and Diplomatic Instructions of Queen Anne, ed. Beatrice Curtis Brown, New York: Funk and Wagnalls, 1935.

Letters and Papers, Foreign and Domestic, of the Reign of Henry VIII, 21 vols., ed. John S. Brewer, James Gairdner, and Robert H. Brodie, London: 1920–32.

[Anonymous], *The Life of Queen Anne*, London: 1721.

Literary Remains of Edward VI, ed. John Gough Nichols, London: Roxburgh Club, 1858.

Locke, John. *Second Treatise on Civil Government (an essay Concerning the True original, Extent, and end of Civil government), and a Letter Concerning Toleration*, ed. J.W. Gough, New York: Macmillan, 1956.

Luttrell, Narcissus. *A Brief Historical Relation of State Affairs From September 1678 to April 1714*, 6 vols., Oxford: Oxford University Press, 1857.

Machyn, Henry. *The Diary of Henry Machyn*, ed. John Gough Nichols, London: Camden Society, 1848.

Macky, John. *Memoirs of the Secret Services of John Macky, esq., During the Reigns of King William, Queen Anne, and George I*, London: 1733.

Manuscripts of the House of Lords, 1702–1704, 1704–1706, 1706–1708, 1708–1710, London: 1910–1921.

The Marlborough–Godolphin Correspondence, six volumes, ed. Henry l. Snyder, Oxford: Oxford University Press, 1975.

Mary II. *Memoirs of Mary, Queen of England (1689–1693)*, ed. R. Doebner, London: David Nutt, 1886.

Mulleneaux, Samuel. *A Journal of the Three Months Campaign of His Majesty in Ireland, Together with a True and Perfect Diary of the Siege of Limerick*, London: 1690.

The Order of the Installation of Prince George of Denmark, Charles, Duke of Somerset, and George, Duke of Northumberland. Knights and Companions of the Most Noble Order of the Garter, London: 1684.

The Parliamentary History of England, vols. 3–6. London: 1762–1810.

[Anonymous], *The Present State of Matrimony*, London: 1749.

Proctor, John. *The Historie of Wyates Rebellion*, London: 1554.

Regesta Regum Anglo-Normannorum, vol. 2, ed. C. Johnson and H.A. Cronne, Oxford: Clarendon Press, 1968.

———. vol. 3, ed. H.A. Cronne and R.H.C. Davis, Oxford: Clarendon Press, 1968.

Reports of the Historical Manuscripts Commission, Ninth Report, part II, London: 1882, Twelfth Report, Appendix, part III, The manuscript of the Earl Cowper, K.G., London: 1889, Twelfth Report, Appendix, part V, The manuscripts of the Duke of Rutland, K.G., ii, London: 1889, Fourteenth Report, Appendix, part IV, The Manuscripts of Lord Kenyon, London: 1894, Calendar of the Manuscripts of the Most Honorable Marquis of Salisbury, K.G. (The Cecil Papers), pts 1 and 2, London: 1896, Report on the Manuscripts of F.W. Leybourne-Popham, esq., London: 1899, Report on the Manuscripts of the Marquis of Ormonde, II, London: 1899, new series, VII, London: 1912, Fifteenth Report, Appendix, part VII, The Manuscripts of the Duke of Somerset, the Marquis of Ailesbury, and the Rev. Sir T.H.G. Puleston, Bart., London: 1898, Report on the Manuscripts of the Duke of Buccleuch and Queensbury, II, parts I and II, London: 1903, Report on the Manuscripts in Various collections, viii, The Manuscripts of the Honorable Frederick Lindley Wood, M.L.S. Clements, esq., S. Philip Unwin, esq., London: 1913.

Rymer's Foedera, ed. Thomas Rymer and Robert Sanderson, 20 vols., London: 1727–35.

Sharp, John, Archbishop of York. *A Sermon preached at the coronation of Queen Anne*, London: 1702.

Sir Robert Peel: From His Private Papers, ed. Charles Stuart Parker, London: John Murray, 1899.

Smith, Thomas. *De Republica Anglorum*, ed. L. Alston, New York: Harper and Row, 1973 (orig. pub. 1584).

Sources of English Constitutional History, vol. 2, ed. Carl Stephenson and George Frederick Marcham, New York: Harper and Row, 1972.

State Papers and Correspondence Illustrative of the Social and Political State of Europe From the Revolution to the Accession of the House of Hanover, ed. John Kemble, London: John Parker and Sons, 1857.

State Papers of Henry VIII, vol. 1, London: 1830.

Statutes of the Realm, 35 Henry VIII, cap.I, 1 Marie, sess. 2, cap. I, 1 Marie, sess. 3, cap. II, 1 William and Mary, sess. 2, cap. II, private, 7 and 8 William III, cap. 30, 1 Anne, sess. 2, cap. 2, 1 Vic, cap. 77.

Stow, John. *Annales, or a Generall chronicle of England*, ed. Edmund Howes, London: 1631.

Swift, Jonathan. *The Prose Works of Jonathan Swift: Political Tracts, 1713–1719*, ed. Herbert Davis and Irwin Ehrenpreis, 8 vols., Oxford: Oxford University Press, 1954.

———. *The Last Four Years of the Queen*, London: 1758.

Tate, N. *A Congratulatory Poem to His Royal Highness Prince George of Denmark Upon the Glorious Successes at Sea*, London: 1708.

Torres, W.M., ed., *Memoirs of Lord Melbourne*, London: Ward, Locke, and Co., 1890.

Trelawny, Sir Jonathan. *A Sermon Preach'd Before the Queen and Both Houses of Parliament at the Cathedral of St. Pauls, Nov. 12, 1702*, London: 1702.

Tudor Royal Proclamations, vol. 2, ed. P.L. Hughes and J.L. Larkin, New Haven: Yale University Press, 1969.

Vitalis, Orderic. *Historia Ecclesiastica*, vol. 6, ed. Marjorie Chibnall, Oxford: Clarendon Press, 1998.

Vives, Juan Luis. *Vives and the Renascense Education of Women*, ed. Foster Watson, London: Edward Arnold, 1910.

William III, King of England, *Declaration of His Highness William Henry, By the Grace of God Prince of Orange, & of the Reasons Inducing Him to Appear in Arms in the Kingdome of England for Preserving the Protestant Religion*. London: 1688.

William of Malmesbury's Chronicle of the Kings of England, ed. J.A. Giles, London: Henry Bohn, 1897.

William of Malmesbury's Historia Novella, ed. Edmund King, trans. K.R. Potter, Oxford: Clarendon Press, 1998.

Wingfield, Robert. "Vitae Mariae Angliae Reginae," *Camden Miscellany*, fourth series, 29, London: Royal Historical Society, 1984, pp. 181–301.

Wrioethesley, Charles. *A Chronicle of England during the Reigns of the Tudors*, ed. William Douglas Hamilton, London: Camden Society, 1877.

Secondary Sources

Alsop, J.D. "The Act for the Queen's Regal Power," *Parliamentary History*, 13, 3 (1994), pp. 261–276.

Ambiguous Realities, ed. Carole Levin and Jeanie Watson, Detroit: Wayne State University Press, 1987.

Amussen, Susan. *An Ordered Society: Gender and Class in Early Modern England*, New York: Columbia University Press, 1988.

Analyzing Gender, ed. Beth B. Hess and Myra Marx Feree, Newberry Park: Sage Productions, 1987.

The Anarchy of Stephen's Reign, ed. Edmund King. Oxford: Clarendon Press, 1994.

The Anglo-Dutch Moment: Essays on the Glorious Revolution and Its World Impact, ed. Jonathan Israel, Cambridge: Cambridge University Press, 1991.

Anglo, Sydney. *Spectacle, Pageantry, and Early Tudor Policy*, second ed., Oxford: Clarendon Press, 1997.

Aram, Bethany. "Juana 'the Mad's' Signature: The Problem of Invoking Royal Authority, 1505–1507," *Sixteenth Century Journal*, 29 (Summer 1998), pp. 331–358.

Ashton, John. *Social Life in Queen Anne's Reign*, London: Chatto and Windus, 1919.

Axton, Marie. *The Queen's Two Bodies: Drama and the Elizabethan Succession*, London: Royal Historical Society, 1977.

Bagehot, Walter. *The English Constitution*, Ithica, New York: Cornell University Press, 1966 (orig. pub. 1867).

Barlow, Frank. *The Feudal Kingdom of England*, second ed., London: Longmans, 1961.

Bartlett, Robert. *England Under the Norman and Angevin Kings*, Oxford: Clarendon Press, 2000.

Bassnet, Susan. *Elizabeth I: A Feminist Perspective*, Oxford: Berg, 1988.

Baxter, Stephen. *William III and the Defense of European Liberty*, London: Macmillan, 1966.

Beem, Charles E. *The Royal Minorities of Medieval England*, M.A. Thesis, Northern Arizona University, Flagstaff, 1990.

Bennett, Judith. "Feminism and History," *Gender and History*, 1 (1989), pp. 259–263.

———. *Medieval Women in Modern Perspective*, Washington D.C.: American Historical Association, 2000.

Benson, E.F. *Queen Victoria's Daughters*, New York and London: D. Appleton-Century co., 1938.

Bindoff, S.T. *The History of Parliament: The House of Commons*, vol. 3, London: Secker and Warburg, 1982.

Birch, Walter de Gray. *A Fasciculus of the Charters of Mathildis Empress of the Romans and an Account of her Great Seal* (reprinted from the *Journal of the British Archaeological Association*), London: 1875.

Bloch, Marc. *The Royal Touch: Sacred Monarchy and Scrofula in England and France*, trans. J.E. Anderson, London: Routledge and Kegan Paul, 1973.

Block, Jeremy, and Evelyn Cruickshanks. *The Jacobite Challenge*, Edinburgh: J. Donald; Atlantic Highlands, 1988.

Bogdanor, Vernon. *The Monarchy and the Constitution*, Oxford: Clarendon Press, 1995.

Bradbury, Jim. *Stephen and Matilda: The Civil War, 1139–1154*, Stroud, Gloucestershire: Alan Sutton, 1996.

Bradford, Sarah. *Elizabeth*, New York: Farrar, Straus, and Giroux, 1996.

Brewster, Sir David. *Memoirs of the Life, Writings, and Discoveries of Sir Isaac Newton*, New York and London: Johnson Reprint, 1965, reprinted from the Edinburgh edition of 1851.

Brewster, Sir David. *Memoirs of the Life, Writings, and Discoveries of Sir Isaac Newton*, New York and London: Johnson Reprint, 1965, reprinted from the Edinburgh edition of 1855.

Briacombe, Peter. *All the Queen's Men: The World of Elizabeth I*, New York: St. Martin's Press, 2000.

Briggs, Asa. *A Social History of England*, New York: Viking, 1983.

Brock, Michael. *The Great Reform Act*, London: Hutchinson, 1973.

Bucholz, R.O. "Nothing But Ceremony: Queen Anne and the Limitations of Royal Ritual," *Journal of British Studies*, 30, (July 1991), pp. 288–323.

———. *The Augustan Court: Queen Anne and the Decline of Court Culture*, Stanford: Stanford University Press, 1993.

Burnet, Gilbert. *History of the Reformation of the Church of England*, vol. 2, New York: D. Appleton and Co., 1848 (orig. pub. 1665).

Cambridge History of English Literature, vol. 9, ed. A.A. Ward and A.R. Walker, New York: G. Putnam, 1908.

Carter, Philip. *Men and the Emergence of Polite Society, Britain, 1660–1800*, Singapore: Pearson Education, 2001.

Cathcart, H. *The Married Life of the Queen*, London: W.H. Allen, 1970.

Chapman, Hester. *Queen Anne's Son*, London: Abdre Deutsch, 1954.

Charlot, Monica. *Victoria the Young Queen*, Oxford: Basil Blackwell, 1991.

Chibnall, Marjorie. *The Empress Matilda*, Oxford: Basil Blackwell, 1991.

———. "Women in Orderic Vitalis," *Haskins Society Journal*, 2 (1990), pp. 105–121.

Churchill, Winston. *Marlborough: His Life and Times*, five vols., London: George C. Harrapond, 1933–38.

Clark, Alice. *Working Life of Women in the Seventeenth Century*, New York: Routledge, 1992.

Clark, Anna. *The Struggle For the Breeches*, Berkeley: University of California Press, 1997.

———. *Scandal: The Sexual Politics of the British Constitution*, Princeton: Princeton University Press, 2003.

Clark, G. Kitson. *Peel and the Conservative Party*, Hamden, Conn.: Archon Books, 1964.

Clark, J.C.D. *English Society 1688–1832*, London: Allen and Unwin, 1985.

Clifford, Henry. *The Life of Jane Dormer*, ed. James Stephenson, London: 1887.

Clio's Consciousness Raised: New Perspectives on the History of Women, ed. Mary S. Hartman and Lois Banner, New York: Harper Colophon, 1974.

Colley, Linda. *In Defiance of Oligarchy*, Cambridge: Cambridge University Press, 1982.

———. *Britons: Forging the Nation, 1707–1837*, New Haven: Yale University Press, 1992.

Coole, Diana. *Women in Political Theory: From Ancient Misogyny to Contemporary Feminism*, New York: Harvester/Wheatshaft, 1993.

Coxe, William. *Memoirs of John, Duke of Marlborough*, London: Longman, Hurst, Rees, Orme, and Brown, 1818.

Creighton, Mandell. *Queen Elizabeth*, New York: Thom Y. Crowell, 1966 (orig. pub. 1899).

Creston, Dormer. *The Youthful Queen Victoria*, New York: G. Putnam and Sons, 1954.

Cronne, H.A. *The Reign of King Stephen, 1135–1154: Anarchy in England*, London: Weidenfeld and Nicolson, 1970.

Cruickshanks, Evelyn. *The Glorious Revolution*, New York: Palgrave-Macmillan, 2000.

Curtis, Gila. *The Life and Times of Queen Anne*, London: Weidenfeld and Nicolson, 1972.

Daly, James. *Sir Robert Filmer and English Political Thought*, Toronto: University of Toronto Press, 1979.

Daughters, Wives, and Widows, ed. Joan Larsen Klein, Chicago: University of Illinois Press, 1992.

Davidoff, Leonore, and Catherine Hall. *Family Fortunes: Men and Women of the English Middle Class*, Chicago: Chicago University Press, 1987.

Davis, R.H.C. *King Stephen*, third ed., London: Longman, 1990 (first pub. 1967).

Davis, W.H.C. "Henry of Blois and Brian Fitzcount," *English Historical Review*, 25 (1910), pp. 297–303.

Dissing Elizabeth: Negative Representations of Gloriana, ed. Julia M. Walker, London: Dale University Press, 1998.

Doherty, Richard. *The Williamite War in Ireland, 1688–1691*, London: Four Courts Press, 1998.

Doran, Susan. *Marriage and Matrimony: The Courtships of Elizabeth I*, London and New York: Routledge, 1996.

——. "Elizabeth I: Gender, Power, and Politics," *History Today*, 53, 5 (2003), pp. 29–35.

Doyle, Daniel. "The Sinews of Hapsburg Governance in the Sixteenth Century: Mary of Hungary and Political Patronage," *Sixteenth Century Journal*, 31, 2 (2000), pp. 349–60.

Dunham, William Huse Jr. "Regal Power and the Rule of Law: a Tudor Paradox," *Journal of British Studies*, 3 (May 1964), pp. 24–56.

Earenfight, Theresa. "Maria of Castile, Ruler or Figurehead?" *Mediterranean Studies*, 4 (1994), pp. 45–61.

Elton, G.R. *England Under the Tudors*, New York: Barnes and Noble, 1965.

——. *Reform and Reformation*, London: Edward Arnold, 1977.

Emson, H.E. "For Want of an Heir: The Obstetrical History of Queen Anne," *British Medical Journal*, 304, May 1992, pp. 66–67.

The English Court: From the Wars of the Roses to the Civil War, ed. David Starkey. London and New York: Longman, 1987.

English Masculinities, 1660–1800, ed. Tim Hitchcock and Michele Cohen, London: Longman, 1999.

Erickson, Carolly. *Bloody Mary*, New York: St. Martin's Press, 1978.

———. *The First Elizabeth*, New York: Summit Books, 1983.

Erickson, Mary Louise. *Women and Property in Early Modern England*, New York: Routledge, 1993.

Evan, Eric J. *Sir Robert Peel: Statemanship, Power, and Party*, London: Routledge, 1991.

Ezell, Margaret J.M. *The Patriarch's Wife*, Chapel Hill, N.C.: University of North Carolina Press, 1987.

Fell, Christine. *Women in Anglo-Saxon England*, London: Colonnade, 1984.

Fletcher, Anthony. *Gender, Sex, and Subordination in England*, New Haven Conn.: Yale University Press, 1995.

Foord, Archibald. "The Waning of the Influence of the Crown," *English Historical Review*, vol. 62 (Oct. 1947), pp. 484–507.

———. *His Majesty's Opposition*, Oxford: Clarendon Press, 1964.

Fox-Genovese, Elizabeth. "Placing Women's History in History," *New Left Review*, 133 (May/June 1982), pp. 5–29.

Foyster, Elizabeth A. *Manhood in Early Modern England*, London: Longman, 1999.

Frankle, Robert J. "The Formulation of the Declaration of Rights," *Historical Journal*, 5, 3 (June 1974), pp. 265–79.

Fraser, Antonia. *The Warrior Queens*, New York: Vintage Books, 1988.

Frost, C. *Coronation June 2 1953*, London: Arthur Hacker Ltd., 1978.

Froude, James Anthony. *History of England*, vol. 5, London: Longmans, Green, and Co., 1893.

———. *The Political History of England, 1547–1603*. London: Longman, Green, and Co., 1910.

———. *The Reign of Elizabeth*, 5 vols., London: J.M. Dent, 1911.

Frye, Susan. *Elizabeth I: The Competition for Representation*, New York: Oxford University Press, 1993.

Fulford, Roger. *The Prince Consort*, New York: Macmillan, 1945.

———. *The Wicked Uncles*, London: Duckworth, 1933.

Gammon, Samuel Rhea. *Statesman and Schemer: William, First Lord Paget, Tudor Minister*, Hamden, Conn.: Archon Books, 1973.

Gash, Norman. *Sir Robert Peel*, London: Longman, 1972.

Gernsheim, Helmut, and Alison Gernsheim. *Victoria R*, New York: G. Putnam and Sons, 1959.

Gillingham, John. "Love, Marriage, and Politics in the Twelfth Century," *Forum for Modern Language Studies*, 25 (1989), pp. 292–303.

Given-Wilson, Chris. *The Royal Household and the King's Affinity: Service, Politics And Finance in England, 1360–1413*, New Haven: Yale University Press, 1986.

Graves, Michael. *Early Tudor Parliaments*, London: Longman, 1990.

Green, David. *Sarah Duchess of Marlborough*, London: Collins, 1967.

——. *Queen Anne*, London: Collins, 1970.
Green, Judith. *The Government of England Under Henry I*, Cambridge: Cambridge University Press, 1986.
——. "Aristocratic Women in Early Twelfth Century England," *Anglo-Norman Political Culture in Early Twelfth Century England*, ed. C. Warren Hollister, Woodbridge, Suffolk: Boydell Press, 1997, pp. 60–72.
Gregg, Edward. *Queen Anne*, London: Routledge and Kegan Paul, 1980.
Guy, John. *Tudor England*, Oxford: Oxford University Press, 1988.
Habermas, Jurgen. *The Structural Transformation of the Public Sphere*, trans. Thomas Burger and Frederick Lawrence, Cambridge Mass.: M.I.T. Press, 1982.
Hackett, Helen. *Virgin Mother, Maiden Queen*, New York: St. Martin's Press, 1995.
Haigh, Christopher. *Elizabeth I*, New York: Longman, 1988.
Hallam, Henry. *Constitutional History of England*, Boston: Wells and Lily, 1829.
Harbison, E. Harris. *Rival Ambassadors at the Court of Queen Mary*, Freeport, N.Y.: Books for Libraries Press, 1970 (orig. pub. 1940).
Hardie, Frank. *The Political Influence of Queen Victoria*, London: Frank Cass, 1963.
Harris, Barbara J. "Women and Politics in Early Modern England," *Historical Journal*, 33, 2 (1990), pp. 259–81.
——. *English Aristocratic Women 1450–1550*, Oxford: Oxford University Press, 2002.
Harris, Frances. *A Passion for Government*, Oxford: Clarendon Press, 1991.
Harrison, Dick. *The Age of Abbesses and Queens: Gender and Political Culture in Medieval Europe*, Lund, Sweden: Nordic Academic Press, 1998.
Heisch, Alison. "Queen Elizabeth and the Persistence of Patriarchy," *Feminist Review*, 4 (1980), pp. 45–75.
Hicks, Philip. *Neoclassical History and English Culture*, London: Macmillan, 1996.
High and Mighty Queens of England: Realities and Representations, ed. Carole Levin, Jo Eldridge Carney, and Debra Barrett-Graves, New York: Palgrave Macmillan, 2003.
Higham, C., and R. Mosesley. *Elizabeth and Philip: The Untold Story*, London: Sidgwick and Jackson, 1991.
Hill, Bridget. *Women, Work, and Sexual Politics in Eighteenth Century England*, Oxford: Basil Blackwell, 1989.
Hoff, Joan. "Gender as a Postmodern Category of Paralysis," *Women's History Review*, 3, 2 (1994), pp. 80–99.
Hogrete, Pearl. *Tudor Women*, Ames, Iowa: Iowa University Press, 1975.
Hollister, C. Warren. "The Anglo-Norman Succession Debate of 1126: Prelude to Stephen's Anarchy," *Journal of Medieval History*, 1 (April 1975), pp. 19–42.
——. *Henry I*, completed and edited by Amanda Clark Frost, New Haven, Conn.: Yale University Press, 2001.

Holmes, Geoffrey. *British Politics in the Age of Queen Anne*, London: Macmillan, 1967.

Homans, Margaret. *Royal Representations: Queen Victoria and British Culture, 1837–1876*, Chicago: University of Chicago Press, 1997.

Hopkins, Lisa. *Women Who Would Be Kings: Female Rulers of the Sixteenth Century*, New York: St. Martin's Press, 1991.

Hopkinson, M.R. *Anne of England*, New York: Macmillan, 1934.

Horwitz, Henry. *Parliament, Policy, and Politics in the Reign of William III*, Manchester: Manchester University Press, 1977.

Houghton, John W. "No Bishop, No Queen: Queens Regnant and the Ordination of Women," *Anglican and Episcopal History*, 67 (1998), pp. 2–25.

Hudson, John. *Land, Law, Lordship in Anglo-Norman England*, Oxford: Clarendon Press, 1994.

Hutchings, Michael. "The Reign of Mary Tudor: A Reassessment," *History Review* (March 1999), pp. 1–21.

Hutton, Ronald. *Charles the Second, King of England, Scotland, and Ireland*, Oxford: Clarendon Press, 1989.

James, Robert Rhodes. *Prince Albert*, New York: Alfred A. Knopf, 1984.

———. "Prince Albert: First Constitutional Monarch?" *Proceedings of the Royal Institute of Great Britain*, 64 (1992), pp. 5–21.

Jenkins, Elizabeth. *Elizabeth the Great*, New York: Coward-McCann, 1959.

Jenkins, T.A. *Sir Robert Peel*, London: Macmillan, 1999.

Johns, Susan M. *Noblewomen, Aristocracy and Power*, Manchester: Manchester University Press, 2003.

Johnson, Allen. *The Gender Knot: Unraveling Our Patriarchal Legacy*, Philadelphia: Temple University Press, 1997.

Jones, Michael. *The King's Mother: Lady Margaret Beaufort, Countess of Richmond and Derby*, Cambridge: Cambridge University Press, 1992.

Jones, R. *The First Whigs: The Politics of the Exclusion Crisis, 1678–83*, New York: Greenwood 1985 (orig. pub. 1961).

Jordan, Constance. "Women's Rule in Sixteenth Century British Thought," *Renaissance Quarterly*, 40 (Autumn 1987), pp. 421–51.

———. *Renaissance Feminism: Literary Texts and Political Models*, Ithica: Cornell University Press, 1990.

Jordan, W.K. *Edward VI: The Threshold of Power*, Cambridge, Mass.: Belknap Press, 1970.

Kantorwicz, Ernst. *The King's Two Bodies: A Study in Medieval Theology*, Princeton, Princeton University Press, 1957.

Kenyon, J.P. *Robert Spencer, Earl of Sunderland, 1641–1702*, London: Longmans, Green and Co., 1958.

———. *Stuart England*, second ed., London: Penguin, 1978.

———. *The Stuart Constitution, 1603–1688*, second ed., New York: Cambridge University Press, 1988.

Kings and Kingship in Medieval Europe, ed., Anne Duggan. London: Kings College London Centre for Late Antique and medieval Studies, 1993.

Kishlansky, Mark. *A Monarchy Transformed: Britain 1603–1714*, New York: Penguin, 1997.

Knights, Mark. *Politics and Opinion in Crisis*, Cambridge: Cambridge University Press, 1994.

Langford, Paul. *A Polite and Commercial People: England, 1727–1783*, Oxford: Oxford University Press, 1984.

Law and Government Under the Tudors, ed. Clair Cross, David Loades, and J.J. Scarisbrick, Cambridge: Cambridge University Press, 1988.

Laynesmith, Jane. *The Last Medieval Queens*, Oxford: Oxford University Press, 2004.

Lee, Patricia Ann. "A Bodye Politique to Governe: Aylmer, Knox, and the Debate on Queenship," *Historian*, 52 (February 1990), pp. 242–262.

Legge, Dominica. "William Marshall and Arthur of Brittany," *Bulletin of the Institute of Historical Research*, 55 (May 1982), pp. 18–24.

Lehfeldt, Elizabeth. "Ruling Sexuality: The Political Legitimacy of Isabel of Castile," *Renaissance Quarterly* 51, 1 (2000), pp. 31–56.

LeMay, G.H. L. *The Victorian Constitution*, London: Duckworth, 1979.

Lenman, Bruce. *The Jacobite Cause*, Glasgow: R. Drew in association with the National Trust of Scotland, 1986.

Lerner, Gerda. *The Creation of Patriarchy*, Oxford: Oxford University Press, 1986.

———. *The Creation of Feminist Consciousness*, Oxford: Oxford University Press, 1993.

Levin, Carole. *The Heart and Stomach of a King*, Philadelphia: Pennsylvania University Press, 1994.

Levine, Mortimer. *The Early Elizabethan Succession Question*, Stanford: Stanford University Press, 1966.

———. *Tudor Dynastic Problems, 1460–1571*, London: George Allen and Unwin, 1973.

Lewis, A.W. *Royal Succession in Capetian France: Studies on Familial Order and the State*, Cambridge, Mass.: Harvard University press, 1981.

Leyser, Henrietta. *Medieval Women: A Social History of Women In England, 450–1500*, London: Weidenfeld and Nicolson, 1995.

Leyser, Karl. *Medieval Germany and Its Neighbors*, London: Hambledon Press, 1982.

———. "The Anglo-Norman Succession, 1120–1125," *Anglo-Norman Studies*, xiii, ed. Marjorie Chibnall, Woodridge, Suffolk: Boydell Press, 1991.

Liberty Secured: Britain Before and After 1688, ed. J.R. Jones, Stanford: Stanford University Press, 1992.

Lindsey, Karen. *Divorced Beheaded Survived: A Feminist Reinterpretation of the Wives of Henry VIII*, Reading, Mass.: Perseus Books, 1995.

Loach, Jennifer. *Crown and Parliament in the Reign of Mary Tudor*, Oxford: Oxford University Press, 1986.

Loades, David. *The Tudor Court*, Totowa N.J.: Barnes and Noble, 1987.
——. "The Reign of Mary Tudor: Historiography and Research," *Albion*, 21 (1989), pp. 547–58.
——. *Mary Tudor: A Life*, London: Basil Blackwell, 1989.
——. *The Reign of Mary Tudor*, second ed., London: Longmans, 1991.
——. "Why Queen Mary was Bloody," *Christian History*, 14 (1995), pp. 4–8.
Lodge, Richard. *The Political History of England, 1660–1702*, London: Longmans, Green and Co., 1910.
Longford, Elizabeth. *Queen Victoria: Born to Succeed*, New York: Harper and Row, 1964.
Macaulay, Thomas Babington. *The History of England From the Reign of James II*, 3 vols., New York: American Book Exchange, 1880.
Maitzen, Rohan Amanda. *Gender, Genre, and Victorian Historical Writing*, New York: Garland, 1998.
Marshall, Dorothy. *Lord Melbourne*, London: Weidenfeld and Nicolson, 1979.
Masculinity in Medieval Europe, ed. D.M. Hadley, London: Longman, 1999.
Mattingly, Garret. *Catherine of Aragon*, Boston: Little Brown, 1941.
McCaffery, Wallace. *Elizabeth I*, New York: Edward Arnold, 1993.
McLaren, A.N. *Political Culture in the Reign of Queen Elizabeth: Queen and Commonwealth, 1558–1585*, New York: Cambridge University Press, 1999.
——. "The Quest for a King: Gender, Marriage, and Succession in Elizabethan England," *Journal of British Studies*, 41 (July 2002), 259–290.
Medieval Queenship, ed. John Carmi Parson, New York: St. Martin's Press, 1993.
Medieval Women, ed. Derek Baker, Oxford: Studies in Church History, Subsidia I, 1978.
The Mid-Tudor Polity, ed. Robert Tittler, and Jennifer Loach, Totowa N.J.: Rowman and Littlefield, 1980.
Mitchell, L.G. *Lord Melbourne, 1779–1848*, Oxford: Oxford University Press, 1997.
Monod, Paul Kleber. *The Power of Kings: Monarchy and Religion in Europe*, New Haven, Conn.: 1999.
Muller, James Arthur. *Stephen Gardiner and the Tudor Reaction*, New York: Macmillan, 1926.
Myers, Henry A. *Medieval Kingship*, New York: St. Martin's Press, 1982.
Namier, Lewis Bernstein. *The Structure of Politics at the Accession of George III*, London: MacMillan, 1957.
Neale, J.E. *Queen Elizabeth I*, New York: Anchor Books, 1957 (orig. pub. 1934).

Nenner, Howard. *The Right To Be King: The Succession to the Crown of England, 1603–1702*, Chapel Hill N.C.: University of North Carolina Press, 1995.

Newbound, Ian. "Sir Robert Peel and the Conservative Party: A Study in Failure?," *English Historical Review*, 98 (July 1983), pp. 529–538.

Newman, Charlotte. *The Anglo-Norman Nobility in the Reign of Henry I*, Philadelphia: University of Pennsylvania Press, 1988.

The New York Times, 11/02/02, v. 152, p. A1.

The Nineteenth Century Constitution, ed. A.J. Hanham, Cambridge: Cambridge University Press, 1969.

Ogg, David. *England in the Reign of Charles II*, Oxford: Oxford University Press, 1956.

Okin, Susan Muller. "Patriarchy and Married Women's Property in England: Questions on Some Current Views," *Eighteenth Century Studies*, 17 (Winter 1983/84), pp. 121–138.

On the Laws and Customs of England, ed. Morris S. Arnold, Thomas A. Green, Sally A. Scully, and Stephen D. White, Chapel Hill, N.C.: University of North Carolina Press, 1981.

The Oxford Illustrated History of England, ed. Kenneth O. Morgan, Oxford: Oxford University Press, 1984.

Packard, Jerrold. *Victoria's Daughters*, New York: St. Martins Griffin, 1998.

Pain, Nesta. *Empress Matilda: Uncrowned Queen of England*, London: Weidenfeld and Nicolson, 1978.

Parker, John. *Prince Philip: A Critical Biography*, London: Sidgwick and Jackson, 1990.

Pateman, Carole. *The Sexual Contract*, Oxford: Polity Press, 1988.

——. *The Disorder of Women*, Stanford: Stanford University Press, 1989.

Pimlott, Ben. *The Queen: A Biography of Elizabeth II*, London: Harper Collins, 1996.

Pitock, Murray. *Jacobinism*, New York: St. Martin's Press, 1998.

Plumb, J.H. *England in the Eighteenth Century*, Harmonsworth, Middlesex: Penguin, 1950.

Pollard, A.F. *The Political History of England, 1547–1603*, London: Longman, Green, and Co., 1910.

Pollock, Frederick, and Frederic Maitland. *The History of English Law Before the Time of Edward I*, 2 vols., Cambridge: Cambridge University press, 1968 (orig. pub. 1898).

Poole, A.L. "Henry Plantagenet's Early Visits to England," *English Historical Review*, 47 (1932), pp. 447–450.

——. *From Domesday Book to Magna Carta*, Oxford: Clarendon Press, 1951.

Prescott, H.F.M. *Mary Tudor*, London: Eyre and Spottiswoode, 1952.

Prochaska, Frank. *Women and Philanthropy in Nineteenth Century England*, Oxford, 1980.

Prochaska, Frank. *Royal Bounty: The Making of a Welfare Monarchy*, New Haven: Yale University Press, 1995.

Queen Elizabeth I: Most Politick Princess, ed. Simon Adams, London: History Today, 1983.

Queens and Queenship in Medieval Europe, ed. Anne Duggan, Woodbridge, Suffolk: Boydell Press, 1997.

Queenship in Britain: 1660–1837, ed. Clarissa Campbell Orr, Manchester: Manchester University Press, 2002.

Read, Donald. *Peel and the Victorians*, Oxford: Basil Blackwe, 1987.

Redworth, Glyn. "Matters Impertinent to Women": Male and Female Monarchy Under Philip and Mary, "*English Historical Review* (June 1997), pp. 597–613.

———. *In Defence of the Church Catholic: The Life of Stephen Gardiner*, Cambridge, Mass.: B. Blackwell, 1990.

Reilly, Bernard F. *The Kingdom of Leon-Castilla Under Queen Uracca*, Princeton: Princeton University Press, 1982.

Remaking Queen Victoria, ed. Margaret Homans and Adrienne Munich, Cambridge: Cambridge University Press, 1997.

Representing the English Renaissance, ed. Stephen Greenblatt, Berkeley: University of California Press, 1988.

Richards, Judith M. "Mary Tudor as a 'Sole Quene'?: Gendering Tudor Monarchy," *The Historical Journal*, 40, 4 (1997), pp. 895–924.

———. "To Promote a Woman to Beare Rule: Talking of Queens in Mid-Tudor England," *Sixteenth Century Journal*, 28 (1997), pp. 101–121.

Richardson, H.G., and G.O. Sayles. *The Governance of Medieval England: From the Conquest to Magna Carta*, Edinburgh: Edinburgh University Press, 1963.

Ridley, Jasper. *The Life and Times of Mary Tudor*, London: Weidenfeld and Nicolson, 1973.

Rose, Sonya. *Limited Livelihoods: Gender and Class in Nineteenth-Century England*, Berkeley: University of California Press, 1992.

Round, J.H. *Geoffrey de Mandeville*, New York: Burt Franklin, 1960 (orig. pub. 1892).

Rowse, A.L. *Expansion of Elizabethan England*, New York: St. Martin's Press, 1955.

Russell, Elizabeth. "Mary Tudor and Mr. Jorkins," *Bulletin of the Institute of Historical Research* 152 (October 1990), pp. 263–76.

Sainty, John Christopher, and R.O. Bucholz. *Officers of the Royal Household*, vol. 1, London: University of London, Institute of Historical Research, 1997.

Scalingi, Paula Louise. "The Sceptre or the Distaff: The Question of Female Sovereignty, 1516–1607," *Historian*, 41 (November 1978), pp. 59–75.

Scarisbrick, J.J. *Henry VIII*, Berkeley: University of California Press, 1968.

Schama, Simon. *A History of Britain: At the Edge of the World, 3000 b.c.–a.d. 1603*, New York: Hyperion, 2000.

Schramm, Percy Ernst. *History of the English Coronation*, trans. Leopold G. Wickham Legge, Oxford: Clarendon Press, 1937.

Schuyler, Robert Livingston. "Recent Work of Richardson and Sayles," *Journal of British Studies*, 3 (May 1964), pp. 1–23.

Schwoerer, Lois G. *The Declaration of Rights, 1689*, Baltimore: Johns Hopkins University Press, 1977.

——. "Women and the Glorious Revolution," *Albion*, 18, 2 (Summer 1986), pp. 195–218.

Scott, Joan Wallach. "Gender: A Useful Category of Historical Analysis?" *American Historical Review*, 91, 5 (December 1986), pp. 1053–1075.

——. *Gender and the Politics of History*, New York: Columbia University Press, 2000.

Searle, E. "Women and the Legitimization of Succession of the Norman Conquest," *Anglo-Norman Studies*, iii, ed. Marjorie Chibnall, Woodbridge, Suffolk: Boydell Press, 1980, pp. 159–170.

Shahar, S. *The Fourth Estate: A History of Women in the Middle Ages*, London: Metheun, 1983.

Simon of Glaisdale, Lord. "The Influence and Power of the Monarchy in the United Kingdom Monarchy," *Current* (September 1982), pp. 56–60.

Singlewomen in the European Past, 1250–1800, ed. Judith Bennett and Amy M. Froide, Philadelphia: University of Pennsylvania Press, 1999.

Smith, Bonnie G. *The Gender of History*, Cambridge, Mass.: Harvard University Press, 1998.

Somerset, Anne. *Ladies in Waiting*, London: Weidenfeld and Nicolson, 1984.

——. *Elizabeth I*, London: Weidenfeld and Nicolson, 1991.

Spall, Richard F. Jr. "The Bedchamber Crisis and the Hastings Affair: Morals, Politics and the Press at the Beginning of Victoria's Reign," *Canadian Journal of History*, 22 (April 1987), pp. 19–39.

St. John, Henry, Lord Bolingbroke. *Remarks on the History of England*, Dublin: G. Faulkner, 1743.

Stafford, Pauline. "The King's Wife in Wessex, 800–1066," *Past and Present*, 91 (May 1981), pp. 3–27.

——. *Queen Emma and Queen Edith: Queenship and Women's Power in Eleventh Century England*, Cambridge, Mass.: Blackwell publishers, 1997.

Starkey, David. *Elizabeth: Apprenticeship*, London: Chatto and Windus, 2000.

——. *The Six Wives of Henry VIII*, New York: Harper Collins, 2003.

Stenton, F.M. *The First Century of English Feudalism*, Oxford: Clarendon Press, 1932.

Stone, Lawrence. *The Crisis of the Aristocracy, 1558–1641*, Oxford: Clarendon Press, 1965.

——. *Family, Sex, and Marriage in England, 1500–1800*, New York: Harper and Row, 1977.

Strachey, Lytton. *Queen Victoria*, New York: Blue Ribbon Press, 1921.

Strickland, Agnes. *The Lives of the Queens of England*, 8 vols., London: Henry Colburn, 1852.

Stringer, K.J. *The Reign of King Stephen*, London: Routledge, 1993.

Stubbs, William. *The Constitutional History of England*, 3 vols., Oxford: Clarendon Press, 1894–97.

Studies in Medieval History: Presented to Frederick Maurice Powicke, ed. R.W. Hunt, W.A. Pantin, and R.W. Southern, Oxford: Clarendon Press, 1948.

Taylor, Arthur. *The Glory of Regality: An Historical Treatise of the Anointing and Crownings of the Kings and Queens of England*, London: 1820.

Thompson, Dorothy. *Queen Victoria: Gender and Power*, London: Virago, 1990.

Tittler, Robert, and Susan L. Battley. "The Local Community and the Crown in 1553: The Accession of Mary Tudor Revisited," *Bulletin of the Institute of Historical Research*, 57, 136 (1984), pp. 131–49.

Tittler, Robert. *The Reign of Mary Tudor*, London: Longman, 1991.

Tosh, John. "What Should Historians Do With Masculinity? Reflections on Nineteenth Century Britain," *History Workshop Journal*, 38 (Autumn 1994), pp. 179–202.

———. *A Man's Place: Masculinity and the Middle-Class Home in Victorian England*, New Haven: Yale University Press, 1999.

Toward an Anthropology of Women, ed. Rayna R. Reiter, New York: Monthly Review Press, 1975.

Trevelyan, George Macaulay. *The Reign of Queen Anne*, 3 vols., London: Longmans, Green, and Co., 1930–34.

Tudor Rule and Revolution: Essays For G.R. Elton From His American Friends, ed. Delloyd J. Guth and John W. McKenna, Cambridge: Cambridge University Press, 1982, 109–123.

Turberville, A.S. *The House of Lords in the XVIII Century*, Westport, Conn.: Greenwood Press, 1970.

Vallone, Lynn. *Becoming Victoria*, New Haven and London: Yale University Press, 2001.

Van Der Zee, Henri, and Barbara Van Der Zee. *William and Mary*, London: Macmillan, 1973.

Vickery, Amanda. "Golden Age to Separate Spheres?: A Review of the Categories and Chronology of English Women's History," *Historical Journal*, 36, 2 (June 1993), pp. 383–414.

Waldman, Milton. *The Lady Mary: A Biography of Mary Tudor*, New York: Scribner, 1972.

Warnicke, Retha. *Women of the English Renaissance and Reformation*, Westport Conn.: Greenwood Press, 1983.

Warren, W.L. *Henry II*, Berkeley: University of California Press, 1973.

Waterson, Nellie M. *Mary II Queen of England, 1689–1694*, Durham N.C.: Duke University Press, 1928.

Webster, C.K. "The Accession of Queen Victoria," *History*, 85 (June 1937), pp. 14–33.

Weil, Rachel. *Political Passions: Gender, the Family, and Political Argument in England, 1680–1714*, Manchester: Manchester University Press, 1999.

Weintraub, Stanley. *Queen Victoria: An Intimate Memoir*, New York: Truman Talley Books, 1987.

Weir, Alison. *The Children of Henry VIII*, New York: Ballantine, 1996.

Western, J.R. *Monarchy and Revolution: The English State in the 1680s*, Totowa N.J.: Rowman and Littlefield, 1972.

White, Graeme J. "The End of Stephen's Reign," *History*, 75 (February 1990), pp. 3–22.

Wilkinson, Richard. "Queen Anne," *History Review*, 31 (September 1998), 39–45.

Williams, Ann. *Kingship and Government in Pre-Conquest England*, New York St. Martins Press, 1999.

Williams, Basil. *The Whig Supremacy*, Oxford: Clarendon Press, 1939.

Williams, E. Neville. *The Eighteenth Century Constitution*, Cambridge: Cambridge University Press, 1970.

Williams, Neville. *All the Queen's Men*, London: Cardinal, 1974.

Wilson, A.N. *The Rise and Fall of the House of Windsor*, New York: Norton and Co., 1993.

Women and Power in the Middle Ages, ed. Mary Erler and Maryanne Kowaleski, Athens, Ga.: University of Georgia Press, 1988.

Women in the Middle Ages and Renaissance, ed. Mary Beth Rose, Syracuse: Syracuse University Press, 1986.

Woodham Smith, Cecil. *Queen Victoria: From Her Birth to the Death of the Prince Consort*, New York: Alfred A. Knopf, 1972.

Woodward, E.L. *The Age of Reform*, Oxford: Clarendon Press, 1939.

Woolfe, D.R. "Two Elizabeths? James I and the Late Queen's Memory," *Canadian Journal of History*, 20 (1985) pp. 167–191.

The World of William and Mary: Anglo-Dutch Perspectives on the Revolution of 1688–89, ed. Dale Hoak and Mordechai Feingold. Stanford: Stanford University Press, 1996.

Ziegler, Philip. *William IV*, London: Collins, 1971.

———. *Crown and People*, New York: Alfred A. Knopf, 1978.

INDEX